"Sunita Noronha brilliantly presents the lived experiences of intercultural couples, highlighting positives with appreciation, as well as negotiating differences regarding personal space, identity, values, family traditions, specific cultural orientations, political inclinations, belief systems, and behavioral patterns. Dr. Noronha successfully integrates psychology, theology, therapeutic techniques, cultural studies, and sociology of religion in her pastoral theological method. . . . A valuable resource not only for intercultural couples but also for therapists engaged with multicultural family education and therapy."
    —Joseph George, secretary, International Council
        for Pastoral Care and Counseling

"Choosing a life partner is a major event that impacts every facet of one's being. Noronha offers thoughtful reflection on the questions that matter in these relationships, drawing from both her research and her personal experience. . . . There is an increasing number of couples for whom intercultural issues are significant parts of their presentation. The global village now includes all of us. Welcoming the stranger will sometimes include our spouse or partner."
    —Skip Johnson, pastor, Cannon United Methodist Church

"You need to read this book: (a) if you are engaged in a marriage relationship that has been disturbed by the culture and are trying to resolve the concerns and issues emerging from cultural value and belief systems; (b) if you are willing to journey with 'help-seeking couples' to re-create the possibilities of the 'first couple in the garden of Eden' through psychotherapeutic approaches and skills informed by pastoral theology; (c) if you are a person who believes in the healing of family relationships."
    —A. Israel David, professor, Pastoral Care and Counseling,
        Union Biblical Seminary

Doing Therapy
with Intercultural Couples

Doing Therapy with Intercultural Couples

A Pastoral Theological Study of Premarital Counseling

SUNITA NORONHA

Foreword by Emmanuel Y. Lartey

☙PICKWICK *Publications* · Eugene, Oregon

DOING THERAPY WITH INTERCULTURAL COUPLES
A Pastoral Theological Study of Premarital Counseling

Copyright © 2022 Sunita Noronha. All rights reserved. Except for brief quotations in critical publications or reviews, no part of this book may be reproduced in any manner without prior written permission from the publisher. Write: Permissions, Wipf and Stock Publishers, 199 W. 8th Ave., Suite 3, Eugene, OR 97401.

Pickwick Publications
An Imprint of Wipf and Stock Publishers
199 W. 8th Ave., Suite 3
Eugene, OR 97401

www.wipfandstock.com

PAPERBACK ISBN: 978-1-7252-7113-5
HARDCOVER ISBN: 978-1-7252-7114-2
EBOOK ISBN: 978-1-7252-7115-9

Cataloguing-in-Publication data:

Names: Noronha, Sunita, author | Lartey, Emmanuel Y., foreword.

Title: Doing therapy with intercultural couples : a pastoral theological study of premarital counseling / by Sunita Noronha; foreword by Emmanuel Y. Lartey.

Description: Eugene, OR: Pickwick Publications, 2022 | Includes bibliographical references.

Identifiers: ISBN 978-1-7252-7113-5 (paperback) | ISBN 978-1-7252-7114-2 (hardcover) | ISBN 978-1-7252-7115-9 (ebook)

Subjects: LCSH: Marital psychotherapy—United States. | Cultural psychiatry—United States. | Interethnic marriage. | Intercountry marriage. | Cultural relations. | Interracial marriage. | Marriage counseling.

Classification: HQ1031 N67 2022 (print) | HQ1031 (ebook)

Table of Contents

Abstract xiii
Foreword by Emmanuel Y. Lartey xv
Acknowledgments xvii
Preface xix

Chapter I: Understanding Intercultural Ethos 1
  Introduction 1
  Statement of the Problem 5
  Statement of Purpose 8
  Issues and Challenges 8
  Research Questions 9
  Sub Questions 9
  Overview of Methodology 10
  Rationale and Significance 11
  Role and Subjectivity of the Researcher 12
  Research Assumptions 15
  Research Limitations 17
  Organization of the Research 18

Chapter II: A Pastoral Theological Framework for Intercultural Premarital Couples Counseling 19
  Introduction 19
  Pastoral Theological Perspective on Marriage 20
  Pastoral Theological Perspective
    on Intercultural Marriage 21
  Pastoral Theology and the Correlation Method 27
  Psychological Theoretical Framework 36

Contribution of Kohut's Theory to Intercultural Premarital Counseling 39
Summary 40

Chapter III: Exploring Clinical Literature and Structural Frameworks for Intercultural Premarital Couples Counseling 42
Introduction 42
Review of Literature 42
Conceptual Framework for Research 56
Summary 58

Chapter IV: Describing Research Methodology for Intercultural Premarital Couples Counseling 60
Rationale for Qualitative Research Approach 60
Research Setting/Context 61
Research Sample and Data Sources 62
Research Protocol Process 63
Data Collection Methods 64
Interviews 64
Data Analysis Methods 66
Risks and Discomfort 73
Limitations 74
Summary 74

Chapter V: Reporting Findings of the Research for Intercultural Premarital Couples Counseling 75
Introduction 75
Demographic Information 77
Cultural Diversity Screening I 78
Cultural Diversity Screening II 78
Description of Findings 79
Summary

Chapter VI: Interpreting the Findings of the Research for Intercultural Premarital Couple Counseling
Introduction 116
SECTION A 118
SECTION B 129

SECTION C 143
SECTION D 153

Chapter VII: Conclusion and Recommendations for Intercultural Premarital Couple Counseling 158
Conclusion 158
Reflections on the Contributions of This Research 166
Recommendations for Intercultural Couples
    in Premarital Therapy: 168
Recommendations for Therapists Engaged
    In Intercultural Couples Counseling 169
Recommendations for Future Research 171

Appendix A: Participant Recruitment: Letter to Therapists 173
Appendix B: Emory University Advertisement 174
Appendix C: RESEARCH PARTICIPANTS WANTED 175
Appendix D: Interview Packet: Tentative Interview Questions 176
Appendix E: Emory University: Description of Research and Consent to be a Research Subject 178
Appendix F: Emory University: Institutional Review Board 186
Appendix G: Demographic Questionnaire 188
Appendix H: Cultural Diversity Screening Questions 192
Appendix I: Research Questions to the Single Partner Participants 194
Appendix J: Research Questions to the Couple Participants 196
Appendix K: Collaborative Institutional Training Initiative 198

Bibliography 199

Abstract

THIS STUDY INVESTIGATES HOW cultural realities can be addressed within intercultural premarital couples counseling.

Four intercultural couples give their perceptions about the kinds of understandings that were helpful during their marital discernment process and recommend what areas could be improved. Using a cultural focus approach couples' stories around their particular culture and relationship were analyzed. Themes related to relationship, family and social ties, and parenting bicultural and biracial children were examined. Issues of religious and social influence, money, race, ethnicity, extended family, immigration, and biases in family of origin were explored as are roles and responsibilities, communication, respect, trust, and gender stereotyping.

The study addresses how these themes relate to the experiences of intercultural couples and provides suggestions for therapists working with intercultural premarital couples. For therapists it is pointed out that there are several characteristics at play that need consideration. These include family upbringing, cultural influences, value systems, traditions, therapists' own understanding of culture and cultural nuances, and prejudices that may help or hinder the therapeutic process. The need to realize that the therapist's personality comes into play in how he/she is received by the client is highlighted.

The research adopts a pastoral theological cycle in working towards a deeper understanding of premarital relationships of partners who represent cultural difference and diversity. In conclusion recommendations to therapists and caregivers for counseling intercultural couples are made, and suggestions for further research are offered.

Foreword

AN INEVITABLE SOCIAL FACT of our globalizing world is that of intercultural relations and especially intercultural marriage. We are thrown together in urban as well as rural contexts in the world today from many different ethnic, cultural and national origins. People from various socio-economic, class, religious, and linguistic backgrounds meet, fall in love, and marry regardless of whether our models of society are "melting pot" or "tossed-salad bowl." This book, based as it is on thoughtful research with intercultural couples, offers us a wealth of important views and ways of interacting which can be of great assistance not only for intercultural couples, but also for *all* married couples whatever their backgrounds.

Doing Therapy with Intercultural Couples is written by a pastoral psychotherapist primarily for therapists providing premarital and marital counseling for couples who clearly identify their different cultural backgrounds as factors in their relationship building. It helpfully approaches marriage and marital therapy from a developmental perspective exploring the paths from families of origin, through courtship and onto maturity in marriage, and in therapeutic terms from premarital therapy through marital conflict resolution. In this way it facilitates a thoroughgoing and systematic approach to what can be a "whirlwind" of emotions, processes, and practices often associated with love and marriage.

By exploring issues brought up by four intercultural couples, all of whom chose to consult an intercultural therapist, the book is grounded solidly not in conjecture or theory, but rather in the lived experience of real couples living what they are talking about on a day-to-day basis. To that extent, therefore, *Doing Therapy with Intercultural Couples* is exceedingly valuable for couples themselves as they attempt to make successes of their marital relationships.

Increasingly, therapists worldwide have begun to take people's religion, faith, or spirituality seriously in their therapeutic efforts and interventions. This is in recognition of the fact that for many people matters of faith, of very different persuasions, are a crucial part both of their culture and of their identity as persons. As such it is noteworthy and a credit to the author that the framework that shapes the entire work is named as a "pastoral theological" one. This is an approach which takes religion, faith, and spirituality seriously. Moreover, pastoral theology being interdisciplinary in ethos and practice, takes disciplines that help to illumine the human condition seriously. As such psychology, especially in this case Heinz Kohut's self-psychology, plays an important part in the approach taken to the matters raised by the couples here. Cultural studies also feature very prominently in contemporary pastoral theological work. Dr. Noronha deftly and appropriately engages in interdisciplinary dialog between theology, psychology, and cultural studies in this engaging text.

The quest for identity runs right through the text. Identity is sought not only by the individual partners in the marriages as they navigate an ambiguous social reality, but also by intercultural couples as complex units within global and communal nexuses that are not always understanding of the challenges they face. This search for identity is also a matter of importance in the raising of biracial children, which is considered in the book.

Attention to psychological, social, cultural, ethnic, economic, and religious factors in the weaving of harmonious relationships, as well as in conflictual situations, makes this book a unique example of the much-needed intercultural skill required by therapists and indeed all persons who wish to successfully navigate the challenges of our increasingly contentious global reality.

Emmanuel Y. Lartey, PhD
Charles Howard Candler Professor of Pastoral Theology & Spiritual Care
Candler School of Theology
Emory University,
Atlanta, GA, USA.

Acknowledgments

I WANT TO THANK all who helped me with love, encouragement, support, guidance, on my doctoral journey and research project. I am very grateful for all the words of wisdom, prayers, and mentorship that allowed me this opportunity to stretch myself and explore the parts of me that I had not paid sufficient attention to in my life's journey.

First of all I am very grateful to my dissertation committee Chairperson Dr. Emmanuel Y. Lartey, for his continued and sustained guidance and mentorship in my research work for two years. I am also grateful to my dissertation committee members Dr. Paul (Skip) Johnson and Dr. Karen D. Scheib for their encouragement and support in helping me sustain interest and motivation to complete this research work.

I am grateful to the Staff and Administration, the Registrar, and all the distinguished Professors in my ThD studies program for their sustained guidance in my incredible academic journey. They showed me the way to find my voice, to explore and to examine various social, cultural, political, racial, ethical, ethnic, immigration, and other systems, nuances of my own worldview that impact and influence who I am in the world, that inevitably shapes my personal identity and my overall wellbeing.

I am thankful for the understanding and caring clinical practicum supervisors at the Care & Counseling Center of Georgia, Decatur, GA, for their continued guidance in helping me hone my skills and expertise in counseling and to pay attention to various theories and approaches available for psychotherapy with my individual and couple clients in order to help them on their journey of healing, wholeness and transformation. Thank you for your challenging but thought-provoking questions and comments that enabled me to reflect objectively to be a mature and robust clinician.

I am grateful for the nurturing presence of my near and dear friends and well-wishers who continually were there to lift me up and compel me to keep going.

I am very grateful to all of the four participating couples who were my true inspiration. Your energy and encouragement was the stepping stone that helped me continue deliberating on this research to discover approaches that aid the therapy of intercultural couples. Your contribution to this research is precious and I deeply value your contribution. Even though you will remain anonymous to the world, I will always hold you dear to me. I trust that your views and experience will serve to encourage other intercultural couples in their relational journey as well as other intercultural therapists to draw inspiration and insight to do a much deeper work with intercultural couples, especially premarital couples who need support and direction about discernment.

I am grateful to my extended family in India who are always praying and encouraging me from a very far place and yet are closer than ever. I am grateful to God for my late parents who wanted the best for my life, however they probably never imagined that their youngest determined child will reach such heights. I am the first female with a doctoral degree in my family. I wish you both were present here with me.

I am extremely grateful to an ever-present loving presence and participation of my two lovely daughters Shalini Roy and Preeti Noronha who were willing to give me space and time to work on this project and supported me with their prayers and love. Most of all I am thankful to my beloved husband Niranjan of thirty-nine years who dreamed this dream with me and sometimes for me. He stood by me like a rock, never letting me give up on me. He truly is a trusted friend and delightful guide who had my back. I have lived the intercultural couple dream in my own personal life and that is my biggest reality—that it can be done. I am grateful to God for your love and support. I love you all very much.

I am thankful to my beloved pet dog Benji who was my stress buster but sadly has since passed. He was sent only to support and encourage me and I am grateful to God for his life and his gift to me.

Most of all I am thankful and grateful to God for God's Shadow over me. God was my "cloud by day" and my "pillar of fire" by night. I was energized by God's "still small voice" whispering in my ear to never give up. God was with me every step of the way. This research is a piece of God's own heart for God wants us to "love one another" because God is the Creator and Sustainer of all humankind.

Dr. Sunita Noronha, July 15, 2020

Preface

My "American Dream" seems fulfilled with the publication of my doctoral dissertation submitted to Emory at the Candler Theological Seminary in the United States in 2016. It was with a deep sense of humility and gratitude that I began this journey of doctoral studies in pastoral counseling five years ago. And now this dream seems to be fulfilled in another way as I publish this as a book for wider reading. However, the seeds of the dream were sown way back in 1983 while I was doing my graduate studies in theology. All through these many years, trying to honor my family and my commitments in ministry, my dream seemed to be fading away. Just when I thought I had completely given up, while doing my CPE (Clinical Pastoral Education), my supervisor in Atlanta urged me to dream again, "to dream a new dream." "How can that be?" I asked in desperation. "How can I dream a new dream? There's only one dream in a person's life and mine has been shattered," I lamented. But I heeded her advice and encouragement and in 2010 I applied for the Th.D. program at Emory. With the support and encouragement of many, here I am at the last stages of a very worthwhile journey, sitting down to write a preface for my doctoral dissertation and getting it published.

The vision to carry out this research came from my clinical work at the Care & Counseling Center of Georgia. In the first two years I began to see clients who sought me out on the internet and wanted to come in for couples counseling. Most of them were young couples in an intercultural relationship, unmarried and experiencing difficulty. They were not necessarily looking for premarital counseling as they were still in the discernment phase, wanting to know if moving forward in their current relationship was a viable option. The cultural differences that they were experiencing did not necessarily appear cultural to them but they were significant enough to warrant an outside intervention. Interestingly they were looking for an ethnic therapist who could understand them. There were several others, for whom culture was not a major issue, who were not concerned about the ethnic background of their therapist. They just wanted help. But for me, cultural difference in these relationships mattered as they would impinge on the counseling therapy.

My romance with intercultural marriage began when I decided to marry a man who was from a different culture. Even though my husband and I are Indians, he is from the South and I am from the North. The differences in language, food, traditions, music and the like between us are very significant and from time to time they posed a real challenge. There was a lot to negotiate and work with. We did have to work at reciprocity and understanding with each other. This personal experience of mine had already impressed upon me the need for counseling intercultural couples. Furthermore, being an immigrant here in the United States and being constantly faced with many cultural challenges, I seemed to have the needed groundwork and the motivation to work with intercultural couples. And so here I am, ushered into a new dimension in my romance with intercultural marriage. It has been a very enriching experience working with intercultural couples. They have been much held and sustained and nurtured. I have learned many valuable lessons from them. This research is a testament to my love and respect for them and for all other such couples I might meet in the future.

I admit the limitations of this study as it is set in the United States, working with intercultural couples in the United States, and so the implications of this study may not be fully appropriate in other cultural contexts. Despite this, the comprehensive treatment of intercultural and ethnic problems among the people in marital and premarital crisis in the United States needing therapeutic assistance is well documented.

CHAPTER I

Understanding Intercultural Ethos

Introduction

IN A WORLD WHERE marriage seems to be the end-all of most Indians, especially a girl if she is of marriageable age and a boy if he is an eligible bachelor, there are innumerable hurdles to cross over to fructify the same in marriage. These hurdles may be in terms of parental approval, matching horoscopes, cultural compatibility, language, region, and so on. As matrimony is a question of money, the couple in question need to be suitably and financially matching too. Cultural and ethnic differences are varied as India has a multicultural community of different religions, eating and dining habits, dresses, etc. With all these, the question of caste, class, and clan can also creep in to further clarify the suitability of marriage. Since marriages are traditionally arranged, love marriages are not rare now. Even when the marriage takes place, as per the horoscope, the question of dowry haunts the bride and her parents for a long time. And the problems thus continue over. As such there is hardly any counseling at the proposal stage or even after marriage. This in brief is the Indian situation.

The situation in America is very different for obvious reasons. For one, interracial and interethnic marriages have come to stay among the locals and the immigrants among the opposite sex. Same-sex marriages too have been not rare in recent years, approved as such by the church. And also premarital relationships and live-ins are not rare.

In terms of their living and contributions to the local social activity interracial or interethnic couples make a significant contribution to the diversity of US society according to the US Census Bureau. In 2010, there were 5.4 million opposite-sex interracial or interethnic married-couple households. These married couples were 9.5 percent of all married-couple households, i.e., approximately one in ten of all married-couple household are interracial. This is an increase of 28 percent since 2000, when 7.4 percent of married-couple households were interracial or interethnic and intercultural couples.[1] There is a higher percentage of unmarried partners who are interracial or interethnic than married couples. Nationally, 10 percent of opposite-sex married couples had partners of a different race or Hispanic origin, compared with 18 percent of opposite-sex unmarried partners and 21 percent of same-sex unmarried partners.[2] This is a clear indication that mixed racial marriages are on the increase and people are faced with the new reality of intercultural and interfaith marriages and raising bicultural and biracial children. This is also the century of advancement in various walks of life, intermingling of cultures, opportunities to meet together as world students, working together in various fields such as medicine, information technology, and social networking sites, as well as a surge in the tourism industry. This is making it relatively easier to get to know people from different backgrounds and cultures than before. Hundreds of immigrants are choosing to come to America every day to pursue the "American Dream" and make America their home. The influx of immigrants, refugees, students, families of immigrants, and new citizens and fiancées from all over the world, is a recurring phenomenon and not a temporary event.

Immigrants can be categorized in the following ways: The first-generation immigrant as it applies to one's nationality or residency can be understood in two ways. One as in a "foreign-born citizen" or "resident" who has immigrated to a new country of residence as in "first-generation migrant" or a "native-born citizen" or "resident" of a country whose parents are foreign born as in "first-generation American" but "second-generation immigrant." According to Rumbaut and Portes, professors and prominent Cuban-American sociologists and leading experts on immigration and refugee resettlement in the United States, the term 1.5 generation or 1.5G refers to people who immigrate to a new country with their parents or alone during their early teens (thirteen to seventeen years

---

1. http://www.censUS.gov/prod/cen2010/briefs/c2010br-14.pdf.

2. https://www.censUS.gov/newsroom/releases/archives/2010_censUS/cb12-68.html.

of age).³ They are not born in the country of adoption but immigrate bringing with them traits and traditions from their country of birth. They continue the process of assimilation and socialization into their new adopted country thereby forming a new identity of a third culture. They are considered halfway between their country of birth and country of adoption thus halfway between the first generation and second-generation. Such individuals are often bilingual and find it easier to be assimilated into the local culture and society than their parents. Many 1.5 generation individuals are bicultural, combining both cultures—the culture of the country of origin with the culture of the new country.⁴ The second generation refers to the second generation of a family to inhabit or else be native born in the new country. These are often referred as US-born children of foreign-born parents. Generally, if they are born in the United States they cannot be considered as immigrants. Intercultural couple partners can make up any of the above combinations and bring with them any number of concerns pertaining to their specific immigration status.

It is imperative to begin to sit up and take notice of the growing reality of intercultural, interfaith, and interethnic marital alliances. American Professor of Social Work, educator, and therapist Judith Mishne states that, "these newly arrived populations compel us to consider and examine the impact of the migration experience, as part of a culturally sensitive response to race and ethnicity."⁵

Couples invariably find themselves intermingling with individuals from other cultures. After a while they realize that this is not going as expected, that there are several hurdles to cross and begin to look for someone who will understand them and provide guidance and support. They often feel "stuck" and search for a professional whom they can go to and who will help them move forward. In the last five years this is why many intercultural couples have come for premarital couples counseling. In my clinical experience, these couples are not necessarily looking for premarital counseling but they are at the crossroads, and are seeking "discernment" about their relationship in the light of the differences and difficulties that they may be experiencing. Dugan Romano, a cross-cultural trainer and counselor, lists several potential trouble spots for intercultural marriages. These are values, food and drink, sex, male-female roles,

---

3. Rumbaut and Portes, *Ethnicities*.
4. Rumbaut, "Ages, Life Stages, and Generational Cohorts," 1160–205.
5. Mishne, *Multiculturalism and the Therapeutic Process*, 17.

time, place of residence, politics, friends, finances, in-laws, social class, religion, raising children, language and communication, responding to stress and conflict, illness and suffering, ethnocentrism, the expatriate spouse, and coping with death and divorce.[6] Romano argues that most of these are potentially problematic to all marriages and not just to intercultural marriages. However, in intercultural marriages some of these concerns appear to be not just trivial but much more dramatic and problematic. In intercultural marriages, these concerns "involve cultural identity and thereby are unconscious and more difficult to resolve. And the more different the cultures, the more difficult the job."[7] Kyle D. Killian, American scholar, researcher, counselor, and instructor asks, "the U.S. Census says interracial couples are on the rise. But are clinicians ready?"[8]

Professor of Human Development and Family Studies Terri Karis and licensed couple and family therapist Kyle Killian define cross-cultural couples or intercultural or interracial couples as: "consisting of partners from different countries, nationalities, ethnicities, and religions who may possess quite divergent beliefs, assumptions, and values as a result of their socialization in different socio-cultural spaces."[9]

Intercultural premarital couples' counseling provides couples with skills to enhance communication, to work through problems and decrease conflict, increase understanding, care, and nurture. It helps in addressing expectations even in their discernment process if they should move towards marriage. In recent times we have seen a steady lowering in both the age of marriage for couples as well as the ability to sustain a marriage over a long term. One question that I have heard intercultural couples often ask is, "What problems can we expect to encounter along the way and can we have some level of certainty about the longevity of our marriage so as to proceed further with our commitment to each other?" Generally speaking, premarital counseling programs, though helpful to couples, often present a Western approach to assisting all couples, including intercultural couples. This hinders understanding in relation to culture and related issues and concerns.

There seems to be a good amount of published material in terms of multicultural marital counseling, but a lack of attention in the literature

6. Romano, *Intercultural Marriage: Promises and Pitfalls*, 35–36.

7. Romano, *Intercultural Marriage: Promises and Pitfalls*, 36.

8. https://www.psychologytoday.com/blog/intersections/201311/guess-whos-coming-therapy-interracial-couples.

9. Karis and Killian, *Intercultural Couples*, xviii.

to appropriate approaches within intercultural premarital counseling seems glaring. The discussion in the following chapters addresses how the cultural themes within the relevant literature relates to the research questions of the current study and provides suggestions for therapists working with intercultural premarital couples as well as to the intercultural couples themselves.

Statement of the Problem

In my clinical experience with intercultural couples, I find that most premarital couples tend to look for advice and suggestions about how to work through their decision making process and to better understand their partner. They often find themselves at a loss to address some of the stressors stemming from the culture of their family of origin. Some of them try to make sense of their mate by assuming that this is because of a personality disorder rather than culture. They begin to think, and want to change their partners as if it was a mere temperamental thing, not realizing that the roots of those worldviews are deep and strong. What one experiences as a positive trait in one culture can be considered very negative in another culture and this can lead to misunderstanding and create mistrust and inability to accept the other.

It would thus seem that intercultural couples are even more in need of premarital counseling as they begin their own discernment process. Intercultural couples in my clinical practice go through a myriad of doubts, such as, "Is this worth it?" "Will I/we be able to sail through our marriage or will the cultural differences overwhelm me/us and force me/us to give up?" In the midst of such dilemmas, decision-making seems a very tedious task. Even if they get past the decision making process, there would be still a lot of cultural aspects to address. Many feel that they have tried their best and cannot handle the relationship discord that results from cultural diversity. They think they are now in a situation where professional help can make a significant difference in their relationship.

The growing need for intercultural premarital counseling was realized by professional counselors following the rise in divorce as a means of dealing with marital discord, and the harmful effects that divorce has on individuals, couples, and families.[10] The significance of marital dis-

---

10. Brotherson and Duncan, "Rebinding the Ties That Bind," 459–68. (S. E. Brotherson is a researcher and family life specialist.)

cord was felt so greatly that most states in America require some form of premarital counseling prior to a wedding.[11] For example, in the State of Georgia, it is recommended by law to receive "premarital education" of at least six hours of instruction involving marital issues, that may include but is not limited to topics such as conflict management, communication skills, financial responsibilities, child and parenting responsibilities, and extended family roles. The premarital education is to be completed within twelve months prior to the application for a marriage license and the couple is expected to undergo the premarital education together. Furthermore, it is to be noted that a couple can be married with court order at age sixteen if both parents and legal guardians give their consent.[12] This can be a very tender age for any type of a relationship or marriage, let alone for an intercultural alliance. The couple need to be equipped with insights about the life-changing commitment they are about to make and about the future that they are choosing.

Understanding the Terms:

Interculture

According to Ibanez B. Penas, specialist in semiotics, pragmalinguistics, and American literature, and Carmen López Sáenz, a senior lecturer in philosophy, interculture refers to "support for cross-cultural dialogue and challenging self-segregation tendencies within cultures. Interculturalism involves moving beyond mere passive acceptance of a multicultural fact of multiple cultures effectively existing in a society and instead promotes dialogue and interaction between cultures."[13] Intercultural premarital counseling is gradually but surely moving towards becoming an accepted way to assist couples in establishing a healthy marriage.

Marriage

A healthy marriage for the purpose of this research is defined in the following terms: (1) where both partners recognize that they belong to two different cultures and that there are particular characteristics that are unique to them; (2) the couple should be willing and able to make necessary changes that are best suited for their growth and nurture, both

---

11. Murray, "Professional Responses to Government-Endorsed Premarital Counseling," 53–67. (C. E. Murray is a mental health professional.)

12. US Marriage Laws: https://theamm.org/marriagelaws/georgia; see also /http://www.USmarriagelaws.com/search/united_states/georgia/.

13. Penas and López Sáenz, *Interculturalism*, 15.

individually and relationally; (3) it is for the couple to come to a rising awareness that, while some cultural features need to be allowed to stay and be respected, some cultural features need to be subjected to modification or negotiation, to maintain the well-being of the relationship. Brenda Lane Richardson, an American journalist and active public speaker, offers intercultural couples this very positive outlook that "multicultural relationships, though challenging, can be rich, vibrant, and full."[14]

Culture

Sociologists have broadly defined culture as a human characteristic that uniquely encompasses an individual's life from birth to death. A particular culture consists of a way of life of individuals and groups of individuals with the same or similar language/dialect, social mores, customs and traditions, religion, religious rituals and beliefs, festivals and observances, ways of being in the world, worldview, decision-making, problem-solving, familial bonds and ties, music, arts, literature, dress, food habits, and many other things. Distinguished African scholar and pastoral theologian Emmanuel Lartey defines culture as:

> Culture of a group of persons is the particular and distinctive way of life of the group. This includes ideas, values and meaning embodies in institutions and practices, in forms of social relationship, in systems of beliefs, in mores and customs, in the way objects are used and physical life organized.[15]

It is to be noted that many, who believe in culturally specific treatment, point to differing standards across cultures for what is deemed normal and what is psychopathological. For example, in some cultures, actions such as worship or deep respect of elders are considered normal but in some other cultures it may be considered irrelevant. Those who believe in culturally appropriate therapy, contend that these practices and behaviors need to be accepted as relevant in their cultures and that what is necessary is to work towards finding a middle ground if the partner is from another culture. However, neither of them should be judged from the other's perspective. Those that support cultural specificity also point to the problem of power in defining what is normal or pathological.

---

14. Richardson, *Guess Who's Coming for Dinner*, 23.
15. Lartey, *In Living Color*, 34.

Statement of Purpose

In my clinical practice thus far, I have observed that certain deeply integrated and communal family systems belong to a particular culture, wherein they do things together, make decisions together, and each one seems to be intricately bound with the other. Terms like "enmeshment" and "differentiation" seem like alien concepts to some because enmeshment or communal bonding is the norm that they are quite comfortable with. We might miss these nuances and become stereotypical in our approach and consider such bonding as backward or irrelevant if we are not culturally sensitive. In such cases, marriage can easily fall apart. However, if some work on culture is done and both are able to respect culture then there is a possibility of working out these differences in ways that are mutually enriching to both.

I believe that therapists need to take this concern seriously if they wish to improve the quality of their work with their clients from different cultural backgrounds. It is important to investigate individual cultures and the impact of each culture on individuals and couples throughout their life. This study on intercultural premarital couples counseling seeks to investigate how different approaches can assist in determining ways that cultural aspects can be addressed within intercultural premarital counseling. Following are the issues that this study seeks to explore in order to help counseling:

Issues and Challenges

1. Intercultural premarital couples' insights about their own respective cultures and cultural upbringing are needed to enable and enrich mutual respect and relationship. Counseling to be made more culturally relevant in terms of therapeutic approaches in dealing with intercultural marital issues and concerns.

2. Suitable and appropriate techniques, theories, dynamics, or approaches that work best to be chosen in premarital couples counseling.

3. Suggestions/recommendations for exploring and understanding cultural diversity insights need to be provided to faith leaders,

therapists who deal with clients seeking intercultural premarital couples counseling.
4. New themes that emerge for future research with intercultural premarital couples counseling need to be explored.

Research Questions

1. What are intercultural premarital couples' insights about their own respective cultures and cultural upbringing? What has stayed with them and what shapes them as individuals and as potential mates?
2. What aspects of culture are important for sustaining and thriving in a given relationship?
3. How can intercultural premarital couples counseling be made more culturally relevant in terms of therapeutic approaches in dealing with intercultural marital issues and concerns?
4. What techniques, theories, dynamics, or approaches work best in premarital couples counseling?
5. What suggestions/recommendations for exploring and understanding cultural diversity insights can be provided to faith leaders, therapists who deal with clients seeking intercultural premarital couples counseling?
6. What themes emerge for future research with intercultural premarital couples counseling?

Sub Questions

1. Since each culture is different, would one cultural therapy be a good fit for the other?
2. How does one discern what works best for what culture?
3. What is it that helps make a connection between the client and the therapist knowing that at face value there may be three different cultures and many subcultures present in the therapy room? What does it take to sustain the therapy in the face of this cultural mix?

4. Is homogamy or the idea of sameness in culture required to sustain a relationship? Or, can acceptable sameness in terms of worldview, likes and dislikes, hobbies, value system, and ideologies be equally satisfying?
5. How do couples resolve conflict or difference of opinion? Do they always blame culture, upbringing, or personality?
6. Do clients prefer individual counseling or dyadic?
7. Do they feel free to discuss their innermost feelings in front of their partners?
8. How and when do couples feel ready to commit to marriage?
9. How much time is typically required for intercultural counseling?

Overview of Methodology

Selection of Samples

For the purpose of this study on intercultural premarital couples counseling, I selected four intercultural couples to provide their perceptions about their understanding of their own culture and how it plays out in their day-to-day life. I wanted to discover what therapeutic approaches were beneficial to couples in their own discernment process and recommend what areas can be improved. Two of these couples were recently married, one had been married for a period of eight years, and one couple was in their premarital stage of counseling. All four of these couples had received a minimum of ten to twelve sessions and a maximum of fifty sessions of premarital counseling, except for the one married couple of eight years who had received only four sessions of premarital counseling.

Therapists

My intent was to work with at least three therapists who were engaged in intercultural counseling for over a year, however, despite my best efforts I was unable to find such therapists. As such I had to be content with peer debriefing with three therapists who were interested in intercultural premarital couples counseling.

Approach

I primarily used cultural focus to formulate my questions and also briefly employed a narrative approach in interviewing, to analyze couples' stories around their particular culture and marriage. I looked for major themes in their narrative related to their relationship, marriage, family and social ties, raising intercultural and biracial children, communication and listening skills, problem-solving or conflict management, financial responsibilities and planning, child and parenting responsibilities, and extended family roles and other related issues and concerns.

I also focused on discovering premarital counseling approaches that are effective in participant couples moving forward to marriage and to sustaining their marriage.

Rationale and Significance

Intercultural premarital couples counseling, whenever undertaken, is carried out by many different professionals, including clergy (pastors, *imams* (Muslim priests) and *pujaris* (Hindu priests), chaplains, faith leaders, spirituals directors, clinicians, teachers, and paraprofessionals. Studies in premarital counseling have shown that clergy were found to provide the majority of premarital counseling. However, clergy members have little training in intercultural premarital counseling and also provide services for the least amount of time.[16] On average, the maximum duration for a premarital couple's counseling services provided by a clergy is about four to five hours, whereas premarital couples counseling services provided by a therapist or a counselor can extend from approximately two to thirty hours. There is a need to extend the hours for intercultural premarital counseling as there are relatively more issues and concerns that need to be addressed as compared to same-culture counseling.

Therefore, the question arises as to how therapists, paraprofessionals, and leaders in the faith community can be helped to become more culturally sensitive and relevant in their task so as to offer effective counseling services to intercultural premarital couples. The first significance of this study then is the better understanding of how the insight of their own culture varies among intercultural couples. Moreover, this study develops an understanding of how intercultural premarital counseling can be made more responsive to culture.

16. Silliman and Schumm, "Improving Practice in Marriage Preparation," 23–43.

For the purpose of this study on intercultural premarital couples counseling, cultural background is understood as being "profoundly influenced by social class, religion, migration, geography, gender oppression and racism, as well as by family dynamics."[17] Attention to culture is seen as an approach needed in order to assist therapists in understanding the impact of culture and related topics to discuss within intercultural premarital counseling. Additionally, culture encompasses customs, race, geographic area, traditions, food, rituals, language, shared values, family of origin, and ethnicity. Another aspect of the significance of the study lies in ascertaining how aspects of culture impact one's worldview thereby impacting one's expectations of one's partner and the relationship. The study seeks to provide an understanding to therapists and others about the importance of considering culture and cultural approaches within intercultural premarital counseling based on intercultural premarital couples' wants and needs and thereby to suggest recommendations for future intercultural premarital couples counseling.

Role and Subjectivity of the Researcher

It is very true that biases of the author could impact the findings and interpretations of the research. Renowned American family therapist, Director of Family Institute and writer McGoldrick encourages therapists and researchers to become more culturally competent by questioning and exploring the values and the cultural identities they possess. She also persuades therapists to incorporate multicultural understanding into their theories and therapies so that clients who are not of the dominant culture will not feel lost, misplaced or mystified.[18] In the following section, I take a closer look at my own aspects of culture and how they relate to the current study.

On a Personal Note:

There are several factors contributing to the cultural values that I hold today. For the purpose of this study, I have narrowed the explanation of my cultural background to those surrounding my beliefs and values regarding marriage and diversity. I grew up in a city that emphasized community, culture, language and faith diversity, participating with my

---

17. McGoldrick, "Culture," 240.
18. McGoldrick et al., *Ethnicity and Family Therapy*, 4.

neighbors and celebrating multi-faith festivals. These beliefs compelled my aspiration to help others within my career and personal life. Some of the values and customs that I carry from my family background include eating together at the dinner table, sharing holidays with extended family members, and holding the commitment of marriage to a high but healthy standard.

The community in which I grew up consisted of middle- and upper-class multi-faith neighbors with college-level education. My friends were from Muslim, Hindu, Sikh, and Zoroastrian faith. Even though we were all Indians, culturally we were very different. The community I lived in had come to India from Pakistan after the 1947 partition and Indian Independence. They were refugees but were given hospitality in India. When I was five years old we moved to this neighborhood as my mother wanted to open a school in that locality. Apparently we were the only Christian family in my community. We too felt displaced as we also had recently moved from the safe confines of a "Christian mission compound" to a totally new place with people of other faiths. My friends, growing up, were girls and families of other faiths particularly of Hindu religion. I grew up participating in their festivals and even going to their places of worship and participating in most religious functions in homes and in the community. I was eager to learn from them as much as they were eager to learn from me. As my mother ran a school in the community, that gave me more access to the homes of my peers and other children studying in the school. All the teachers in the school were from different faith traditions and I was privy to their homes and rite-of-passage celebrations as well as to their weddings. I also had several aunts and first cousins who married into other cultures or other faith traditions and this added another variation in the diversity of my understanding and experience. On a more personal note, I hail from North India and my mother tongue is Hindi. My husband hails from South India and his mother tongue is Kannada. Our common language at home is English. My husband and I are from different cultural backgrounds with diverse food habits, music, traditions, and dress. We have worked hard to learn and appreciate each other's cultural biases and differences and it is a constant work in progress. Through this exploration of varying cultures, I have been exposed to a myriad of diversity. I have experienced much stress at times as it meant stepping out of the comfort of my own native culture and relating to other cultures, which at times seemed very strange and did not seem to make any sense to me. Understanding and appreciating other cultures is a journey that I have undertaken all through my life and I know will continue for the rest of my life. As a result, my views have been broadened. I have learned that it is important to be true to my own culture and relate to other cultures with respect and integrity.

My interest in becoming a marriage and family therapist began as I was engaged in clinical pastoral education while serving as a chaplain at one of the hospitals in the United States. I began to meet patients who were married to persons from another culture, race, religion, ethnicity, and or country. I was able to spend time with my patients and several of them gave me the opportunity to listen to their marital/relationship narratives and learn of their relationship adjustments. I also came across single clients who were contemplating marrying someone from another culture. This work experience has been a learning process that has opened my eyes to challenging life events that have impacted individuals and families.

One emphasis within my Masters of Theology training both in India and at Candler was on understanding the effects of culture and ethnicity both clinically and in everyday life. I felt compelled to understand this impact in greater detail. As an immigrant for fifteen years in this country I have met many intercultural couples who are either seeking answers or struggling to make sense of their parents' opposition to their intercultural partner or those who are already married, trying to balance cultural diversity and live in peace with each other. Other married couples are learning to face the challenges of bringing up biracial children in a society that is biased racially. It has opened my eyes to privileges, roles, biases, and discrimination that occur on individual, dyadic, and societal levels. My training in diversity has led to my understanding of how important culture can be within intimate relationships. For this reason, I believe that intercultural premarital counseling should address the influences of culture on a couple.

I believe that marriage is a significant commitment that two people make with one another, and this commitment needs to be fostered through education, love, and understanding. This was the case for me and my husband, young and in love, not understanding the intricacies of marriage let alone intercultural marriage. This misunderstanding caused a great deal of hurt within our relationship. Even though my husband and I both went through premarital counseling it was through a psychiatrist who was also a clergy and counselor at our church. He used a more technical approach and made us fill some forms and tabulated it and showed us the results. According to the data, he said that we were mostly compatible. That's all the premarital counseling that we received. We were left to figure out for ourselves where we were in this relationship and how to sustain it. To say the least, it has not been an easy journey and over the last thirty-five years we have worked hard to understand the cultural nuances that shape and make our life. As a result, I believe that all couples should partake in intercultural premarital counseling with a trained professional who understands the complexity of couple's issues. Understanding marriage from culturally diverse perspectives is crucial for therapists and intercultural premarital couples.

I believe diversity issues, especially culture, should be addressed within intercultural premarital counseling. Very often clinicians fall short of understanding the impact of culture on couples. And couples do not recognize the ways that culture has impacted their own lives. This can have a detrimental effect for couples' relationship in future. Counseling professor Zagelbaum and licensed psychologist Carlson note that global economic and political concerns are causing hundreds and thousands of people to relocate from the confines of their own comfortable worlds to alien countries. They are relocating in search of better financial opportunities and higher quality of life. According to Zagelbaum and Carlson, "The competent therapist is not only aware of these concerns but also acts and applies this awareness to the work and clientele that he or she encounters."[19] As such, this study seeks to explore gaps in the literature by analyzing people's perspectives on intercultural premarital counseling who are from varying cultural backgrounds.

Prior to each interview for this study, I briefly shared about my background (i.e., being from India, living here for the past fourteen years, education, work, and my own intercultural marriage) and my current biases (i.e., about the importance of intercultural premarital counseling).

Research Assumptions

Culture

The therapist needs to look into the complex ways culture shapes the experiences of "couplehood"(a harmonious match between two partners in a relationship),[20] with the awareness that cultures are not static entities;

19. Zagelbaum and Carlson, *Working with Immigrant Families*, 18.
20. http://www.urbandictionary.com/define.php?term=Couplehood.

they are always in a flux, as are individual members of these cultures. Associate professor Shibusawa suggests that, for any same-culture couple, therapists need to take into account "the history of the relationship, the move as a possible crisis, family life cycle stages, conflicts over intimacy, power dynamics, and each partner's goals for therapy despite offering foci based on their theoretical orientation."[21]

It is not just the couples or the partners, or the therapist but also the family members who are at different levels of acculturation and or different stages of development. Shibusawa further states that it is important for therapists to note that, cultures do not remain constant. They are forever changing. It is important for intercultural clinicians to understand that no matter the level of acculturation in the country of adoption it is very likely that both the clinician and the client maybe at two different levels in their understanding of their worldview.[22] Shibusawa states that it is difficult for Asian clinicians to do full justice to couples as the clinical theories about functional marriages and "couplehood" are based on Western assumptions and values.[23] A son or daughter may consider fulfilling their parents' dream and for him or her that may be the most ideal thing to do, however, this according to a Western perspective may be an example of "enmeshment" or lack of individuation. Thus there is a need for bicultural and bilingual therapists.[24]

Research assumptions for this current research on intercultural premarital couples counseling were:

1. That there are very few, if any, documented theoretical approach(es) for intercultural premarital couples counseling.
2. That most therapists, both White and non-White, are not engaged in intercultural premarital couples counseling and so lack firsthand experience and thus shy away from accepting such clients or that clients themselves are reluctant to go to therapists who do not show signs of multicultural understanding.
3. That most therapists, both White and non-White, do not have an in-depth exposure to people from other cultures and so assume that

---

21. Shibusawa, "Interracial Asian Couples," 378–88.
22. Shibusawa, "Interracial Asian Couples," 384.
23. Shibusawa, "Interracial Asian Couples," 384.
24. Shibusawa, "Interracial Asian Couples," 384.

they are all the same and so continue with the application of Western theoretical framework.

4. That there are effective psychotherapy approaches that are pertinent to intercultural premarital couples counseling which this research will bring to light.

Research Limitations

1. This research on intercultural premarital couples counseling initially set out to examine at least eight couples, four couples who were currently in premarital counseling and four who were now married but previously received premarital counseling. However, I was unable to find eight couples and had to select the four couples that responded.

2. I also wanted to interview three therapists currently engaged in intercultural premarital couples counseling with at least one-year experience. Despite my best efforts I was unable to find a therapist who had counseled intercultural couples.

3. The research was limited to participants currently living in Georgia only.

4. The participants had to be well-versed in written and spoken English.

5. No particular limitation was set for a given ethnicity or cultural background. The research had to be left open as the researcher was unsure of who will respond to the request to participate in the research. As a result, the research content turned out to be more general than specific.

6. The current research does not seek to analyze any particular theory or theorist or programs but seeks to examine integrated approaches that may be helpful in intercultural premarital couples counseling.

Organization of the Research

This research seeks to aid therapists in understanding the needs of counseling for intercultural premarital couples and provide an initial rubric on which therapists can further enhance and apply strategies that will benefit intercultural premarital couples.

Chapter 1 provides an overview of what to expect from the study and how the researcher has arrived at her conclusions and recommendations for future therapists. The chapter includes the problem statement, statement of purpose, research questions and, sub questions, overview of methodology, rationale and significance, role of the researcher, research assumptions, and organization of the dissertation.

Chapter 2 offers a theological reflection on intercultural premarital couples counseling. It looks into pastoral theological methodology in general and the correlation methodology in particular and explores implications of bridging the gap between intercultural and interfaith marriages within and outside the church. This chapter also looks at the theoretical basis for therapists or faith leaders as intercultural couple counselors. It offers responses to the following questions: What characteristics are required in therapists or caregivers to be engaged in intercultural counseling? What are the ways in which one can understand the significance and relevance of this topic in the current geo-political, cultural scenario wherein the world is becoming a "global village"?

Chapter 3 takes a deeper look into the clinical literature providing an integrated conceptual and theoretical framework for therapists and other caregivers who work with intercultural premarital couples counseling.

Chapter 4 focuses on the methodology of the research and looks into the following: rationale for research approach, research setting/context, research sample and data sources, data collection methods, data analysis methods, software used for data analysis, issues of trustworthiness, and limitations of the research.

Chapter 5 describes the findings of this research on intercultural premarital couples counseling.

Chapter 6 gives an analysis of data and reflection upon the data in the light of the literature reviewed.

Chapter 7 provides the conclusion. It makes recommendations to caregivers and therapists as well as some pointers to the intercultural couples themselves. It also offers suggestions for further research.

CHAPTER II

A Pastoral Theological Framework for Intercultural Premarital Couples Counseling

Introduction

AMERICA FEELS LIKE A miniature world, a global village with millions of immigrants descending on its soil from all around the globe. In such a world it is to be expected that the phenomenon of intercultural marriages would be on the increase. There may be a tendency among faith community leaders and pastoral caregivers to shy away from acknowledging the reality of intercultural marriage and the unique challenges it poses. I believe that there needs to be pastoral theological reflections on intercultural marriage and the development of pastoral care practice that addresses the challenges. As a pastoral theologian, it is important for me to take what I learn from those who have experienced it firsthand to the centers of faith and other social and cultural platforms. We need to foster this into a movement of public learning because economic or political issues or even social issues such as interculturalism, immigration, interracial, and interfaith marriages that concern us as human beings are to be voiced and worked on openly in the public arena.

Using culture as a lens, this chapter will lay out a pastoral theological framework and an integrated theoretical framework for intercultural premarital counseling. Much organized work is already going on to help immigrants adjust to their new adopted country, however, as pastoral counselors how can we better prepare ourselves for the task of providing sustainable psychological assistance? What is the most ethical thing for me to do? How much and how far are we willing to journey with the immigrants in their wilderness experience so as to help them reach some level of sanity and comfort?

Pastoral Theological Perspective on Marriage

As a pastoral counselor belonging to the Christian faith tradition, I do believe in marriage as a divine institution that should be respected and cherished. The book of Genesis records the establishing of the marriage covenant between Adam and Eve. The scripture says, "Therefore a man leaves his father and his mother and clings to his wife, and they become one flesh."[1] These are two distinct persons coming together as one. There is a union, and that union is based on commitment to make it work. The nature of this union is in some ways similar to the union that Jesus referred to when he said, "The Father and I are one."[2] Marriage is a covenant relationship and it provides a glimpse of the eternal Triune God. This involves a commitment to one's mate and the maintenance of trust and fidelity. The terms *commitment* and *covenant* are very significant. These concepts originate in God—who God is and how God relates to humans. God is a covenant-keeping God. God is faithful and God promises to be with us forever. God does not break God's covenant and forsake us. The character of God is pure love and fairness in all God's dealings. Likewise, apostle Paul admonishes us, "In the same way, husbands should love their wives as they do their own bodies. He who loves his wife loves himself."[3] New Testament scholar Johnson and Christian theologian Jordan identify five themes or commitments in marriage namely fidelity (sexual exclusivity), reproduction (having and raising children), mutual self-giving (mutual exchange of ownership), self-control (chastity) and social order (well-regulated marriage for a stable society).[4] I also believe in equality and mutual submission among both partners, "Be subject to one another out of reverence for Christ."[5] Witte et al., practical theologian and leading scholar of marriage in America, utilizes Don Browning's term "equal-regard" to describe a relationship between husband and wife

1. Gen 2:4 NRSV.
2. John 10:30 NRSV.
3. Eph 5:25–28 NRSV.
4. Johnson and Jordan, "Uneasy Embodiment," 86–88.
5. Eph 5:21–33 NRSV.

as characterized by mutual respect, affection, practical assistance and justice—a relationship that values and aids the self and the other with equal seriousness.[6]

A committed marital relationship is built into the nature of reality and serves several important functions. Distinguished American Practical theologian, Browning describes marriage as a multidimensional reality and claims marriage as a natural institution that fulfills affective, sexual, and procreative purposes and a contractual institution of two consenting adults contributing to the public welfare, as well as a religious institution with covenantal or even sacramental significance.[7]

This study on intercultural premarital couples counseling is important to me because marriage itself is of value to me. Family life and family values are important to me, mates and children and their happiness are important to me. Infidelity, mistrust, disrespect of the other, breakup, divorce and other aspects of life are painful experiences that often lead to sadness, loneliness and depression. Thus, I do believe in marital monogamy, fidelity, and equality that stems from my Christian faith.

Pastoral Theological Perspective on Intercultural Marriage

In today's context of America as a melting pot of many different races, cultures, languages, and worldviews it is becoming commonplace to find intercultural couples all around us. Faith communities are yet to take seriously into consideration this unique phenomenon in planning and executing their mission and ministry. Often the tendency in faith communities is to take note of the differences or diversity that intercultural couples are faced with but fail to understand and embrace the differences and facilitate transformation. Diversity in cultures, when disrespected or not addressed with understanding and care, and this can result in discord and dissension among couples. Culture can play a very powerful role in keeping persons restricted to their beliefs and practices and cause them to resist any changes. Thus, there is the experience of struggle and pain when couples who are from two different cultures with fixed beliefs and practices try to relate to each other. American Christian psychotherapist and pastoral theologian, Brian Grant points out how the rigidity of our

---

6. Witte et al., *Equal-Regard Family and Its Friendly Critics*, ix.
7. Browning, *Fundamental Practical Theology*, 207.

thoughts and actions keep us bound and that "the more tightly we restrict ourselves to any set of patterns, the more likely we are to feel the distress of psychological symptoms, physical discomfort or illness, and relational sterility."[8] Browning et al.[9] and Bidwell and Marshall[10] claim that all care has spiritual dimensions and when caregivers bring in their allegiance to their spiritual traditions and to particular sacred texts, values, worldviews and spiritual practices their care can be spiritually integrative.

The experience of distress or pain can motivate couples to seek healing and wholeness. This is where therapy can give them hope. Both pain and hope work together to bring to the surface the memory of the reason that caused them pain. This awareness can be either liberating or binding. How one responds to it can either keep one bound with the pain or help one identify the resources to find freedom from the past and experience freedom from chronic emotional pain.

Premarital intercultural, and more so interfaith couples, are faced with the challenge to keep the lines of communication open between them about their culture and belief system. Differences in faith issues can be much more difficult to bridge than differences in culture. The willingness to bring into the open long-held and cherished belief systems and enter into an honest and non-judgmental dialogue with one's partner is indispensable in building bridges. Grant rightly points out that the initial opening of the seal of the unconscious in people is indeed a gift of God, even in the midst of pain. Grant believes that memory is a vehicle for the grace of God. He believes, "God wills human beings and communities to be in constant dialogue with an orienting narrative, connecting them into history and describing a trajectory into the future."[11]

Interfaith and intercultural dialogue has the potential of helping one get a better understanding and appreciation of one's religious beliefs and practices and also to better understand and appreciate the partner's beliefs and practices. As a Christian pastoral theologian, it is imperative for me and others engaged in pastoral counseling, to become facilitators of such a dialogue and bring people together in harmonious relationships. Bidwell and Marshall aptly describe this in the following words:

---

8. Grant, *Theology for Pastoral Psychotherapy*, 92.
9. Browning et al., *From Culture Wars to Common Ground*, 2.
10. Bidwell and Marshall, *Empowering Couples*, 5, 6.
11. Bidwell and Marshall, *Empowering Couples*, 94.

Simply by talking in a different way than the usual relational partners, talking about different things, the therapist creates a different environment, which increases the chances of a different response. As such the therapist performs a prophetic function, regardless of that person's skill, theoretical base, or personal style.[12]

The therapist helps each one to remain true to his or her own belief system even as each one seeks to embrace the belief system of the other. The relationship between the therapist and the client is vital in providing the safety and the security to address these conflicting issues. The therapeutic space becomes a sacred and a safe space in which these personal and meaningful issues can be opened up. "God best uses the therapist as vehicle when the therapist conveys that this is a special place, and that we are together in a different way, for a different purpose, than we could be in any other context."[13] This is an important aspect for the therapist to acknowledge. The therapist provides the space for the client to remember his/her own faith and belief system, to know that God loves him/her and supports his/her decision. Reflecting theologically, I prefer to adopt the perspective that the awareness and experience of hope, while engaged in the therapy process, is a grace and gift of God to help sustain in the growth of the client. This growth process is not just for the client but also for me as a therapist. It is by the divine initiative that I have been placed as a therapist in the community of love and trust to grow alongside my client. I experience within myself safety and security as a result of my understanding of the role of God in the therapy process. Internally, I consider it a divinely created opportunity for me as a therapist to play a vital role in transferring to them the safety and security that I am experiencing. In this process, I become a safe container myself, surrounded by the divine love that is unconditional and eternal that wants the best for my life and for the client.

The context of counseling intercultural couples, including interfaith couples, demands an approach where the culture and faith of each one, including that of the therapist, is equally respected and affirmed with a non-judgmental attitude. It is the context in which cultures are called to intermingle and support each other and not in any way minimize each other. Professor of religion, Anselm Min uses the phrase "solidarity of

---

12. Bidwell and Marshall, *Empowering Couples*, 94.
13. Bidwell and Marshall, *Empowering Couples*, 98.

others,"[14] where all are for others and to one another, and there is no privileged perspective, that we as others to one another are equally responsible for each other and that all are subjects, not objects. He joins Levinas in asserting that solidarity with others does not negate and exclude others who are marginalized because they have been reduced to a system of identity. Min believes that solidarity with others has been the very essence of Christian faith.[15] The Trinitarian understanding of God is a community, a solidarity of three persons, truly different as persons yet truly united as divine. This is a very important model, a community of three, equality within diversity. To practice solidarity of others is to live the tension between two poles, without attempting to abolish either, between solidarity and otherness. It is not necessary to either be in complete agreement with the other or even to be fully accepting of the other but to be in a place of transcending the difference so as to find new ways of knowing and becoming.[16]

In my practice and also in my general observation, I have noticed that many of the partners in intercultural relationships/marriages are second-generation immigrants. In some ways, second-generation immigrants, along with all the recent immigrants to the United States, can be viewed as strangers. And so there is the opportunity to fulfill the biblical mandate to extend hospitality to the stranger. The practice of "solidarity with others" becomes absolutely essential in providing authentic hospitality. In Scripture, the stranger is often characterized by the condition of vulnerability. Their vulnerability reminds us of our own dependence on the kindness of God and instructs us to act towards the stranger as God has acted towards us.[17] The ethical responsibility of extending hospitality to the stranger is a key requirement of faithfulness to the Christian faith.

In welcoming the stranger, the people of God are required to establish justice on their behalf. Given the vulnerability of undocumented migrants in the United States, the role of churches advocating for the stranger is a crucial matter of justice and a corporate expression of our faith. Political advocacy is a legitimate aspect of the mission of the church for it affirms the human dignity of migrants and seeks to ensure their equal access to economic, social, and political resources. Justice for the

14. Min, *Solidarity of Others*, 3.
15. Min, *Solidarity of Others*, 83.
16. Min, *Solidarity of Others*, 86.
17. http://www.nationalcouncilofchurches.US/common-witness/2008/immigration.php.

stranger means that those who contribute to our communities should be given opportunities for full membership in these communities. This teaching is imperative for churches and for places of worship in general and homes and families in particular, for only then will intercultural couples be willing to reach out to faith leaders and feel accepted by their family members and find support and encouragement.

The church is faced with an increasing challenge to work towards change and inclusiveness in order to provide pastoral care for all persons who may be suffering in their soul and need healing and wholeness. In order to be successful in addressing this challenge the church needs to embrace a new paradigm in pastoral care that is truly liberative and transformative. Lartey has provided us with a critical review of the pastoral care paradigms of the past and has found that they have tended to be colored by patriarchy, hierarchy, power and privilege, authoritarianism and individualism. In the revised approach that Lartey proposes, pastoral care is viewed as social action and it engages the voice of Latin American liberationist Leonardo and Clodovis Boff to explore the implementation of the same.[18] The new approach is liberative in nature and it addresses the need for spiritual healing and "cure of souls." Lartey quotes Leonardo and Clodovis Boff's words: "It is the theology that sheds the light of the saving world on the reality of injustice so as to inspire the church to struggle for liberation."[19]

Pastoral care of intercultural couples has the responsibility of not only respecting and affirming the uniqueness of each culture but also of recognizing and bringing to awareness the similarities and connectedness that may not be apparent. Lartey writes about four different approaches to Pastoral Care that I think are important for all caregivers to be aware of in a multicultural context. They are: monoculturalism, cross-culturalism, multiculturalism and interculturality.[20]

Firstly, the monoculturalist care basically claims to work in a "color-blind, culture-free way." In other words, stressing the fact that "we are all really the same" or negating the fact that we live in a diverse world with differences that arise from cultural or social background. Thereby, monoculturalist caregivers/therapists assume that the therapeutic frame they choose to work with is suitable and applicable to all human persons.

---

18. Lartey, *In Living Color*, 57, 115–18.
19. Lartey, *In Living Color*, 57–58.
20. Lartey, *In Living Color*, 163–77.

According to Lartey, based on this understanding they hardly ever offer a cultural critique or cultural "fit."[21] It also denies and suppresses cultural expressions that do not appear to conform to this mould. For example, any form of counseling that appears to be directive is shunned and condemned as "advising" or "informing."[22] Often those practicing monoculturalism are blissfully ignorant of its use as culturally violent and coercive.[23] The practitioners continue to insist on privacy, intimacy, confidentiality, developmental psychology, articulate, autonomous, independent and self-directing, which may be true of Western culture but is certainly not true of many other cultures of the world.[24]

Secondly, concerning cross-culturalism in pastoral care, Lartey speaks about pluralism and its generalization. Cross-culturalism recognizes cultural differences and that we are all not the same. However, they stretch it to fact that those who are different from us are totally different from us. According to Lartey, they also believe that the boundaries around groups are fixed, and impenetrable. And they view identity as shared by all within the group, and every member in the group is like everyone else.[25] The disadvantage of this mentality, according to Lartey, is that it creates a "them" and "us" and alienates us from others completely.[26] He further warns us that a very real danger of the cross-cultural approach is the encouragement of division through the essentializing of cultural difference. Essentializing occurs when we make particular characteristics the only real expression of a people.[27]

Thirdly, multiculturalism for pastoral care, according to Lartey, is based on the need for accurate and detailed information to provide the basis for relevant policy and social action and to keep away from stereotyping. Stereotyping, according to him, involves perceiving and treating any particular individual member of a racial or cultural group as bearing the presumed characteristics of that group. Lartey argues that there is a need to approach any client from the communities surveyed, with

---

21. Lartey, *In Living Color*, 164.
22. Lartey, *In Living Color*, 164.
23. Lartey, *In Living Color*, 164.
24. Lartey, *In Living Color*, 165.
25. Lartey, *In Living Color*, 166.
26. Lartey, *In Living Color*, 167.
27. Lartey, *In Living Color*, 168.

the respect, awe, and wonder that all clients deserve.[28] Borrowing from Kluckholn and Murray, Lartey emphasizes that because of our humanity all possess human characteristics ("we are like all others"), as in physical, cognition and psychological capabilities. The cultural ("we are like some others") refers to characteristic ways of knowing, interpreting and valuing the world which we receive through the socialization processes we go through in our social groupings. These include worldviews, values preferences, and interpretive frames, as well as language, customs, and forms of social relationships. The individual ("like no other") or personal indicates that there are characteristics both physical and psychosocial which are unique to individuals.[29]

Fourthly, intercultural pastoral care is based on the maxim, "Every human person is in some respects like all others, like some others and like no other." Intercultural caregivers need to exercise flexibility and creativity in responding to needs as well as in promoting health. Lartey rightly proposes intercultural pastoral care as the most suitable lens for pastoral counseling.[30]

Pastoral Theology and the Correlation Method

Pastoral theology is concerned with the practical application of the study of theology in the context of regular church ministry. Pastoral theology seeks to give practical expression to theology, regards cultural pluralism as both a challenge and an opportunity, and affirms cultural, philosophical, and religious differences as a source for further dialogue and development. This may be achieved through the method of correlation. Correlation methodology assumes that though theology is an internal discourse of Christian identity, it is to be conducted in public.

Dialogical-Making Relevant

The correlative method conceives of theological reflection as occurring via a process of conversation (or "correlation") between Christian revelation and surrounding cultures. Christianity did not spring up in a vacuum. Historically it developed in a particular pluralistic religious context

---

28. Lartey, *In Living Color*, 169–70.
29. Kluckhohn and Murray, *Personality in Nature, Society and Culture*. In Lartey, *In Living Color*, 171–75.
30. Lartey, *In Living Color*, 171–75.

and from its inception its task was and has been to make its norms and theology meaningful and relevant to its faithful disciples. Therefore, to be relevant Christian theology must necessarily continually re-examine itself in the light of the cultural, religious, social, political, and other backgrounds. The assumption here is that a new mixed culture of sorts is emerging in our neighborhoods, places of work, and schools and colleges and a new scenario is unfolding before our very eyes, that of intercultural couples. Should we just close our eyes and ears to this new dynamic or can the church be the beacon bearer for the society creating a voice for the voiceless? This research on intercultural premarital couples counseling seeks to briefly look at the relevance of a revised correlation method for pastoral theology.

Experiential-Building Rapport

As a therapist, the lived experience of my clients is very important to me. Each individual, each family, each culture, and each relationship is unique and has a myriad of overt and covert cultural dynamics that takes many sessions to uncover or name. Building the trust between the client and the therapist is crucial for this openness to occur. In the beginning of my work as a therapist with intercultural couples counseling I saw myself only as a therapist with a client, with little regard for gender, culture, language, color difference, and them as clients, as if these were the only two dynamics present. Gradually, as an Indian American therapist working as a pastoral theologian, sitting with clients from different cultures and different nationalities, I learned more about race, culture, religion, nationality and gender. I was awakened to the need for intercultural sensitivity, of who I was in the room and who they were and where each of us was coming from, what was our objective and what is the groundwork that needed to be done in terms of acceptance, mental embrace, and love for the truth to find space to emerge and therapy to flourish.

Building Trust—Being Correlative

In the light of the above, I acknowledge that there is an urgent need for Christian theology to respond with openness and honesty to the intellectual, political, social and cultural realities of each generation. Elaine Graham et al., citing American feminist scholar and a Catholic theologian Rosemary Radford Ruether, states the belief that the Christian tradition stands in need of a radical corrective through the inclusion of extra-theological voices. It is in the application of the correlation method that Ruether is able to work towards a Christian theology that is relevant to the present context. She argues that the essence of the Christian gospel is equality, human dignity, reconciliation, and justice but the same has been distorted by the andro-centric nature of the Christian doctrine and the structures and practices of the church. She proposes the need for a critique of the points where tradition has misrepresented the spirit of the gospel and then the development of a reconstruction of theology according to emancipatory principles. She argues that all theology derives from human experiences and understanding.[31] In the context of acceptance of the other in interfaith marriage between a Christian and a person of other faith what should be the church's stand? Will the church perform such a blessing within the church or just perform a blessing without the marriage rituals. A refusal of the church to perform such a ritual breaks many a heart, both of the couple as well as the families involved.

Building Confidence-Relationality

In my personal experience of counseling couples, two of the most neglected themes in marriage are "communication" and "relationality." The couples often report that they are experiencing difficulty in the area of communication and relationship leading to lack of intimacy. This understanding gives us a framework to build on premarital counseling so as to re-invent communication and relationality. Additionally, race, class, and gender dynamics play a very significant role in our life today. There is much hatred going on in the world in the name of religion and tradition. Often we read about killings and honor killings in the context of interracial or interethnic and interfaith love affairs or marriages, and it certainly makes us cringe. There is a lack of acceptance of the other. If the church herself will practice discrimination and excommunication, then how can we expect her members to be accepting and embracing others in the family or society? In order to understand humanity's core problem of exclusion, we turn to God for reconciliation that is found in the embrace of God, since we are embraced by God, we are to embrace others. Protestant theologian, Miroslav Volf sets out to explore the root of human identity in order to understand human beings' core problem of

---

31. Ruether, *Sexism and God-Talk*, 19, in Graham et al., *Theological Reflection: Methods*, 163–66.

exclusion. For him, reconciliation is to be found in the embrace of God and so the end result of our knowing God is this that if we are embraced by God, we are to embrace others. Volf recognizes that the main problem of humanity today that has been for centuries is exclusion.[32] We create boundaries between groups, leading to inclusion and exclusion. Oftentimes we are more comfortable with distancing and separation than with coming together and embracing difference. It is time for the church and the religious leaders to shun their piety and dominance and move to a God-like character that God is the God of all cultures and God wants us to embrace all.

Building up Trust—A Cultural Need

The task of theology, according to American Roman Catholic scholar and theologian, David Tracy's critical correlational approach, is to locate itself at the interface between human experience and culture, and Christian truth-claims, for faith and confession precede reason; our thoughts are situated and historically shaped before they become conscious and critical. Tracy envisions theology as a mutually critical dialogue between interpretations of the Christian message and the interpretations of contemporary cultural experiences and practices.[33] So the questions arise as to how do we decide between faith and culture or more specifically Christian faith versus other faiths? How do we proceed to discover what and where is truth in such a situation and are we called to embrace difference even religious difference?

Pastoral theologian James Whitehead and developmental and social psychologist Evelyn Whitehead help us in answering these questions. According to them, theological reflection helps us bring the process of practical decisions of ministry to align with the resources of our Christian faith.[34] "Such a process of theological reflection is problem-centered, transformative and correlational"[35] "and the sources and norms for pastoral action are drawn from three sources of information, namely, Christian tradition, personal and corporate experience and cultural information."[36]

---

32. Volf, *Exclusion and Embrace*, 225.
33. Tracy, *Analogical Imagination*, 64.
34. Whitehead and Whitehead, *Method in Ministry*, 6.
35. Whitehead and Whitehead, *Method in Ministry*, 14.
36. Whitehead and Whitehead, *Method in Ministry*, 1.

Whitehead and Whitehead propose a three-stage method of theological reflection in ministry:[37] Firstly, attending: to seek out the information on a particular pastoral concern that is available in personal experience that links Christian tradition, and cultural sources. Secondly, assertion: to engage the information from these sources in a process of mutual clarification and challenge in order to expand and deepen religious insight and, thirdly, decision: to move from insight through decision to concrete pastoral action. This helps us to correlate our experience of interacting with others and our theological understanding of dialogue as the model that God and Christ have set before us.

Emmanuel Levinas was a Jewish philosopher whose major field of philosophy was that of ethics. His work, in my opinion, has special meaning for building acceptance and caring for all people particularly for and with immigrants or people who are different from me/us. His philosophy about the face-to-face relation refers to a concept in his thought on "human sociality," and "Other," which usually translates the French word *autrui*, meaning "the other person," "someone else," i.e., other than oneself.[38] It is the personal other, the other person, that each of us encounters directly or experiences traces of every day. "Living presence," for Levinas, would imply that the other person is exposed to me and expresses himself or herself simply by being there as an undeniable reality that I cannot reduce to images or ideas in my head. He or she is the stranger who comes to me in my mundane, self-centered existence demanding from me a "Here I am." That challenge includes the "Thou shalt welcome the stranger in thy midst," of Jewish law. Levinas' theory makes sense in that, I am responsible for the Other without knowing that the Other will reciprocate and whether or not Others reciprocate is their affair not mine. According to Levinas, I am subject to the Other without knowing how it will come out. And in this relationship Levinas finds the meaning of being human and of being concerned with justice.[39] Ethical proximity is the most original form of relation, whereby the Other is truly Other and the "I" becomes "me" here for you! Fraternity manifests itself as ethical solidarity. "It is my responsibility before a face looking at me as absolutely foreign that constitutes the original fact of fraternity."[40]

---

37. Whitehead and Whitehead, *Method in Ministry*, 22.
38. Levinas, *Totality and Infinity*, 174.
39. Levinas, *Totality and Infinity*, 213–16.
40. Levinas, *Totality and Infinity*, 215.

Ethical solidarity does not arise from the free initiative of the "I." Even before I make myself responsible for the Other, I am before my knowing and doing already made responsible for the Other. I am already linked with the Other even before I willingly link with the Other. I am involved with the Other before I choose to involve myself with the Other. I am already my brother's keeper even before I ask "Am I my brother's keeper?" Psychotherapy, as we know, has its roots in the face-to-face encounter with the Other. As a matter of fact, psychotherapy has its origins and is sustained by the research with the Other. Emanuel Levinas helps us understand the prime significance and respect for the Other. It is appropriate that we face our clients in therapy. Our clinical practice often calls our clients to look inward and backward but it is for both of us to look faceward. To behold one another for it is in the presence of the Other that we are mutually enriched and enlightened. In this day and age, we are constantly surrounded by the Other and it is important that we take time to reflect on our reality with the Other's lenses. I am intrigued by the simplicity of Levinas' idea that in the human face is found the original ethical code. From a look into the face of the Other we become aware of basic human responsibility and meaning. Thus to become ethical is to affirm the primacy of the Other. Levinas is critical of a society in which people are depersonalized, in which they move around side by side rather than meet face to face. It is this "Face of the Other" that draws me out of my egoism, complacency, and my indifference.

As a pastoral theologian and a pastoral counselor, it is imperative for me to understand this theology of the other because I have both a moral and an ethical responsibility for the other that God places in my life. In clinical practice, this other is my client. Alistair McFadyen, an American systematic theologian and a theological anthropologist, who works on the theme of humanity and what it means to be human, both in theory and practice, points out that individuality is socially structured and that individuals are formed through social processes. This is what forms their identity. According to him, the biblical theme of creation is not about cosmology but about relationship between God and God's creatures.[41] He believes that the divine-human relationship is structured from God's side as a dialogue and human being is intended in this communication to be God's dialogue-partner and this initiative of God is

---

41. McFadyen, *Call to Personhood*, 18.

grace.[42] McFadyen also talks about human beings created in the image of God not just in our internal attributes of reason and consciousness but in our total personhood. This theology is the same for all people regardless of color, race, or religion. He explains that just as the Persons in Trinity receive and maintain their identities in three persons in relation with others, we too need to be relational human beings.[43] This realization, on both ends, will help us to engage in dialogue and well-being for each other. According to McFadyen, "In our social relationships, we become fully centered personal identities through moving beyond ourselves in dialogue with others. Living out the fullness of God's Image involves relation in both dimensions."[44] In this way, we can help individuals who are either stuck or experiencing stunted growth in the development of a healthy identity and self-acceptance. McFadyen iterates that Christ is God's address to us; but from the human side he is the perfect human response to that address. Christ, he says, is the enacting of the image in its fullness. Therefore, he adds that to be fully in God's image, is to make a right response to God and others, is to be conformed to Christ.[45] Thus McFadyen believes that the process of call and response must be considered a moral discourse and therefore the call and response to one another is also loaded with moral content and implication. This leads to one's moral responsibility for one another which in my opinion is similar to Levinas' ethics. I think that the realization of a moral responsibility is essential in enabling us to see our valid contribution in the life of the other. McFadyen asks the question, "Is a person a physical or a social 'thing'?"[46] It is undeniable that social life and communication including speech and hearing requires a body, for body is important in the public recognition of personal identity. This concept is similar to Levinas face-to-face, and is the first tool in personal identification. However, a person is formed not just by having a body but by communication and relation.[47]

Jewish and Christian Scripture is a very integral part of my life as a human being and as a therapist. Scripture teaches me to be a better human being, to be concerned and caring, to be accepting and admiring,

---

42. McFadyen, *Call to Personhood*, 19.
43. McFadyen, *Call to Personhood*, 31.
44. McFadyen, *Call to Personhood*, 45.
45. McFadyen, *Call to Personhood*, 47.
46. McFadyen, *Call to Personhood*, 73.
47. McFadyen, *Call to Personhood*, 78.

to count others better than myself, to be humble and to offer empathy to those in need or seeking counsel in time of need. When I look at the Scripture for answers to accept others I find, "'You shall love your neighbor as yourself.' There is no other commandment greater than these." Or "for I was hungry and you gave me food, I was thirsty and you gave me something to drink, I was a stranger and you welcomed me,"[48] take care of the "wounded Samaritan,"[49] "When an alien resides with you in your land, you shall not oppress the alien. The alien who resides with you shall be to you as the citizen among you; you shall love the alien as yourself, for you were aliens in the land of Egypt: I am the LORD your God."[50] "Thus says the LORD of hosts: Render true judgments, show kindness and mercy to one another; do not oppress the widow, the orphan, the alien, or the poor; and do not devise evil in your hearts against one another."[51] Bless the "Syro-Phoenician woman and her family,"[52] care for the "strangers," "Do not neglect to show hospitality to strangers, for by doing that some have entertained angels without knowing it."[53] Though these verses may not directly apply to intercultural premarital counseling they do give me a framework as a pastoral counselor to offer kindness and hospitality and offer positive regard to all my clients, particularly those who do not have anyone else to whom to turn.

I believe that more often than not, in reality, our assumptions about people under our care do not correspond to the reality that they are experiencing. Sometimes we may think we are doing our best but we may actually be hurting their faith or their sentiments. We must let them help us to know them as they would like to be known. This knowing brings me to the next dynamic.

More than fifty years ago, the approach of Anton Boisen, the father of the Clinical Pastoral Education Movement, was to learn not just from written documents but also from 'living human documents' which was more personal and dynamic. His concept of the client as a "living human

---

48. Matt 25:35 NRSV.
49. Luke 10:25–37 NRSV.
50. Lev 19:33–34 NRSV.
51. Zech 7:9–10 NRSV.
52. Mark 7:25–30 NRSV.
53. Heb 13:2 NRSV.

document"⁵⁴ was enlarged to a concept of "living human web"⁵⁵ by professor of psychology, religion and culture, Bonnie Miller-McLemore. I agree with her when she states, the "living human web" suggests itself as a better term for the appropriate object for investigation, interpretation, and transformation. Public policy issues that determine the health of the human web are as important as issues of individual emotional well-being. Miller-McLemore iterates that a "living human web" cannot simply be read and interpreted like a document. She strongly believes that those within the web who have not yet spoken must speak for themselves such as the underprivileged, the outcast, the underclass and the silenced.⁵⁶ "If knowledge depends upon power, then power must be turned over to the silenced."⁵⁷ This lesson that we must hear voices of the marginalized from within their own contexts is one that pastoral theologians have known all along, but perhaps never articulated in quite this way. We often do not include immigrant women and men as marginalized or voiceless. There is a definite need to realize that they have been silenced for long and need to be heard. Miller-McLemore states that her focus is less on who offers care (clergy or laity) or how care is offered (hierarchically or collaboratively) and more on what care involves today.⁵⁸ She also talks about "thick description," meaning seeking a multilayered analysis of human strife, including detailed experience of readings of the "living human document" which is so helpful in our understanding of the immigrant.⁵⁹ Practical theologian Rick Osmer talking about Miller-McLemore's work of "living human web" adds that, "just as the strands of a spider's web are interconnected, so too are the bonds that link individuals, families, congregations, communities, and larger social systems."⁶⁰ I agree with Miller-McLemore that laity needs help in formulating theory and thereby need the clergy and the academicians, thus it is a living human web where all play a part. I suggest that this web is expanded by including the laity and the immigrants. The immigrants are not mere objects of receiving help for then it would be patronizing, but are those who participate in their

---

54. Dykstra, *Images of Pastoral Care*, 2.
55. Miller-McLemore, "Living Human Web," 16.
56. Miller-McLemore, "Living Human Web," 21.
57. Miller-McLemore, "Living Human Web," 21.
58. Miller-McLemore, "Pastoral Theology as Public Theology," 51.
59. Miller-McLemore, "Living Human Web," 24.
60. Miller-McLemore, "Feminist Theory in Pastoral Theology," 93.

own well-being for they set the agenda and the tone of what help they will receive.

Psychological Theoretical Framework

My theological and ethical reflection as a pastoral theologian has provided me with the understanding that I have a responsibility for the other that God places in my life. This understanding has shaped my work in such a way that I am able to employ clinical practices consistent with my pastoral theological and ethical commitments. As an immigrant therapist I am the "other" and most of my clients are also "other" to me. I have found the work of Heinz Kohut, informing of my relationship with my client as a therapist. Specific concepts in Kohut's work help me to answer the questions: How do I engage in respectful, ethical regard with my clients, that is, empathic and liberative? How might my therapeutic reception of the client facilitate a greater receptivity in the client for the partner who is the other?

One of the ways of understanding a client is through the use of empathy. Generally, empathy can be defined as "the ability to identify with and experience another person's experiences. This is accomplished by suspending one's own frame of reference in order to enter the perceptual and emotional world of the other."[61] Since 1959 Kohut and his followers have transformed the practice of psychoanalysis and psychotherapy by deepening the therapist's empathic attunement to the patient and describing fundamental human needs for healthy development, particularly idealizing, mirroring, and twinship (or "alterego") needs.[62] The Intersubjectivity school of thought, pioneered by Kohut, has empathy as one of its key concepts. Kohut moved away from the prevailing concept of "ego psychology" to "self-psychology" which emphasized a shift from the traditional notions of the therapist as a blank screen or a neutral observer, in favor of an empathic stance that attempted to enter into the patient's own inner experience. This self, including one's sense of self-worth and well-being, can only develop in relationship with others. "Empathy, from Kohut's point of view is not sympathy or warmth, but rather the most effective source of information about the patient, a form of data

---

61. Massey, "Empathy," in Hunter, *Dictionary of Pastoral Care and Counseling*, 354.
62. http://www.selfpsychology.com/whatis.htm.

gathering through vicarious introspection."⁶³ Kohut believed this adoption of an empathic stance was necessitated at least in part by a changing patient population. Kohut developed his theory based on the narcissistic self, wherein the patients cover up their low self-esteem by talking highly about themselves. This may not be necessarily true of all clients, however, it is possible that they may not want to project their failures and shortcomings and therefore may not come out to get help. But who can resist genuine empathy, when realistically clients are struggling with their own worthlessness?

Kohut thus introduced the concepts of "idealizing" and "mirroring" into psychodynamic psychotherapy. Mirroring is not merely a good feedback but involves positive, warm expressions of pride and admiration. Idealizing involves modeling wholesome values and behaviors and tolerating and not deflecting the client's idealization of the therapist. In his first book, *The Analysis of the Self*, "Kohut described the therapist's role as a '*self-object*' for the patient—that is, an object used for the maintenance of a fragile sense of cohesion and equilibrium of the most central, irreducible core of the personality, or 'self.'"⁶⁴ While empathy plays a major role in therapy, Kohut was also aware of the patient's experience of empathic failure by the therapist. This is where tolerance and continuity come into play.

Cooper-White writing about the role of empathy in the therapeutic work states that, "Genuine empathy usually does not mean more activity on the part of the therapist but, rather, more attunement to what is occurring in the transference-countertransference continuum."⁶⁵ She goes on to explain well when she says,

> Empathy works primarily through the medium of the countertransference, as the therapist experiences affects, resonances, fantasies, and images that are drawn from the pool of unconscious material and "shared wisdom" in the intersubjective dynamic of the therapy.⁶⁶

Kohut's concept of healthy narcissism conveys a self that embodies a sense of internal solidarity, personal confidence, and an ability to use

---

63. Kohut, "Introspection, Empathy and Psychoanalysis," 459–83, and Kohut, "Introspection, Empathy, and the Semi-Circle of Mental Health," 395–407.
64. Cooper-White, *Shared Wisdom*, 23.
65. Cooper-White, *Many Voices*, 186.
66. Cooper-White, *Many Voices*, 187.

one's talents to achieve personal goals. Self-psychological theory proposes that healthy self-development proceeds from adequate responsiveness of caregivers to the child's vital emotional needs, including alter-ego needs, idealizing needs, and mirroring needs. As a pastoral counselor my role is to foster healthy self-development in my clients, thus supporting their participation in healthy and meaningful relationships, which evolves their ability to receive the "other." Clinical psychologist Mitchell and psychoanalyst Black writing about Kohut state that "He tried to put himself in his patient's shoes, to understand the experience from the patient's point of view."[67] Kohut described this approach as empathic immersion and vicarious introspection.[68] Through these practices, the therapist empathically receives the "other" in the client, which facilitates the client accepting the other in him or herself as well "others" outside of oneself.

Kohut believed narcissistic clients see the therapist as an extension of themselves and their own subjective experience. He identified three basic types of *self-object* transference that parallel the three childhood *self-object* experience, which he argued could bring about a healthy change in a client.[69] The first is the mirroring transference when the client needs the therapist to affirm and reflect back their experiences both good and bad. In this scenario the client can begin to develop trust in a substantial way. Secondly, idealizing transference when the client regards the therapist as being perfect and feels him/herself to be growing stronger because by virtue of the connection with the therapist. Thirdly, an alter ego or twinship transference when the client feels an essential yearning to be like the therapist, not in terms of external resemblance but in terms of substance or function.

According to Kohut, a central role of the therapist is to take on the role as a "self-object" for the client that is, an object used for the maintenance of a fragile sense of self right at the core of one's inner personality. Often, the intercultural couples that come for therapy are at the end of their rope of patience. They feel helpless and often feel rejected by their lover or partner. The therapist can be a great help by being their *self-object* so that they maintain self-esteem and enough motivation to change things in their life. Idealizing involves modeling wholesome values and

---

67. Mitchell and Black, *Freud and Beyond*, 157.
68. Kohut, "Introspection, Empathy and Psychoanalysis," 459–83.
69. Mitchell and Black, *Freud and Beyond*, 161.

behaviors and tolerating and not deflecting the client's idealization of the therapist.

While empathy plays a major role in therapy, Kohut was also aware of the client's experience of empathic failure by the therapist. This is where tolerance and continuity come into play. The therapist who displays shortcomings and imperfections actually helps to create a realistic relationship where the client is "reborn" and establishes a healthier sense of self that is more cohesive and able to manage disappointment and imperfections.[70] Self-psychology acknowledges our profound dependence on others for developing the self we become, as therapists. In my experience as a clinician, I feel that it is easier to build an empathic regard with my client when I am "more normal" and do not hesitate to share my shortcomings. It helps them relax and this also helps build mutual trust.

Contribution of Kohut's Theory to Intercultural Premarital Counseling

I believe that Kohut's theory can work to ease the stress and sense of loss experienced by immigrants through the healthy understanding of the therapist. I do, however, want to say that using this theory with immigrants does not or should not put those who are providing the care in a superior position, for it needs to be a position of equal regard.

Premarital counseling may lower the risk of divorce. However, marital stressors will always be there. Premarital counseling does help prepare the couple for what is coming and so they are better prepared to face reality. In other words, premarital counseling will not prevent stressors from happening but will give tools to couples to know what to do should they face a trying situation.

It is true that developing a separate self is primary to the overall growth and development of an individual. Much has been written about the need for individuation in psychotherapy wherein the need to develop the "self" is of immense importance in the light of the fact that the "self" is often dwarfed because of the over importance of "others" in the family and or community. When a significant individual or a significant community takes up a lot of space in our heads and is present as an audience to our decisions, behaviors and thoughts, there is interference in the process of individuation. When we have not developed a secure sense of

---

70. Mitchell and Black, *Freud and Beyond*, 161.

self, we feel vulnerable to the judgments, demands, and expectations of others. Allowing ourselves to be loved or to love, can feel like it requires giving ourselves over to the other. This creates a tremendous amount of anxiety in the person so much so that they are unable to develop their full potential as an individual and live in constant fear of being suppressed. Thus, both the individual and the other are constantly in a tug-of-war. There is a constant play of power dynamics, restlessness, and waste of energy. Negative fear can be crippling in itself, thus, for a person to be continuously fearful of the other can be both damaging and degrading. So, how can we so live as to live in peace and harmony with each other?

I believe *I am the change* I am expecting to see in others. I need to exercise empathy with all my clients and understand their culture, their longings, and their brokenness from their perspective without judgment. I am in the room with them with a purpose and I must be aware of their realities and seek to help them in a way that is relevant to their reality. We are in the midst of multiple cultures, ethnicities, races, and mindsets. We cannot ignore the realities of our growing neighborhoods and even our clients. We live and work and have our being in multiplicity and diversity and our task is relational, living together in respectful solidarity in a diverse community is the need of the hour. The concept of building inclusive communities is the key to fulfilling the *agape* love of God for all.

Summary

Most religious practitioners view marriage as a sacred and holy institution between two people for life. Marriage is an intimate relationship between two adult partners who make a loving and binding commitment to each other and is to be held with pride and honor. There are many stressors that every couple encounters in their life's journey, and intercultural couples are no exception. With intercultural couples this stress is often multiplied and partners falter and fail and marriages break. However, it is possible that bringing God into the equation early even at the premarital stage might help the couples in finding motivation to work at their relationship and not quit when the going gets tough.

The therapist holds a key position in intercultural premarital couples counseling. The assumption is that the therapist has a deeper and wider understanding of various cultures and is able to discern the differences or points of contention within the relationship being experienced by the intercultural couples. Putting into practice empathy, as discussed by Kohut, the therapist is able to offer tangible and relevant interventions that can both lead to a better cognitive plus emotional understanding of culture and cultural issues, thereby enabling the premarital couple to resolve their differences and conflicts.

CHAPTER III

Exploring Clinical Literature and Structural Frameworks For Intercultural Premarital Couples Counseling

Introduction

THE CLINICAL AND THEORETICAL literature that is reviewed below provides insights into various aspects of intercultural premarital counseling. Those aspects include structural elements of intercultural premarital counseling with a discussion on the influences of individual and dyadic characteristics of clients, role of culture, delivery of intercultural premarital counseling services, therapy and culture, premarital counseling and culture, and other related issues. The literature demonstrates how it is essential for intercultural premarital counseling providers and caregivers to understand these factors, as they provide guidelines, knowledge, and awareness of the clients' needs. In my experience with intercultural marital couples counseling I have realized that getting married is one thing but sustaining a marriage is quite another. For most part, couples come for premarital counseling because they not only want to get married but they are eager to explore how they can stay married and raise healthy children and happy families.

Review of Literature

Intercultural premarital couples counseling can be defined as a specific type of systemic therapy aimed at assisting couples that are considering marriage. Interventions help improve our understanding of the interactions of the couple that can influence both the quality and the stability of the premarital or marital relationship.[1] Scholarly research in understanding pastoral care and cultural realities in relationships does acknowledge the fact that all relationships are inherently complex. However, dimensions of differences are magnified for intercultural couples and families because they combine more than one distinct cultural reference group, different levels of acculturation, and influences on social location such as family, peers, school, and work.[2] To sustain the relationships of intercultural couples it is important to work towards cultural adjustment that helps foster positive relationship outcomes. This in turn assists in adapting and integrating with others in the areas of cognitive flexibility, improved social competence, acceptance,[3] increased self-awareness, upward social movement and personal growth.[4] There is substantial research on clinical populations that reinforces cultural difference as a source of instability, conflict,[5] or dissatisfaction and mental-emotional impairment for couples.[6] On the contrary, we find much less research evidence on positive traits and behaviors or actions that bring about an opportunity for transformation.[7] Does this mean there is very little room for flourishing in intercultural relationships? There is no denying that intercultural couples face a higher degree of marital discord;[8] and with little or no moral, psychological, emotional, familial and social support they are more prone to failure.[9] Intercultural couples are faced with several stressors that affect them in numerous ways such as familial, social, and national allegiances and worldview, family structures, and patterns of communication, ideals and value systems.[10] They are seeking help and help needs to be given to them. Therefore, premarital counseling for

---

1. Holman et al., "Assumptions and Methods," 29–45.
2. Molina et al., "Cultural Communities," 139–147.
3. Ting-Toomey, *Communicating Across Cultures*, 246.
4. Kim, *Becoming Intercultural*, 169.
5. Cottrell, "Cross-National Marriages," 151–69.
6. Hsu, "Marital Therapy for Intercultural Couples," 225–42.
7. Crippen and Brew, "Intercultural Parenting and the Transcultural Family," 107–15.
8. Crohn, "Intercultural Couples," 295–308.
9. Gurung and Duong, "Mixing and Matching," 639–57.
10. Perel, "Tourist's View of Marriage," 178–204.

intercultural couples whether interracial, interethnic, or interfaith is of utmost importance today.

Culture

Definition and understandings of culture are constantly changing. In American society historically, the need to define or even describe culture was largely minimized.[11] With the advancement in understanding of other cultures, world news, and the opportunity to hear the voices of "other" people, in recent years, American society is gradually being more accepting of persons from other cultures and their worldviews. Culture encompasses many different facets of everyday life. It is the way in which groups of people develop distinct patterns of life and give expressive forms to their social and material experience. The culture of a group of persons is the particular and distinctive way of life of that particular group. This includes ideas, values and meaning embodied in institutions and practices, in systems of belief, in mores and customs, in forms of social relationship, in the way objects are used and physical life is organized.[12] One important consideration is that culture and cultural beliefs are fluid and can change over time.[13] For the purpose of this study culture encompasses customs, traditions, food, ritual, language, shared values, family of origin, and ethnicity. According to Laird, "Culture is an individual and social construction, a constantly evolving and changing set of meanings."[14] The meaning of culture is manifested through customs, beliefs, traditions, values and roles.

In working with intercultural couples with one partner of African American descent, Wimberly's suggestions may be very useful. Professor of pastoral care and counseling Wimberly talks about the model of joining, assessment, and intervening in African American marriages and families. Joining has to do with a therapeutic intervention within a marriage or family and building a relationship in order to allow the therapist to help the couple discover who they uniquely are and to recognize that the key to success is to connect emotionally with those present in the therapeutic session and to demonstrate empathy (attempting to see the world through their eyes). Since religion plays an integral role

---

11. Cornell and Hartmann, *Ethnicity and Race*, 26.
12. Lartey, *In Living Color*, 31.
13. Laird, "Theorizing Cultures," 20–36.
14. Laird, "Theorizing Cultures," 28, 29.

in African American families, it is easier for them to be more comfortable with clergy who have therapeutic skills, therefore, joining with them is relatively easier. Wimberly suggests that generally speaking, African American families respond well to time-limited, child-focused, problem-solving-oriented approaches, and are less likely to be engaged in deeper personal issues related to marital or family difficulties and or issues of family of origin.[15]

Lena Robinson, professor of social policy and social work in the United Kingdom, addresses the issue of racial identity development and its relationship to interethnic communication from a Black perspective.[16] She adopts the argument that Black people go through several stages of racial identity development, and that one's stage of racial identity may have a stronger impact on the communication process than issues of "race" alone. She analyzes the way in which prejudice and stereotypes function as a barrier to effective communication between social and healthcare workers and Black clients. In the therapeutic context this can be true between a therapist and a client as well as between an intercultural couple.

There has been some research in the area of the importance of culture and relevance of dealing with cultural understanding in intercultural premarital counseling. Clinical and psychological family systems theory and practice helps us understand that the family of origin provides the blueprint for a person's understanding of conflict management, relationship interaction, and communication styles and this blueprint influences the worldview held by individuals.[17] When each partner's values regarding aspects of the blueprint do not coincide, or are not understood by the partner, greater levels of conflict and lower relationship satisfaction occur.[18] For example, escalating conflict is likely to occur if the man in the relationship is raised to believe that the man is the head of the household, the breadwinner, and so demands the wife's obedience and submission but the woman is raised to believe that it is expected to be an egalitarian relationship where both share household chores and share in family spending and decision-making, where both trust and practice mutual obedience and nurturing.

---

15. Wimberly, *Counseling African American Marriages and Families*, 64–68.
16. Robinson, *'Race,' Communication and the Caring Professions*.
17. Halford et al., "Best Practice in Couple Relationship," 385–406.
18. Halford et al., "Best Practice in Couple Relationship," 385–406.

Larson emphasized the significance of the cultural context for the individual and the couple. The context in which an individual is brought up has implications for the assumptions, expectations, and belief system, incongruent expectations of roles, rituals, socialization, and communication. In addition, individuals who are brought up in a traditional manner are more prone to be conventional and thus more likely to participate in rituals such as wedding ceremonies, honeymoons, couple rituals that positively correlate with marital satisfaction in one culture, whereas in another culture all this may be frowned upon and replaced with a more modern style of functioning.[19]

Intercultural couples are defined as "the bringing together or the meeting of two different cultural backgrounds into one relationship."[20] Intercultural couples present their own unique dynamics that affect the premarital and marital relationship. It is a well-known fact that culture has a significant influence on an individual and on a couple in their upbringing and personality formation throughout their whole life.[21] Culture also plays an important role in shaping how couples communicate with each other, solve problems, and make meaning together.[22]

Interactional processes between partners are to be taken in together with the influences of the clients' cultural background. Most marriage and family therapists strive to help clients to create and maintain healthy premarital and marital relationships.[23] It is important for therapists to understand the breadth of factors that contribute to functional and stable relationships and marriages, such as individual strengths and vulnerabilities.[24] For the last two decades human services professionals have increasingly been looking for understanding of the impact of culture on marriage[25] as they see an urgent need to discard stereotypical approaches in counseling intercultural couples.

We are at a point in history where change is taking place in every direction. As therapists, we too need to expand our horizon, integrate new perspectives and techniques, and begin to look at a multilevel contextual

19. Larson, "Clinical Update," 36–42.
20. Crippen and Brew, "Intercultural Parenting," 107.
21. Halford et al., "Best Practice," 385–406.
22. Holman et al. "Assumptions and Methods," 29–45.
23. Bradbury and Karney, "Understanding and Altering," 862–79.
24. McGoldrick and Hardy, "Re-Visioning Family Therapy from Multicultural Perspective," 4.
25. Asai and Olson, "Culturally Sensitive Adaptation," 411–26.

model. There is a need to explore culturally-centered approaches in order to assist therapists in understanding the impact of culture within intercultural premarital couples counseling. There is a definite need to develop a cultural psychotherapy that would better serve the foreign and ethnic clients who seek psychotherapy.[26] Family therapist Almeida argues that when cultural competency focuses on the "White" or about White systems of service delivery, or an analysis of the "White therapist," it obscures and or disintegrates the complex personal, social, and political intersect of couples' lives from diverse cultures. She states that, "too frequently, the impact of culture is dangerously misunderstood by therapists, embedded within the treatment systems guided by dominant or White-centric theories."[27] She rightly points out that when "culture" is taken in as an "added on" characteristic, it serves to minimize the full meaning and impact of culture. She talks about the misguided presumption of a White therapist saying, "Those people are just like us (Whites) except for certain idiosyncratic patterns that one needs to keep in mind." Or, "Let's understand how this culture lives their lives." There is no structural power analysis between "their" lives and cultural intersections with mainstream cultural adaptations and lifestyles.[28]

According to social worker, anthropologist, and psychotherapist Seeley, "It is increasingly being realized that universalizing psychotherapeutic models and the therapeutic requirements of culturally diverse psychotherapeutic clients do not make a good fit and what is needed, is culturally enriched approaches to psychological treatment."[29] Since no two people are identical, a universal model fails to pay attention to the functioning of cultural dimensions of human psychology, and they disregard the ways in which significant cultural differences between client and psychotherapist affect the progress and outcomes of psychological treatment for "how do we treat people who describe themselves as having two separate cultural selves?"[30] It is also important to note that, between clients and therapists, when cultural and linguistic backgrounds differ based on different nationalities and ethnicities that they cannot be expected to share culturally shaped worldviews, assumptions, habits or

26. Seeley, *Cultural Psychotherapy*, 9.
27. Almeida, "Couples in the *Desi* Community," 279.
28. Almeida, "Couples in the *Desi* Community," 279.
29. Seeley, *Cultural Psychotherapy*, 9, 10.
30. Seeley, *Cultural Psychotherapy*, 9.

patterns of thought. As a result of their varying histories and conceptual frameworks, clients and therapists are likely to experience difficulties in creating the shared, culturally organized meanings on which successful psychotherapeutic treatments depend.[31] Consequently, I wanted to discover what it is that brings a client and or couple to a particular therapist? What does it take to sustain the therapeutic relationship amidst cultural differences? And also what does it take for two people from two different cultural backgrounds to stay united?

We now know that lack of cultural understanding between the client and the therapist results in premature terminations, mutually uncomprehending and mutually incomprehensible relationships. Evaluating and assessing through Western norms and standards and thereby interpreting clients' culturally normative behaviors may serve to impede achieving Western ideals of selfhood. Often in Eastern cultures, asking clients to reveal intimate personal material or to recount family histories or to express emotional reactions, or else to air interpersonal disputes, can be seen not just as intrusive by the clients but also as a betrayal to parents and elders or the whole family. When a therapist over-pathologizes behaviors that are identified as normative in the client's native culture then he or she can be perceived as subjective and uninformed in his/her understanding.[32] It is clear that the "voices of the clients ought to be given importance in building cultural psychotherapy."[33] This is what this research tries to do—to listen to the voice of the clients and to see what approach works best for them. In my experience with clients I have noted that psychoanalysis does not always work with clients of South Asian origins. Due to their deep roots in respect for elders and parents they find it difficult to reveal secrets of abuse and neglect caused by the above and thereby minimizes the negative impact. They would rather suffer in silence than talk about their parents or relatives which to them amounts to discrediting the family name.

Gottman's research indicates that healthy communication,[34] among intimate partners is a strong predictor of relationship and marital satisfaction.[35] Healthy communication is defined by one's openness with his/

---

31. Seeley, *Cultural Psychotherapy*, 14.
32. Seeley, *Cultural Psychotherapy*, 20.
33. Seeley, *Cultural Psychotherapy*, 21.
34. Gottman, *What Predicts Divorce?*, 131.
35. Gottman et al., "Predicting Marital Happiness and Stability," 5–22.

her partner, the ability to discuss particular issues and behaviors that bother him/her, and request changes without being negative or critical.[36] Homogamy means couples having similar traits and expectations of the marital relationship. Higher levels of homogamy means higher levels of marital satisfaction.[37] Couple traits may include race, ethnicity, age, cultural background, level of education, and socioeconomic status.[38] Needless to say, family of origin plays a very important role in one's behavior and day-to-day functioning or way of life such as gender roles, parenting roles, and household responsibilities that were carried out in the family of origin,[39] for these influence expectations of roles within the current marital relationship.[40] One's cultural background influences how much one is "like" his/her partner. This is often said to help bring about cordiality and togetherness in partners. Consequently, levels of homogamy impact how couples communicate. For example, in some cultures men are often seen as the dominant figure within the relationship and may be expected to financially provide for the family. This expectation may never be communicated verbally as it has been engrained into the individual from observing family and community members. My aim through this research was not only to gain insight into the cultural background of each individual participant but also to delve deeper into their "thick" narrative and flesh out needs and concerns that often get overlooked. Through the use of face-to-face dyadic interviews I was also able to observe how they relate to each other, which culture is more dominant and how they reduce stress by how they manage conflict. Very often one's body language or nonverbal communication speaks louder than one's verbal communication.

There has been an inconsistency in research in showing outcome differences for couples based on length of intercultural premarital counseling and who provides intercultural premarital counseling. Intercultural premarital counseling has been delivered via group and individual counseling settings. Silliman and Schumm reported that couples prefer individual counseling over group settings. Research indicates that couples who receive intercultural premarital counseling four to twelve months

---

36. Nichols, *Family Therapy*, 246.
37. Larson, "Clinical Update," 36–42.
38. Larson, "Clinical Update," 36–42.
39. Holman et al., "Assumptions and Methods," 29–45.
40. Larson, "Clinical Update," 36–42.

prior to their wedding are helped. Each program for counseling varies in length, format, timing, and topics of sessions of intercultural premarital counseling.[41]

This study followed the path of recent literature, in that participants were asked to define culture and how their cultural background may have influenced their insights into marriage and aspects that they believe are important to intercultural premarital counseling. One's comprehension of the world is manifested through one's interactions (e.g., support, feedback, communication, relationships) with others.[42] Within therapy, culture impacts the therapeutic relationship, the process of therapy, and goals.[43] Kennedy et al. state that

> There is growing awareness that although psychology attempts to make timeless and universal claims about human behavior and consciousness, it is rooted in specific social, cultural, and historical circumstances; that although psychology aims to be value free, it is embedded in Western ideals of the individual, of the family, and of the mind; and that although psychology wishes to be the authoritative voice on human behavior and consciousness, it typically studies a narrow segment of the human population.[44]

In order to address the impact that cultural issues can have on varying aspects of mental health and the services provided in a therapeutic setting this study sought to explore ways culture can be addressed within intercultural premarital counseling.

Individual characteristics are defined by historical and personal experiences and take into consideration each partner's relationship history, family of origin structure, physical and mental health, ability to manage stress, emotional readiness, sociability, flexibility, self-esteem, interpersonal skills, conventionality, and context.[45] Relationship history refers to the parental relationship that the couple observed in childhood, adolescence, and the present day. Ineffective stress management is related to lower levels of relationship satisfaction.[46] Several factors such

41. Silliman and Schumm, "Improving Practice," 23–43.
42. Jones, *Family Systems Therapy*, 3.
43. Ponterotto, *Handbook of Multicultural Counseling*, 139.
44. Kennedy et al., "Our Monocultural Science," 996–97.
45. Bodenmann and Shantinath, "Couples Coping Enhancement Training (CCET)," 477–84.
46. Bodenmann and Shantinath, "Couples Coping Enhancement Training

as emotional readiness, sociability, flexibility, self-esteem, reciprocity, interpersonal skills, and conventionality have all been linked to increased relationship satisfaction, and thus reduced levels of stress. Emotional readiness is defined as the individual's willingness to commit to a marriage. Sociability, flexibility, and self-esteem contribute to how individuals relate to one another.[47] Higher levels of these traits create reciprocity among couples, which is correlated with greater levels of relationship satisfaction.[48] Dyadic traits are defined by interactional processes that two people engage in.[49] In intercultural premarital counseling these processes include couple interaction, support, communication styles, interracial challenges, and homogamy which provide the premarital counselor with a better understanding of the couple's patterns.[50]

There has been some support for intercultural premarital counseling within the clinical and social community, however there has not been a sufficient amount of research in explaining the effectiveness of relevant therapeutic approaches for intercultural premarital couples counseling. Relational psychoanalyst Nancy McWilliams believes that the main theme among psychodynamic approaches to helping people is that the more honest we are with ourselves, the better our chances for living a satisfying and useful life. However, that honesty about our own motives does not come easily to us. Therapeutic approaches help us to bring to consciousness what is difficult or painful to see in ourselves, namely: a sense of weakness, vanity, conflict, moral deficit, lust, greed, competition, and aggression.[51] For many decades the ethic of honesty was personified in the image of a therapist who was supposed to have attained high self-awareness through personal analysis and was somehow expected to translate the same achievement to the client. However, in current therapeutic writing the responsibility is mutual. Transference and countertransference are important aspects of intercultural counseling. As the saying goes, a therapist can only take a client where he/she himself/herself has gone. If the therapist is self-aware about his/her own biases and prejudices he/she can help his/her clients reflect on them by naming and

(CCET)," 477–84.
    47. Holman et al., "Assumptions and Methods," 29–45.
    48. Holman et al., "Assumptions and Methods," 29–45.
    49. Holman et al., "Assumptions and Methods," 29–45.
    50. Bodenmann and Shantinath, "Couples Coping," 477–84.
    51. McWilliams, "What Defines a Psychoanalytic Therapy?," 1–26.

acknowledging them and help clients do something about them as well. It is important for the therapist to be culturally relevant to his/her clients. He/she does not have to belong to the same culture but needs to have a cultural mindset that is open and accepting of difference and diversity.

McWilliams comments that, while theorists differ in the task of promoting their favorite paradigms, ordinarily practitioners tend to be more synthetic. She respects the fact that there are numerous effective ways to help people and thus a diversity of perspectives opens possibilities for finding specific effective approaches for specific difficulties. However, alternative approaches do not necessarily shorten the time needed to help people.[52] The "classical" technique in psychotherapy involved Freud's reflection on how he personally had come to conduct treatment and were condensed into a set of "rules" that supervisors handed down to trainees (e.g., "You never answer a patient's question; you explore it" and "Always analyze; never gratify" and "Coming late must be interpreted as resistance" and "You can't tell the patient anything about yourself"). Beginning therapists, according to McWilliams, can feel discouraged and get a sense that, "they are not doing it right" and sometimes they lose clients because they are unwilling to be flexible.[53] Oftentimes, they do address their clients' individual needs with adaptations that are empathic, intuitively sound and effective but then they get anxious whether they can safely reveal the same to their supervisors or classmates; this, she believes, delays their maturation as therapists. She does believe in the time-honored principle that one needs to master a discipline before one seeks to deviate from it. However, she agrees that therapy should be "client-driven rather than rule-driven."[54] This is so true in intercultural counseling. Each culture is different and as revealed in this research one of the participants was upset with his partner because she would always be late and he saw it as a personality issue rather than as cultural. A similar dynamic can play out in the therapeutic environment if the therapist is very time-driven and ends the session exactly at a given time even if they are in the midst of an emotionally tense situation. It is best to give time for the couple to relax a bit and end the counseling session feeling better rather than worse.

---

52. McWilliams, "What Defines a Psychoanalytic Therapy?," 1–26.
53. McWilliams, "What Defines a Psychoanalytic Therapy?," 1–26.
54. McWilliams, "What Defines a Psychoanalytic Therapy?," 1–26.

Waldegrave, while talking about intercultural therapy, suggests that a therapist must make some consideration with regard to the following questions: How does culture dictate the structure of each family? What is the level of each family member's acculturation? What additional cultural considerations must be addressed to be effective and culturally sensitive to the family? What change needs to occur for greater functionality?[55]

Theories are developed to guide us through the therapeutic process. A theory is based upon hypotheses and is supported by evidence. It is mostly concepts and ideas based on research, and provides understanding of human thoughts and behaviors and emotions and even predicts future behavior. According to the American Psychological Association, psychologists generally draw on one or more theories of psychotherapy.[56] Psychotherapeutic theories act as a road map for psychologists. They guide them through the process of understanding clients and their problems and assist them in developing solutions.

Each client is different and has their own set of unique characteristics and needs. We may use one theory or several to help receive the desired result. For example, in working with intercultural couples using Family Systems theory, a look at the genogram of both families is always helpful. It is constructed by the therapist and helps bring out facets that were left uncovered. It looks at past relationships and events and what impact or influence they have had on the individual's current emotional state. A culturally sensitive therapist will be able to look at that and ask questions that will uncover deeper dynamics and nuances that the couple may have failed to take into consideration. The therapist also looks at the style of communication practiced within a particular family, what is functional and what is dysfunctional communication, thereby helping the individual to work on the pattern of communication that will work for them. Communication is often made up of cultural nuances that need to be paid attention to. Also to look into the sibling order of each partner is helpful and may reveal a ton of information about what the sibling order does to the personality, character and behavior of the partner. Any combination of the sibling order within an intercultural couple will have many cultural themes to wrestle with. This is the case also with other theories such as cognitive behavioral therapy, attachment therapy, emotionally focused therapy, psychoanalytic therapy, intersubjective therapy,

55. Waldegrave, "Cultural, Gender and Socioeconomic Contexts," 85–111.
56. http://www.apa.org/topics/therapy/psychotherapy-approaches.aspx.

psychodynamic therapy, and multicultural therapy, to name a few. Each therapy offers a different conceptual framework and steps or guidelines that are helpful to reach a desired result. An approach is a way of dealing with something such as method or methodology, procedure or perspective, tool or technique, access or style or way, factors or framework, system or strategy, tactic, paradigm and manner or means. An approach can be many different things. In other words, a theory is a prediction or an idea about a certain situation but an approach is a practical way of dealing with that situation, or the way we might implement a theory.

Approaches to psychotherapy fall into five broad categories:[57]

Psychoanalysis and psychodynamic therapies

These approaches focus on changing problematic behaviors, feelings, and thoughts by discovering their unconscious meanings and motivations. Psychoanalytically oriented therapies are characterized by a close working partnership between therapist and client. Clients learn about themselves by exploring their interactions in the therapeutic relationship.

Behavior Therapy

The focus of this approach is on the role of learning in developing both normal and abnormal behaviors. A therapist might help a client through repeated exposure to whatever it is that causes anxiety.

Cognitive Therapy

It emphasizes what people think rather than what they do. Cognitive therapists believe that it is dysfunctional thinking that leads to dysfunctional emotions or behaviors. By changing their thoughts, people can change how they feel and what they do.

Humanistic Therapy

This approach emphasizes people's capacity to make rational choices and develop to their maximum potential. Concern and respect for others are also important themes. Humanistic philosophers like Jean-Paul Sartre,

---

57. Kazdin, *Encyclopedia of Psychology*. In http://www.apa.org/topics/therapy/psychotherapy-approaches.aspx.

Martin Buber, and Søren Kierkegaard influenced this type of therapy. Three types of humanistic therapy are especially influential namely:

Client-centered therapy rejects the idea of therapists as authorities on their clients inner experiences. Instead, therapists help clients change by emphasizing their concern, care and interest.

Gestalt therapy emphasizes the importance of being aware of the here and now and accepting responsibility for yourself.

Existential therapy focuses on free will, self-determination, and the search for meaning.

Integrative or holistic therapy

Many therapists blend elements from different approaches and tailor their treatment according to each client's needs.

All of the above can be helpful in intercultural couples counseling.

Multicultural Ethos and Therapy

A multicultural couple therapist, be it premarital or marital, often uses family therapy. The therapist begins by asking the clients about their family of origin, family history, significant events, childhood, growing up, sibling position, and other significant members of the family or extended family, their influence on the individual, roles and responsibilities, relationships and rules in their particular culture. All of these may vary in each culture. Thus it is not right to assume that because they come from the same country that their culture is the same. The therapist himself or herself cannot assume that just because he/she comes from the same culture as that of the clients that he/she may be free of biases. Cultural stereotyping is not helpful in intercultural counseling. We derive our self-concept from our cultural upbringing. Our ethnic heritage shapes our attitudes and beliefs. Thus it is important to understand how family and cultural factors affect one's worldview.

Multicultural family therapy emphasizes the importance of language and loyalty to one's own cultural group. It provides information on many different topics such as acculturation and oppression, the significance of gender roles, facets of identity development, self-esteem and self-awareness, and an understanding of our total worldview. A multicultural theory enables the therapist to examine his or her own racial beliefs and attitudes, in order that they are able to discuss racially relevant topics and are willing to work on issues of anger or hurt or even shame. A multicultural family therapist views clients on two levels: individual and as members of a group. They take a deeper look at several psychodynamic questions: What are the important personal and interpersonal aspects of their culture? They are mindful of the research done in that field and are eager to notice the recommendations given and to use them in concrete situations. A significant part of any session needs to address the issues of significant others, and their cultural, environmental and contextual issues, self in relation to, connectedness, relationship and interdependence.

Conceptual Framework for Research

The literature review above provided me with a conceptual framework to proceed with the research on intercultural premarital couples counseling. It is a fact that in all marriages or relationships one has to constantly work on the dynamics of being oneself, of being liked and accepted by the other, of negotiating differences and the like. These differences can be magnified in intercultural couples more so when they are in the phase of negotiating their relationship. A culturally conscious therapist can help the couple by culturally relevant interventions and thereby influence the relationship to become more stable and enjoyable. Adjusting to each other, adapting and integrating values and belief systems, is required all through one's life but particularly in the initial phase of the relationship.

To achieve complementarity with the other, each partner has to simultaneously work both on oneself and the relationship that may include both cognitive and emotional flexibility, reframing of fixed social ideas or norms and sustained work on self-growth.

It can be said with a relative amount of acceptance that whenever cultural issues and concerns are neglected that there is a possibility of conflict or dissatisfaction within the couple. They are unable to appreciate each other's background and upbringing and this gives rise to mistrust or being misunderstood. Relationship is less about survival and more about flourishing. The objective of being together is to understand, appreciate, and enjoy each other's company and not to find fault, belittle, or feel hampered or hindered by the other. Relationships flourish in the midst of mutual respect and admiration of the other and of one's upbringing in the family of origin. How can one keep oneself from being misunderstood or made fun of by the one person who means the world to them? This is where cultural understanding comes to aid the couple. A culturally sensitive therapist plays an important role in helping the couple sift through the concerns and make sense of why a person behaves in a particular manner. This, more often than not, helps resolve stress and conflict among couples.

There are a plethora of areas in which intercultural couples need help including communication, parenting, managing finance, dealing with in-laws, place of residence, visits to native place, learning language, or what language the children should speak, political ideology, vacation, belonging to a community, and the like.

Clinicians have realized the need for culture-based therapies but have not been able to come up with any specific theory for intercultural premarital couples counseling. There is an urgent need for cultural psychotherapy. However, in developing a cultural psychotherapy for intercultural couples, questions such as the following must be faced: Since each culture is different, would one cultural therapy be a good fit for the other? How does one discern what works best for what culture? So what is it that helps make a connection between the client and the therapist knowing that at face value there may be three different cultures and many subcultures present in the therapy room? What does it take to sustain the therapy in the face of this cultural mix?

Is homogamy, or the idea of sameness in culture, required to sustain a relationship or can acceptable sameness in terms of worldview, likes and dislikes, hobbies, value system, and ideologies be equally satisfying? How do couples resolve conflict or difference of opinion? Do they always blame culture, upbringing, or personality?

Do clients prefer individual counseling to dyadic? Do they feel free to discuss their innermost feelings in front of their partners? How and when do couples feel ready to commit to marriage? How much time is typically required for intercultural counseling? These questions are addressed in this research.

Sollod, in writing about Carl Rogers, states that Carl Rogers talks about unconditional positive regard, congruence of "being real," acceptance of others, and empathic understanding. Rogers established a client-centered counseling and was of the opinion that the counselor's "acceptance" of the client's impulses provided the setting for self-acceptance and growth.[58] Likewise, I believe if people are willing to accept others into their life without prejudice and anxiety then it is possible that both lives are enriched simultaneously. Shurman rightly points out that the community of faith is necessary to provide a context of meaning and values for guiding and disciplining the unfolding of human potential. He laments that the secular growth movements often lack this perspective of accountability to the community which is a necessary check and balance for individual development.[59] There is power in belonging. Human hearts often yearn to be cared for, accepted, and loved.

Summary

Currently there is a dearth in the premarital counseling literature regarding how to directly address culture. This deficit inhibits premarital counselors from assessing and providing effective interventions to assist couples in understanding and working through issues regarding culture. More specifically, clinicians are potentially unaware of how to attend to premarital issues related to specific aspects of culture. For example, a premarital couple disagrees on what gender roles each person in the relationship should play. The man believes the woman should do all the cooking and cleaning, as the wives/mothers did this when he was growing up. The woman believes that the household chores should be equally divided between the man and the woman. This issue directly relates to the culture in which the two individuals were brought up. The man may feel that his role is the monetary provider for the family, whereas the wife is the organizational provider for the family. In order to address this issue the therapist would need to be knowledgeable of the cultural patterns, values, emphases, and meaning of the roles for each partner.

As shown in the literature review, there is a deficit in understanding and implementing culturally sensitive and useful approaches within intercultural premarital counseling. Additionally, literature has shown that there are culture specific aspects that relate to marriage. This study aimed to explore cultural insights as well as what approaches are effective or ineffective in dealing with premarital counseling. Interviews and the researcher's interpretations of interviews provided participants with a

---

58. Sollod et al., *Beneath the Mask*, 476.

59. Shurman, "Being/Becoming Relationship," in Hunter, *Dictionary of Pastoral Care and Counseling*, 81–82.

voice, and provided clinicians and researchers with a better understanding of clients' needs surrounding the topic of culture within intercultural premarital counseling.

CHAPTER IV

Describing Research Methodology for Intercultural Premarital Couples Counseling

Rationale for Qualitative Research Approach

THE PURPOSE OF THIS study on intercultural premarital couples counseling is to understand how couples feel about culture and what approaches were beneficial in intercultural premarital counseling. As discussed in the previous chapter, some research is available on culture and its significance in each individual's life. However, not much research is available in terms of how couples practically negotiate each other's cultural demands and facets that are different than theirs. The focus in my research methodology was to learn more about these negotiations as well as what aspects of culture the intercultural couples find useful to keep and what, if any, to break away from. I was primarily interested in finding out what approaches are helpful in intercultural premarital couple counseling that could be of interest to therapists and other counselors and faith leaders who are engaged in premarital couples counseling.

To explore the research questions above, a qualitative approach was used. As we are aware, a basic qualitative research design attempts to uncover the experiences of the participants. In this case it was their lived-out story of how culture impacts their everyday life. Qualitative research design also helped me to rediscover the meaning that each participant ascribes to those lived-in experiences, making each experience real and unique. In this case it was to know how culture impacts, is impacting, or has impacted their relationship, how they begin to recognize it, and what steps they take to deal with it in a way that is helpful to them. Qualitative research is also a process that helps to uncover facts and dynamics over a period of time. Thus building trust with the participants and helping them to open up to their life story was the most interesting part of the research. According to Bloomberg and Volpe, qualitative research provides a deep comprehension of people's perspectives of a particular event.[1] This study on intercultural premarital couples counseling posited that culture is a topic that needs further research in order to help therapists provide intercultural premarital counseling to clients with relevant interventions and assistance regarding the impact of culture in their relationship. In the sections below, I further discuss participants' recruitment and data collection, subjectivity of the researcher, data analysis, and ethical considerations.

Research Setting/Context

For the purpose of this research, I primarily used an interview technique and my own journaling in engaging four intercultural couples, one of them in their own premarital counseling and three of them now married but who have received premarital counseling. Four couples were interviewed in a total of twelve interviews. There were eight individual interviews—one interview with each of the eight participants. Then there were four dyadic interviews, one with each couple. Interviews were conducted in a semi-structured format. This allowed room for some structure as well as space for additional areas of concern to be addressed or to elaborate on topics that were of particular importance.

In order to select participants, I used purposeful sampling.[2] Purposeful sampling is conducted by seeking out participants who have been through specific experiences and can provide insight on the experience.[3] I used four couples that responded positively to the email sent out to them in the State of Georgia. I sought out a culturally diverse sample in which at least one member of the couple considered him or herself to be intercultural. In turn, the Emory Institutional Review Board (IRB) approval to move forward with the study including recruitment of participants was received. Recruitment methods involved contacting therapists

---

1. Bloomberg and Volpe, *Completing Your Qualitative Dissertation*, 69.
2. Creswell, *Research Design*, 178.
3. Merriam, *Qualitative Research in Practice*, 20.

in the Atlanta area, particularly through the Care and Counseling Center of Georgia (CCCG), and informing them of the purpose of the study and requesting that they post flyers in their office and satellite offices to inform current clients about the study (see Appendices A, B, C).

Research Sample and Data Sources

The prime criteria for selecting the four couples was that each of the couples have received some form of premarital counseling, that they understand and speak English, that one of the partners considers himself or herself as intercultural, and that they reside in the State of Georgia. In order to conceal their identities all couples were assigned numbers.

The first couple is A111, a thirty-three-year-old female who is second-generation immigrant of South Asian descent and practices the Hindu faith. She was born and raised in Canada. She had never previously been married. Her boyfriend B112 is a thirty-seven-year-old male and is of African American descent and he practices the Christian faith. He was born and raised in Georgia. He also had never previously been married. Both share a common profession in that they both are radiologists. They met each other while doing their internship. They received counseling for about twenty sessions as part of the discernment process towards making a choice for marriage.

The second couple is made up of C113, a thirty-six-year-old female who was born and raised in Georgia. She is a lawyer by profession. Her husband D114 is a thirty-eight-year-old male, born and raised in Canada. He is a corporate marketing professional. He has had to adapt to American culture after marriage. Both are practicing Catholics and have been married to each other for ten years and this is their first marriage. They met each other through a community dating program. They received four sessions of premarital counseling.

The third research participant couple is E115, a male of thirty-two years. He is a Caucasian and was born and raised in Georgia. He describes his profession as English language teacher. F116 is a female of thirty years, born in Ghana and migrated to America at age eleven. Her profession is school psychologist. She is a Catholic and he is a Protestant Christian. They met each other in college. Both of them have not been married before. They were in premarital counseling for about two years with more than forty sessions and they also took part in counseling sessions as part of discernment towards making a choice for continuing their relationship.

My last research participant couple was G117, a female who is forty-seven years old of South Asian descent and was born and raised in India. About seven years ago she came to America as an adult to seek employment. She works as a program officer/Sr. relationship officer in a nonprofit organization. She has never previously been married. H118 is a fifty-year-old male. He is a Caucasian and was born and raised in Georgia. He was married previously and has two grown children. He works as a systems architect. Both are practicing Messianic Jews and have been married for two months. They met at the Synagogue they attended. Both received individual counseling for about thirty sessions each. A few of those sessions were devoted to individual premarital counseling.

Research Protocol Process

The researcher informed the participants of the structure that will be used in research to get the desired outcome. They were informed that during the study they may expect the following study procedures: First, that they will complete a form describing their demographic information and an initial screening survey to determine their appropriateness for the study. They will also be emailed or mailed a set of tentative interview questions. Second, they will be contacted within one week of the screening by the primary researcher via phone or in person to let them know if they have been selected for the study. If they have been selected for the study the researcher will set up a time and place for the individual interviews with both partners. Third, approximately one week prior to the interview they will receive the interview questions via email or via mail. They are invited to look over the questions, reflect on potential answers. Fourth, the interview will consist of individual partners present for an hour each time, to talk on the topics of culture, premarital counseling, and marriage. Fifth, after the individual interview correspondence about findings, researcher interpretations and presentation of findings will occur on an as-needed basis either in person, via telephone, or via email. The researcher may ask them a few short questions in order to confirm or clarify interpretations from the interview. Interviews will be recorded using a digital audio recorder. The recordings will be stored in a locked office cabinet at the Care and Counseling Center of Georgia and will be destroyed after transcription. Sixth, a second couple interview will be scheduled for an hour and both members will be present to answer questions and discuss. Seventh, after the couple interview correspondence about findings, researcher interpretations and presentation of findings will occur on an as-needed basis either in person, via telephone, or via email. The researcher may ask them a few short questions in order to confirm or clarify interpretations from the interview. Interviews will be recorded using a digital audio recorder. The recordings will be stored in the locked office cabinet at the Care and Counseling Center of Georgia and will be destroyed after transcription. Eighth, that they may skip any question throughout the interview or demographic information that they do not wish to answer or that makes them feel uncomfortable.

Data Collection Methods:

Prior to conducting the interview, an initial telephonic consultation with participants was conducted. After the initial consultation, participants were emailed a copy of the interview packet that consisted of tentative interview questions (Appendix D), the description of research (Appendix E), informed consent (Appendix F), demographic questionnaire (Appendix H), cultural diversity, screening questions I & II (Appendix I), and Emory IRB approval form (Appendix G). Participants were asked to fill out the cultural diversity survey, demographic questionnaire and informed consent and to either mail it to me or scan and send it to me electronically. Interviews occurred in the latter part of Fall Term of 2014 and early part of Spring Term of 2015.

Interviews

As mentioned earlier, approximately a week before the interview, the researcher provided the participants via email with the interview questions, confidentiality statement, demographic questionnaire, and the cultural questionnaire to encourage the participants to think over and prepare for the interview (see Appendices D, E, F, G, H, and I). Sending the participants the interview questions allowed them additional time to contemplate potential answers, as many of the questions required insight and reflection. Prior to beginning the interview, the researcher shared biases, e.g., the importance of therapy and premarital counseling, the importance for therapists to understand culture, and a small summary of her own cultural background and her desire to know more about others cultural background and share the information with the academic and clinical community. As a result of sharing my own background and desire of the study I hoped to establish rapport with participants, thus increasing comfort levels of participants for the duration of the interviews.

Data collection occurred via personal interviews. Interviews are a powerful way of gathering information,[4] and thus serve as a major source of gathering information about participants' insights. According to Sohier,[5] a dyadic interview can provide a richer and more detailed account of certain events as participants can provide one another and the researcher with a more in-depth account of particular events. All interviews were conducted between the principal investigator and the individual participants and or couples.

The researcher interviewed four couples. All interviews occurred in person. Each partner was interviewed once individually and then once as a couple. Saturation was achieved after interviewing these participants until the responses consistently provided no new or conflicting information.[6] I adhered to the following guidelines in the selection criteria for participants—that each couple must have an awareness and a basic understanding of how culture impacts each partner and the marriage; that at least one member of the couple must consider him/herself intercultural; that both members must be able to speak English fluently; that both members of the couple must be present for the individual interview, as well as the couple interview; and that each couple has received at least four to twelve sessions of premarital counseling.

Interview questions were asked in a semi-structured format.[7] Semi-structured interviews are defined by having a predetermined set of questions that guide the interview, but allowing the researcher to deviate from the questions as additional questions or topics emerge.[8] Interviews were recorded with a digital recording device. Initial interview questions and discussion led to probing questions that were not listed. These questions

---

4. Fontana and Frey, "Interviewing," 47–78.
5. Sohier, "Dyadic Interview as a Tool," 96.
6. Bradley, "Methodological Issues and Practices," 431–49.
7. Blee and Taylor, "Semi-Structured Interviewing," 92–117.
8. Blee and Taylor, "Semi-Structured Interviewing," 92–117.

were recorded and considered for possible second interviews and for analytic memos (see point 4 below under data analysis methods).

Interview procedure was as follows: Firstly, each participant was asked to explain the important aspects of their culture in general followed by unique characteristics of the culture. Secondly, in the individual interview, an interview summary sheet was filled out by the participants (Appendix I). Thirdly, in the couple interview, another interview summary sheet was filled out by the participants (Appendix J). These interview summary sheets provided the researcher with information about the interviews and important abstractions that were needed for data analysis. Fourthly, following each interview, coding and data analysis occurred using MAXQDA software for content analysis. Fifthly, following the completion of solidifying of themes, a member check was done with participants where they were asked to look over and collaborate with the researcher on findings and interpretations of their interview as well as other themes that emerged in the interviews.

Data Analysis Methods

Rigor

The use of rigor for data analysis in this study is meant to render the findings trustworthy and valid. Using several different avenues within this qualitative research and various strategies such as triangulation, member checks, researcher reflexivity, peer review, and an audit trail, it was possible to achieve rigor. Triangulation and member checks represent forms of internal validity, while an audit trail represents a form of reliability.[9] Merriam also suggests that external validity of qualitative research be applied by the researcher such that he/she asks how the findings of this study can be related to his/her own work.[10] The quality of rigor thus achieved should make the data provided by clients a reliable source for further research in this area.

---

9. Merriam, *Qualitative Research in Practice*, 22.
10. Merriam, *Qualitative Research in Practice*, 22.

Triangulation

Triangulation is defined as the use of multiple sources to validate the data collected.[11] Strategies that were used for this purpose include individual interviews, dyadic interviews with the couples and member checks. Using of two or more data collection procedures does help in arriving at an interpretation that reflects the couples' feelings, views, and as it relates to various aspects of the intercultural premarital counseling process.

Member Checks

Member check has to do with participants reviewing the researcher's interpretations of the interviews and providing feedback about their accuracy. This spurs additional thoughts or insights about the participants' experiences.[12] Member checks were done at the convenience of the participant (i.e., in person, phone, or email) once the data analysis of the emerging themes had been done. The researcher then revisited and looked at the themes through the lens of the feedback provided by the member-check and made the needed revisions and corrections.

Analytic Memos

Analytic memos or writing supplement journals provide a direct, brief summary of procedures, thought processes, coding processes, choices of the researcher, emergent patterns and categories, themes and concepts within the data, and flow of the research. Topics of the analytic memos include reflection about similarities between researcher and the participant, shared experiences between the researcher and participants, the research questions, purpose of the research, emergent patterns, categories or themes, problems with the study, ethical dilemmas, observations, future directions of research or the study, implications for the field, or a general reflection.

"Rich and Thick" Description/"Thick Theory"

Rich and thick descriptions (same as Thick Theory described under definition of terms) supplied the basis for external validity, as they tend to provide the reader with ample information on a particular subject.[13] I

---

11. Merriam, *Qualitative Research in Practice*, 19.
12. Merriam, *Qualitative Research in Practice*, 24.
13. Merriam, *Qualitative Research in Practice*, 13.

studied aspects of intercultural premarital counseling that highlighted culture and sought to show how understanding culture can potentially enhance the intercultural premarital counseling experience. Through rich and thick descriptions I was able to apply the sense of a narrative so that it can provide voice to the participants of my study.

Audit Trail

An audit trail helps to keep a record of the methods, procedures, emergent themes, emergent interview questions, and the data analysis process. This enables the reader to understand how I (as the researcher) came to my conclusions.[14] The audit trail is made up of a research journal that I keep throughout the process of formulating interview questions, creating a conceptual framework, data collection, and data analysis. I was able to work on a journal, which helped me keep track my own personal journey through the dissertation process. The journal tracked emotions related to interviews, collecting and writing data.

Peer Reviews/Debriefing

Creswell recommends peer debriefing as a means of "enhancing the accuracy of the account" and to add elements of validity to the analysis process and final outcome of the study.[15] Peer reviews were conducted by therapists that have had knowledge of the research process and culture. Three therapists were selected to review transcripts and emerging themes. Each therapist was provided with a summary of themes as well as three transcripts to read over. Therapists provided a feedback via email followed by discussion either in person or via phone. Discussions centered on themes found by the peer reviewer and myself, as well as for future research considerations. Following the peer reviews, I was able to go back and compare the notes and suggestions from the peer review to the themes and subthemes that were previously found. I was able to adjust, move, and change aspects of the study as I saw fit.

14. Merriam, *Qualitative Research in Practice*, 19.
15. Creswell, *Research Design*, 192.

Research Software Use

I used the MAXQDA software[16] for data analysis. MAXQDA is a flexible and easy-to-use text analysis software that helped me do the analysis by evaluating, coding themes and subthemes, and interpreting the data collected. Qualitative data analysis is an inductive process of taking a large amount of data and focusing the data to show certain phenomena by identifying themes and making meaning of people's stories. Firstly, I uploaded on the software the written material on tentative questions and then went over the interview questions and picked out some questions that I wanted some elaboration on. Based on the number of occurrences in the written and transcribed material, I established themes and went on to sort out the content analysis across interviews. To provide participants with a voice, interpretations of participants' narratives was established and the transcribed material was uploaded in the software after being verified with the participants. I also added the information for specific thoughts, actions, communication styles, expectations, and cultural language that related to the research questions for the current study.

Issues of Trustworthiness/Ethical Considerations

As a marriage and family therapist, I am first bound by the ethical code of the American Association of Marriage and Family Therapy (AAMFT), and secondly as a researcher I am bound by the ethical standards of qualitative research.

The American Association for Marriage and Family Therapy (AAMFT 2015) has a Code of Ethics[17] that, although it does not specifically address diversity and culture in an explicit section of the document, contains several principles that articulate the therapist's duty to serve culturally diverse populations. Such principles include the following:

Non-Discrimination

Marriage and family therapists provide professional assistance to persons without discrimination on the basis of race, age, ethnicity, socioeconomic status, disability, gender, health status, religion, national origin, sexual orientation, gender identity, or relationship status.

---

16. http://www.maxqda.com/.

17. http://www.aamft.org/iMIS15/AAMFT/Content/Legal_Ethics/Code_of_Ethics.aspx.

Non-Abandonment

Marriage and family therapists do not abandon or neglect clients in treatment without making reasonable arrangements for the continuation of treatment.

Maintenance of Competency

Marriage and family therapists pursue knowledge of new developments and maintain their competence in marriage and family therapy through education, training, and/or supervised experience.

Seek Assistance

Marriage and family therapists seek appropriate professional assistance for issues that may impair work performance or clinical judgment.

Institutional Approval

When institutional approval is required, marriage and family therapists submit accurate information about their research proposals and obtain appropriate approval prior to conducting the research.

Protection of Research Participants

Marriage and family therapists are responsible for making careful examinations of ethical acceptability in planning research. To the extent that services to research participants may be compromised by participation in research, marriage and family therapists seek the ethical advice of qualified professionals not directly involved in the investigation and observe safeguards to protect the rights of research participants.

Informed Consent to Research

Marriage and family therapists inform participants about the purpose of the research, expected length, and research procedures. They also inform participants of the aspects of the research that might reasonably be expected to influence willingness to participate such as potential risks, discomforts, or adverse effects. Marriage and family therapists are especially sensitive to the possibility of diminished consent when participants are also receiving clinical services, or have impairments which limit understanding and/or communication, or when participants are children. Marriage and family therapists inform participants about any potential research benefits, the limits of confidentiality, and whom to contact concerning questions about the research and their rights as research participants.

Right to Decline or Withdraw Participation

Marriage and family therapists respect each participant's freedom to decline participation in or to withdraw from a research study at any time. This obligation requires special thought and consideration when investigators or other members of the research team are in positions of authority or influence over participants. Marriage and family therapists, therefore, make every effort to avoid multiple relationships with research participants that could impair professional judgment or increase the risk of exploitation. When offering inducements for research participation, marriage and family therapists make reasonable efforts to avoid offering inappropriate or excessive inducements when such inducements are likely to coerce participation.

Confidentiality of Research Data

Information obtained about a research participant during the course of an investigation is confidential unless there is a waiver previously obtained in writing. When the possibility exists that others, including family members, may obtain access to such information. This possibility, together with the plan for protecting confidentiality, is explained as part of the procedure for obtaining informed consent.

Publication

Marriage and family therapists do not fabricate research results. Marriage and family therapists disclose potential conflicts of interest and take authorship credit only for work they have performed or to which they have contributed. Publication credits accurately reflect the relative contributions of the individual involved.

The dissertation committee provided counsel to the researcher and for the development of research methods of this study. Participants signed and were given a copy of the informed consent document which informed participants of their rights as a research participant and about the purpose and topic of the study.

Confidentiality was addressed by giving each participant a study number within the initial contact to be used in the transcription on the screening questionnaire and on the demographic questionnaire. The transcription was completed by this researcher. Participants' names and identities were kept confidential in the final dissertation through the use of the study numbers. Identifying information is not included in the final dissertation. The actual participant names and codes are kept under lock in the researcher's locker at the Care and Counseling Center of Georgia. Transcribed interviews were also kept under lock. Participants' transcripts and participant information will be kept for approximately one year after the interviews, before being destroyed. This timeline of holding transcripts is based on the timeline for the dissertation. Additionally, this timeline allows for information to be kept and revisited if the dissertation is published.

Participants were given the option to withdraw from the study at any time. None of the couples decided this. However, there was provision that if a couple decided to withdraw from the study after the first interview, I would have to let them go and select another couple for participation. Participants were informed at the time of the member checks that if there is any information they wish to be withheld from the final dissertation, they could make the request to withhold that information and their request will be honored. None of the participants made any requests and if they did make the request the information would not be included in this research. Member check provided the basis for asking to withhold certain information.

In addition, I upheld the ethical considerations of qualitative research by avoiding harm to participants.[18] Two dimensions of ethics for qualitative researchers were observed, namely, procedural ethics and ethics in practice.[19] Procedural ethics involves having a dissertation proposal and gaining approval from others in the field such as the dissertation committee and the Institutional Review Board (IRB) prior to collecting data. Ethics in practice refers to managing and dealing with ethical issues that arise throughout data collection and data analysis.[20] The IRB is responsible for reviewing *human subjects' research* and FDA-regulated *clinical investigations*, and ensuring that they are conducted in accordance with applicable federal regulations and institutional policies.

18. Fontana and Frey, "Interviewing," 70–71.
19. Guillemin and Gillam, "Ethics, Reflexivity, and Ethically Important Moments," 261–80.
20. Guillemin and Gillam, "Ethics, Reflexivity, and Ethically Important Moments," 261–80.

The Common Rule defines "research" as *a systematic investigation, including research development, testing and evaluation, designed to develop or contribute to generalizable knowledge.*[21]

This leads to two further explanations. Systematic Investigation: An activity that involves a prospective plan that incorporates data collection, either quantitative or qualitative, and data analysis to answer a question. It often includes surveys, interviews, data analyses, cognitive experiences, or medical chart reviews. Generalizable Knowledge: Knowledge from which conclusions will be drawn that can be applied to populations outside of the specific study population. This usually includes one or more of the following concepts: knowledge that contributes to a theoretical framework of an established body of knowledge; the primary beneficiaries of the research are other researchers, scholars, and practitioners in the field of study; dissemination of the results is intended to inform the field of study (though this alone does not make an activity constitute research "designed to contribute to generalizable knowledge"); the results are expected to be generalized to a larger population beyond the site of data collection; the results are intended to be replicated in other settings.

The Common Rule defines a human subject as a living individual about whom an investigator conducting research obtains (1) Data through intervention or interaction with the individual, or (2) Identifiable private information.[22]

Risks and Discomfort

Participants were informed that while participating in this study if they were to experience the following risks: emotional conflict may arise among the couple. If this does occur and they feel they need counseling, then they may contact C_____ at _____ at (404)_____. That they will pay for it out-of-pocket or through their own personal insurance. That doing this may lead to a breach of confidentiality meaning that if they disclose why they are there to see a therapist they will in effect disclose that they are the research participant. None of the participants reported any risk or

---

21. http://www.hhs.gov/ohrp/humansubjects/guidance/45cfr46.html45 CFR46.102(d).

22. http://www.irb.emory.edu/documents/PoliciesandProcedures.pdf45 CFR46.102(f).

discomfort with the structure or the content of the research or research questions.

Limitations

Soon after receiving the approval from the Institutional Review Board of Emory University in late November 2014, I began the process of sending out the advertisement of this research on intercultural premarital couples counseling to the intercultural couples I knew as well as to fellow Colleagues, both Staff and Residents, at the Care and Counseling Center of Georgia, and posted the flyer at Emory University. I was able to get four positive responses within a month and began the research process hoping to get more participants along the way. However, I was unsuccessful and so continued the research with the existing four couples. I was very keen to find at least three therapists who have been engaged in counseling intercultural premarital couples counseling and sent out flyers to all the Staff and Residents at Care and Counseling Center of Georgia as well as to other intercultural therapists in Georgia. However, the response was that they have never counseled an intercultural premarital couple or that even if they did it was only for a few sessions for marital counseling. They also expressed that they do not have any experience or expertise in intercultural premarital couples counseling. This was unexpected but I realized that this indeed is the reality for at least in the State of Georgia. Intercultural premarital counseling is a new phenomenon and needs to be explored and experienced.

Summary

The methodology I used for the research was appropriate and detailed. It helped me cover various aspects of data collection while assisting me to keep the data collection objective and accurate. It helped cover any loopholes and kept me as the researcher on track. The software that I selected was also helpful in assisting me in assigning codes and themes and subthemes. It was helpful in incorporating all of the data generated which in turn made it very useful for analysis and recommendations.

CHAPTER V

Reporting Findings of the Research for Intercultural Premarital Couples Counseling

Introduction

It was a joy to work with the eight participants (four couples) that I had selected for this research on intercultural premarital couples counseling. They understood what it means to be an intercultural couple. They were very cooperative and attentive to the process and provided a gem of information that I lay down here and that I will analyze in the next chapter. The participants were given sufficient time to read the questions and to deliberate on them and submit the written text to me. I encouraged them to write at length and not just give me a "yes" or "no" answer. I had tried to keep the questions open-ended so that I got more feedback from the participants. I read their answers before they came in for the interview and since time was short on forty-five minutes to an hour duration, I jotted down either points of clarification or any new question emerging from their answer that I would then ask them to clarify or elaborate. I always began the interview with thanking them for giving their time. I met the participants on Saturdays at the Care and Counseling Center of Georgia office space. All the participants were based in Georgia.

This chapter will deal with reporting the findings of the research. As mentioned earlier, I used the MAXQDA software for data analysis. The software enabled me to upload all of the paperwork including the transcription of the individual and couple interviews. After transcription I did email the transcribed copies to the respective participants, both of their individual interview sessions and their couple interview sessions and asked them to take a look and either confirm the material or let me know what corrections to make. I also asked them through email to let me know if there was some material that they did not want me to include in the findings. All of them confirmed the material without any corrections. There was one clarification that I was able to address with the respective participant. I also asked them to send me any other data that they felt they wanted me to include that was relevant to the research but they said that they have said all that they wanted to say. The first step in the process was to consider the "big ideas or themes." The second step was to dissect and classify the data and place sections of the material into categories. An important step was to reduce all that I have collected to a manageable database. This step is essentially what Creswell and others refer to as a "winnowing process."[1] I was able to work this out on the MAXQDA software by assigning the codes based on the material. Codes are primarily segments of data that I consider relevant to my study. These codes were mainly based on emerging themes and so I was able to organize the written material, sentence by sentence, into these codes. I have organized the material, based on these codes, according to a more sequential understanding of the content on intercultural understanding. The material begins with the cultural screening answers of the participants to the understanding of culture and race. Then it dwells on their experience of the same in their everyday life to attractions to their intercultural mate, the support from other intercultural couples and family. Then it moves to issues and concerns they have experienced including raising biracial children, conflict resolution, need for counseling, approaches that were helpful in therapy and the therapist's understanding of them as an intercultural couple. The last part of the material presents recommendations that participants feel will be helpful to future intercultural couples as well as therapists engaged in intercultural couples counseling. Almost all of the material listed below is in quotation as it is what the participants have said. To avoid confusion, I have refrained from giving their number signifying which participant said what as I did not see that to be of significance. What was important was to align the material of each participant according to its content in that particular segment. Wherever necessary, if citing a direct quote from the participant in my

---

1. Creswell, *Qualitative Inquiry and Research Design*, 152, 153.

next chapter on interpretation of findings, I will cite the number assigned to that particular client.

Demographic Information

The researcher selected four couples—four males and four females. Two females were second-generation immigrants of South Asian parents from India, one set of parents coming from South India and the other set of parents from North India. One was born and raised in Canada and the other in Georgia, United States. Another female was an immigrant from Central India married to a Caucasian. The fourth female participant was from Ghana and came to the United States as a preteen. Out of the four males, one was of South Asian descent from Canada a second-generation immigrant, one an African American from Georgia, two were Caucasians from Georgia, as well. In terms of religious faith/denomination of the participants, three of them were Catholics, one Presbyterian, two Messianic Jews, one Hindu, and one Pentecostal.

Two of the participants were radiologists, one a school psychologist, one a teacher, one a lawyer, one a program officer, another a systems architect, and one a real estate agent. Their annual average income was over sixty thousand dollars each. Between them they spoke five different languages: namely, English, Hindi, Marathi, Punjabi, and Malayalam. Five of them had a Master's degree, two were MDs, and one had a Bachelor's degree. The duration they had known each other as couples varied from eight months to eight years. Three couples were married and one was to be married within two months of the research. Three couples had received from five to twenty-five-plus sessions of premarital counseling together. One couple had received individual counseling that included some premarital counseling. They ranged from the age group of thirty-one to fifty-two years of age.

As part of the screening of the participants, they were sent a cultural diversity screening questionnaire (see Appendix I) to discern their level of cultural awareness so as to aid the researcher in the selection of the participants. The following are the findings of the two sections of the cultural diversity screening questionnaire answers received from the selected participants.

Cultural Diversity Screening I

Of the eight participants, three of them indicated that they often tended to be open to learning more about diversity; three of them said that they often like to make friends with people from other culture; two of them indicated that they often liked to attend social or cultural functions from other cultures; three of them said they often tended not to make judgment of other people based on stereotype; three of them indicated that they often like to help people in their neighborhood who are from other cultures; three of them said they often like to look up cultural history of people on websites or books; three of them pointed out they often like to volunteer at refugee centers or after-school programs for culturally diverse children; three of them said they often tended to like learning foreign languages; three of them indicated they often were willing to correct people when they disregard diversity; and one of them indicated tendency to like to talk about diversity with family and friends.

Cultural Diversity Screening II

Three of the participants expressed that they were in the process of giving thought to their personal cultural beliefs, their worldview and their stand on diversity; three of them said they were well aware of the cultural, racial and ethnic diversity in their surrounding and that they have begun to respect diversity; four of them indicated that they were opening up to the idea of celebrating cultural diversity rather than questioning it; three of them said they grew up in a family environment that tolerated diversity; three of them pointed out that they tended to dislike hanging around with peers who make fun of people of other cultures; three of them said they tended not to get very self-conscious when they were in the presence of people who are different from them; three of them said that they are able to tolerate the smell of food that is different from theirs; three of them indicated that they tended to be attracted to people from other cultures; three of them said that they lived abroad for a period of time and enjoyed it. Three of them indicated that they were learning to respect all people and their cultural heritage.

After analyzing the cultural diversity screening questions, since only four couples responded, all were selected. Two weeks before the actual interview each participant was emailed the tentative interview packet, to reflect upon and respond. The packet included the demographic information form and tentative interview questions (see Appendix D). After receiving the answers to the tentative interview questions, a week before the interview each participant was emailed the research questions for the single partner participant (see Appendix J). A day after the actual individual interview the participants were each emailed the research questions for the couple participants. I received the answers in the mail or through email. After a week they came in together for the couple's interview. When they came in for the interviews (both individual interview and later for the couple's interview), I was able to ask them to further elaborate or clarify any of the points that they were making and audio recorded the same which I later transcribed. I am listing the answers below the questions both in the form of specific themes and as questions and answers. As mentioned above the content below in terms of answers is not in a sequential order but is rather based on themes. Some answers from different questions that were similar in nature have been grouped together into one theme. Care has been taken that the same does not allow for either content or its meaning to be lost.

Description of Findings

Understanding of Culture

The participants made the following observations in conveying their understanding of culture. "Culture represents a set of values, traditions, beliefs, attitudes and rituals followed by a group of people." "It is a way of a life." "It is what brings people together through familiarity." "It is something that shapes us and partially forms who we are." "It is something to fall back in times of crisis." "A combination of ethnic origin and upbringing that embodies a person." "Culture is a set of rituals, customs, traditions and shared patterns and behaviors and values that help to define and shape a group of people." "Culture is social practice and language of a group of people." "Like patriarchy, Culture is used to subdue women, dowry system." "I grew up in a home with three girls, a grand-mother and a great grand-mother who were all educated." "Culture is what makes a person belong to a group. This includes language, behavior, food, music, manners of talking, things that matter (Are manners more important than money, for example, or is money unimportant if it does not come with manners)." "Culture provides people with a sense of belonging.

Within a culture one can find people who are similar to them and provide a thread that connects people." "A certain way of thinking, doing life is culture according to me. It is the way I dress, eat, do life with community, the value systems come from that cultural paradigm. It is also the music, dance, poetry and other expressions of the specific group of people." "It is the way we interact with those around United States based on social norms."

Understanding of Racial Divide in Our Society

One female African participant who is married to a Caucasian male observed that in some places such as shopping malls, theaters, pretty much any large group of strangers, they as a couple run into second looks. "It's not malicious, but it is a reminder that we are an unusual couple." They added that in some of the places outside Atlanta they seemed to face difficulties; for example, he said, "some years ago we were in a grocery store at a checkout line-together-in Savannah, where one of the clerks told me she could take me at a different register, or the time we got pulled over in Alabama." He elaborated saying that "White people just aren't with Black people in Savannah like that." "I was more reactive to different thoughts than I am now therefore better in dealing with differences. I suppose the first I remember of racism was in Mark Twain, but I have witnessed racism in my school, neighborhood, and family. There are two kinds of racism: the kind that people have grown up with that is smug but not especially hateful, and then the kind that despises other groups or races of people. I cannot tolerate the latter. When the former occurs in family members or close friends, mostly you try to forgive and forget. Family members especially were born in a different time and it's best to keep in mind you have no idea how you would have turned out or what beliefs you would hold if you had grown up in the same circumstances. My parents were always big on respect in general. I didn't know many Black people or people who weren't White growing up. When I went to college I worked at a cafeteria with several African Americans which was the first I'd really heard people speak ebonics. I knew what it was but it was interesting to hear, and I can't say I looked down on them. Mostly I was interested. When I moved to Atlanta I interacted with many more cultures and types of people—gay, lesbian, foreign, Arab, Jewish, etc.—and I learned from them all."

The male African American participant with the Indian Canadian girlfriend added that "generally, we don't run into a lot of issues but we do get looks at times, especially when we are outside the city. We did not have to deal with this much at other places like school, college, etc.; however, we have had to deal with this with our immediate family. He further observed that "the family is not supportive or tolerant of the couple's relationship and after three years of trying to address the issue, there has been no progress."

"For people, culture is a way of life and when everyone does the same thing it becomes natural and think that some people do things differently and it is OK, even like walking barefoot. Because I have often been 'the other' I am more sensitive to it, for example we were at the band and I said, 'Oh! I am the only Black person here' and my friend who is White said, 'Oh you always notice things like this.' Even though I am a naturalized American I still have my roots in the African culture. Even though I don't speak the language, I feel most comfortable with African people. I will always be different and I am comfortable with it. Growing up, I was often in settings where I was a minority so it automatically made me more aware and accepting/respectful of others' cultures/differences because I appreciated that respect from them."

"Being in public, especially around people who have not met us as a couple. We try to talk about it beforehand if we know we're going someplace that will be uncomfortable for us, and sometimes we talk about it after. Mostly we try to rely on each other while we're in those situations."

"Try and learn from each occasion to learn the positive aspects of each approach to solving problems."

"We are mostly struggling to have my family accept us and involve us in their lives, and this is ultimately related to culture. What I have found works best so far is to let time play its course and not be aggressive. Forcing the matter has not helped. What has not helped and has not worked is trying to have discussions to explain things or discuss the issues." "My family has been unwilling to listen and instead puts both of us down (even if he is not present) and I have found this to be emotionally damaging. The recovery from this type of emotional blackmail/burden is difficult for me and I often fall into bouts of sadness that also then affects my relationship as well. In the end I have learned that these family discussions will not get us anywhere and it has not helped me or worked for us."

"Now that I've been with her these years I've softened my views on some issues of civil rights and equality (e.g., education subsidies) although I still identify as a Republican. These sorts of interactions generally take this form: She or I will mention some hot-button issue. Then either of us will disagree, and at times these will get heated. Usually we both are sure our individual position is correct. Time will pass and I'll think about her position, or she mine. Later we'll happen to bring it up (not purposefully) and see where we stand. Some of these issues we've revisited multiple times over the years and I've been able to watch mine and her position change (or not, sometimes). But mostly we are in tune on the significant issues."

"Yes! I am aware of it. I had to face this in school, very pluralistic background. Being an immigrant, you face it more. My first job in the United States, I had to struggle with a bunch of culturally different people that I had to supervise. I had to negotiate a lot and learn to be tolerant. Having changed religion (well almost) I had to do it! Being married to a man of different culture I had to do the same."

"I think coming from a pluralistic background gave me a good head start, however, there were areas of stereotyping that honest friends have confronted. My husband's actions often make me become aware of my own stereotyping." "Even educated people act on cultural stereotypes and have racial biases."

"Now I have much more access to other cultures so many of the preconceived opinions and stereotypes have been broken."

Learning Experiences from Their Intercultural Exposure

There were different responses from the participants such as: "We all have inherent biases against people, communities, cultures, etc., that likely stem from our faith/culture/background and are hard to get rid of." "Certain communities and cultures have stronger biases towards others." "Even those who are educated and successful have these biases, even if they are not aware that they are wrong or unfair." "It is very hard to change the opinion of others."

"Acting in a calm, rational manner is always better than being emotionally labile or wild and getting upset." "I have also learned that people in my generation are still racist and have double standards and even those I had considered to be open minded and accepting are not necessarily so." Another said, "I have learned that many people say one thing to us but feel differently inside and it has been hard to figure out who is genuine and who is not—it almost feels discouraging at times because I no longer know who to trust, who to believe, who to befriend and who is judging me. It is an isolating feeling and is to the point where I would say I assume everyone disapproves of us but anyone who says they are approving is 'just saying that.'" One of them said, "I've learned greater tolerance from these experiences. These experiences have ranged from being the minority and also being the majority. There are always two interpretations or views when interacting with a person or group. The variance increased with different cultures." "I hope and believe that I've learned from these experiences and it's given me greater insight into how actions or words maybe perceived or misunderstood." "I wouldn't say that I have experienced the divide in an extreme fashion at any time in my life, but I have always generally been very aware of the divide and feel more self-conscious when I am the only person of color in any given place be it school or an event, etc."

"I didn't really know people from other cultures except for African American. I got a job in the kitchen and I began to come across people from other cultures. They were interesting because they had something to offer to me. In Atlanta, I met people from all backgrounds and ethnicities. I learned how to relate to other people. I have always been interested in other people. I had a strong value system that whoever they are they are human beings. That is why I want to live in the city and not in the suburbs." "When I came into her family, I tried different food and her mother just warmed up to me."

"I sometimes held ignorant views that the majority of people are taking advantage like people on welfare. I felt that if people made better choices they would not be poor. She brought understanding about why people make these choices. Now we do not get heated about issues."

Being Culturally Sensitive

"When we are exposed to other cultures we become culturally sensitive. We try to find a balance between the differences. I grew up in a culture in which there was the practice of parents paying for children's education, giving gifts to the mail delivery person, organizing baby showers, giving thank-you notes, packing food in yogurt containers for family to take back, etc."

"We had an interesting conversation as we were driving down here. He said that I don't notice any cultural differences or issues between us and I replied that that's because I am planted in your culture. Just imagine if you were planted in my culture and he agreed that I was right."

"Family interaction (sometimes we have parents who need to be taken care of). She wants my mom to move in whereas I would have put her in a home, finances need to be discussed, decision-making, religious discussion, patriarchy, women's empowerment, conflict resolution."

"I would get offended if he tried to calm me down. But understanding that the culture or family he comes from is quieter, I learned not to take his correction personal. The question of how expressive one is could be culturally conditioned and understanding this will help in accepting each other's way of expressing oneself."

"If a person is part of a majority culture, he or she tends not to be understanding towards the minority culture. "Most White people resent why should there be Black History month. Why don't we have a White history month, like why is there a Black channel. Not realizing that every day everywhere is White channel."

"I have the same problem in finding makeup for my color, whereas all the makeup is for White-skinned people. There is to be a need for majority cultures to be sensitive to minority cultures."

Cultural Expectations

"We have similar value system. Practicing similar traditions is helpful. However what comes up for me from my culture is my self-esteem issues about the color of my skin, physical appearance, and keeping the house clean, different food habits is also an issue. I have to work through the different expectations."

"Cultural issues come up only when we are in cultural settings. Most of the time we get along well. So far there's not a lot of conflict. I accept her as a good human being. I was not looking for a person from a different culture. I just found her and fell in love. Since our religious beliefs are same, we have much in common. I don't believe that man is the head of the house and I give her full right to speak her mind."

"Once in a while when a story in the media comes up or I read something with racial or cultural themes, we will have discussions, sometimes arguments about it. Sometimes we differ in our perspective. I feel I am more tuned in to cultural and racial factors in certain situations whereas, he does not give much thought to it."

Things They Appreciate in Their Culture

"The close-knit aspects, for example, extended family involvement and lots of family support." "The strong sense of family." "The way people in my culture are constantly giving and there is never anything they wouldn't do. Even strangers are family." "The strong sense of pride and belonging." "Strong will to live beyond the normal just getting by and getting through." "I appreciate the history, the way of talking, and the moral conduct of its society." "As an American, we have great freedoms and a country which holds many beliefs that I hold myself: liberty, responsibility, respect for neighbor, education and hard work, and opportunity. As a southerner, I love the outdoors, the emphasis on family, and on being polite and respectful to other people." "It's collectivist way of life (e.g., value in family support), the food." "I love the values of my culture, modesty, hospitality, tolerance, and forbearance are some values that I love about my cultural background." "Familiarity with what is expected." "Satisfaction with understanding what I like." "Individualistic, get it done, attitude." "As an adult, I have somewhat deviated from the traditional Indian cultural aspects and have formed my own version of culture that includes a little bit of everything."

"In my culture I most admire the closeness, sense of family, and sense of belonging. I like that an entire village cares for you and there is no sense of formality. I like that even at the age of thirty-three, an aunt will pack food for me when I leave her house even though I can now cook for myself or buy grocery for myself. It feels safe and secure."

"I have had to negotiate this in my family. I have learned there is a sense of racism that is still alive and rampant in this world. I have learned you cannot easily change the beliefs of someone, especially if the person is older. I have also learned that people do judge a book by its cover, even if unfair, and many have a hard time looking beyond this." "Admire Most: Creativity and resilience." "Like: respect for family, elders, hard working." "Most get things done."

"I am a Malayalee from South India. I most admire the closeness to family, empathetic way of speaking, emphasis on education, and the country landscape."

"I admire most our warmth, manners, humor, pride, writers, emphasis on family, food, love of the land, and music." "I admire the traditional/collectivist nature of my African culture but also admire the individualism aspect of my American culture."

Things They Do Not Appreciate in Their Culture

"Gossiping, double standards." "Too much emphasis on superficial things." "Extended family involvement (sometimes not easy to deal with)." "The rigid way of looking at life (children must be doctors, etc., no real way to deviate from the norm)." "Sometimes choosing immediate gratification over the road less travelled." "Narrow-minded views and the underlying feeling that community members get jealous of each other's progress."

"The southern pride that celebrates the wrong things. That we lost the civil war, racism generally, and close-mindedness is a part of southern heritage. Especially out of Atlanta, people are still very segregated and rustic, and suspicious of progressive ideas of any sort." "Sometimes this collectivist way of life can be overbearing and intrusive."

"I struggled with the place of women in my culture, struggled to live in India as a single woman when I was single. I did not like that the communal aspect of my cultural background made me do things that I did not really have to do. How enmeshed families are in India. I have also struggled with inequality of class in India."

"Racism." "Spoiled attitude." "Wanting free handouts." "In my culture I least admire the double standard of people and the need to always show off. My community seems to emphasize money and material goods and someone who appears genuine is often not. I find it hard to truly have deep meaningful relationships because I am always afraid of saying too much and trusting too much, only to have the person turn on me and then use it against me, as I have seen so often. I feel that the relationships are great for some things and not others. There is no support for you unless you do what they think is appropriate. You cannot be different."

"Various negative stereotypes: Not respected for being intellectual and the constant association to badness whether it be crimes, violence, or finance." "Dislike: Men are in control and women are less valued." "I am least proud of pieces of our history, and the ignorance and close mindedness which accompanies some forms of popular southern culture (and true southerners who are). I do not like most good ol' boy southerners, 'southern pride' frat boys, or 'White trash' southerners."

Expectations of Themselves That Are Culturally Conditioned

"Being obedient and a 'good girl.'" "To 'look good' and to save face." "To please those in the community even if it does not please myself." "To make choices that others would expect of from me or would approve of." "Protecting and caring for my family and close friend." "Male being the dominant figure and the importance of language's empathetic demeanor."

Researcher: Elaborate "Male being the dominant figure." Where do you get that from? "Just the way my father and my brother behave and the reaction of their wives."

Researcher: Who is more rigid, she or you? "Hmm. There is rigidity on both sides. Our parents' generation has a different culture and today it seems to be in contradiction with our value system."

"To be manly and strong for my wife is number one. In fact, I think that might be the only one, as most of my other expectations I feel have been reflected upon. My parents always advocated independent thinking and consideration, respect for others and yourself, and work."

"This is a good question. My culturally conditioned mind says I have to be a good housewife, which according to me I am not, which was due to my career path. It makes me feel guilty that I am not a proficient home maker. (Example: Ironing shirt, keeping a clean home, making sure everyone is fed, etc.)" "To be a performer, to get things done, can do attitude."

Expectation of Their Partner That Is Culturally Conditioned

One of the participants said "education and career" were important to her. She also added that as parents it was important for her to "pay for college tuition of kids," as well as "always contributing financially for kids, i.e., helping pay for weddings, etc." Another said, "Taking part in family activities; family vacations." He added, "Treating even friends like family." Another added, "being more emotionally tuned in and nurturing" to each other. Another said that she wanted her partner "To be a leader and caretaker and responsible."

"He grew up American but Southern and he already fits into my cultural ideation of my man. We have similar values. He has become more open and accepting of me wanting to entertain guests. I want someone to understand that I have (family) responsibilities and he is understanding." The participant from India said, "I love poetry and Hindi music and *gazals* (Indian classical song). My heart ached that I can't share it with my husband. However, I do get a lot out in the relationship and so I don't make a great deal of it."

Culture vs. Personality

"Personality is shaped by culture. Sometimes it is hard to find a middle ground." "We viewed things like stubbornness or arrogance as being part of personality rather than as behavior conditioned by culture." "We had difficulty in understanding the different ways each of [our] cultures handled the issue of punctuality. It was easy accepting knowing that not being very punctual is culturally conditioned. I have changed a lot of things now. I am late to more things now (laughs)."

Exposure to Other Interracial Couples

The responses of the participants are as follows: "Yes, many of our friends are in mixed relationships and we interact with them regularly. My brother is in a mixed marriage as well, however, the remainder of my extended family is homogeneous and this concept is foreign to them." "Having friends in a similar situation has been helpful because it does not make us feel like we are doing something completely crazy. Our friends have kids and some have been married for ten years plus. It is helpful to have them as role models and to go to when we have questions. It is also helpful to have them to use to see what does and doesn't work, i.e., how we would do something and how we wouldn't."

One of the couples stated that, "One set of friends has emphasized language (French and Chinese) for their kids and we think this works well. Another couple has completely disregarded the particular cultural aspect of one of the partners and we have seen how this upsets the in-laws and why this doesn't work." "There are a few intercultural couples in my family but they do seem more isolated and don't attend family events as much." "Many of our friends are intercultural couples and it's very encouraging to see them happy and prospering." "Yes, many of our good friends are intercultural. Our next door neighbors were an intercultural couple, Black husband and White wife. I was in high school at the time, and I didn't know them that well. I didn't think much one way or the other about it, really." "We have friends that are in intercultural relationships and we have interacted with friends who are interracial couples." One male Caucasian participant observed that he has "only Jewish and Gentile" friends and that he has not had much exposure to intercultural couples.

Identity as an Intercultural Couple

"We do discuss racial/cultural/ethnic issues, especially when there is an action or behavior that is explained by our background. We also discuss how this will affect our children and what we will need to do in order to minimize the difficulties or how we will protect them from it/explain the issues to them."

"The interactions happen usually when I am being more concerned and my partner is being less concerned. This could be because he has dealt with this all his life (being a minority) whereas it is relatively new to me, even though I am also non-Caucasian but not necessarily a minority where I grew up. Either way, the interactions are usually addressed and brought up by me and we do discuss them together but it is he who provides more reassurance to me."

"As a couple, we would describe our identity just as 'mixed.'" "We are Malayalee Catholic—discussing our own racial/ethnic/cultural issues is not generally problematic, but we don't see eye to eye when discussing such issues generally." "We tend not to focus so much on racial issues but we do discuss cultural differences and try to really learn from each other. Issue of living in Atlanta is always our primary issue.... Mostly the cultural stuff isn't an issue. Not trying to avoid the question, it's just not a big deal anymore."

"In the past we argued a lot about being on time. I took it as a sign of disrespect that my wife would never be on time for anything when we both agreed to be there at a particular time. It took a long time to figure that one out."

"We used to argue a good deal about minority issues: Does racism still exist? Are all Black people one particular way? What sorts of things are true to say about people, and what is a stereotype?" Most of that was years ago, though, and we usually resolved it by reminding each other we were in love and I was with a Black woman (in spite of the fact I sometimes held views that were based on my ignorance about race/culture)."

"We don't discuss racial/cultural issues right now not a lot. We've been together for a long time and have worked out a lot of our difference. We sometimes have discussions about race, gender issues but nothing that significant."

Benefits of Intercultural Relationship/Marriage

One participant observed that the present President of the United States is a good example of what multicultural parents bring to you. "Growing up I saw biracial kids as coming from good, educated families, you have a plethora of opportunity and exposure that a lot of other kids will not have." Most of the responses were positive. "One gets the best of two different worlds, you really are a lot more diverse, open-minded, you are not pigeon-holed into being a certain way, you have more opportunity. One jokingly pointed out, "Nice having a minority background for scholarships." "Being an intercultural couple is a help because we bring very different attributes and perspective to our relationship." "I've found that the main hindrance occurs during some cultural activities and the other person is completely unfamiliar with the situation. Some people are so interested in us and tend to stare, which is uncomfortable."

Stating their reservations, one of them added, "Marriage is already so difficult that adding more differences will just make it harder if a couple doesn't have a strong relationship." Another said, "Socially speaking, intercultural relationships are not as easy as being with the person of the same skin color, so you know you're in it for the right reasons." "Living in a city, and in Atlanta no less, makes it pretty easy to be in a counter-culture type of relationship." "We bring different strengths to each other and that makes us together a stronger unit."

Researcher: Do you think intercultural couples have to work harder than couples of similar cultures to make their marriage work? "Probably it is a little hard but if you are in it for the right reasons then it is not."

Raising Bicultural or Biracial Child(ren)

Researcher: What are the joys or privileges for a child to be biracial? How will you contribute to their well-being? What is required in terms of attitude or mindset in bringing them up? "Biracial children are positively impacted because you have not made race as a big deal, though you live in two cultures. You do not show whether culture was either an attraction or a challenge." "If the worst thing that I will do to my child is to have them biracial but healthy then I will take it. They will get the best of both worlds. They will have different worldviews and they can make their choice."

"Our children will be mixed which is an odd idea, but I don't think it's going to matter once I have a son or daughter." "I am concerned about the acceptance of our kids by others and people treating them poorly." "I am nervous about them having no identity and not feeling like they belong to either mine or my partner's community." "I am concerned about them not having a childhood rich of culture, in whatever form, or tradition or learning our languages." "I wonder and hope that if we have children they will be able to associate to both our cultures and not be too one sided."

"My wife worries most about raising our children, and she sometimes worries the views I hold are ignorant. I'm from the south, was raised Republican, and many issues that minorities view in one perspective I view (or viewed) differently." "I have two concerns. One, I wonder how I will be able to help my children with issues of racism. But I don't think it will be that much of an issue. Two, I wonder that perhaps my child will one day identify more with one race than the other, and push one parent out. I don't know how common this is."

"I don't have significant fears but I do think about how to provide an environment that is diverse. I want to make sure that our children are exposed to both cultures and races equally." "They get the benefit of parents who are open and exposed to different cultures and raise their child of teaching them that all people are good. To make sure they are loved and accepted and take a strong positive place."

"It is strange for me to think that my child is going to be Black and will not look like me. I am not too worried about it but it will be a question of identity for them in terms of where do they belong." "How we see them is not how the world will see them. They will be seen as Black. We have not given it much thought. When we get to it we have a counselor guide us through it."

Researcher: Do you want them to learn your language and will you support her? "I don't speak the language but I would like them to be around my sisters and parents so that they will learn." Her partner replied, "I will support her. Her culture is important and I would like for her to teach them about food, cultural values, etc." "Sometimes these cultural issues are related to us having children and how they will be raised and our expectations of them. The expectations of our kids are different because in the Indian culture that I was brought up in parents do a lot for their kids in the early years but maintain that type of mentality throughout life."

Resolving Political Differences of Opinion

One participant indicated that he became rebellious and radical after being raised in a very conservative environment. Another participant defied convention in taking the step to come to us and also in marrying a man from another culture. One of the participants who did not receive premarital counseling together, wished to have brought this up before they got married. They suspect that issues that they did not address together could potentially become a struggle later when they face big decisions. Another female participant affirmed that she is very comfortable with her own evolution and she is not looking for his approval. She said that an investment in her own growth gave her the freedom to express who she was and even if he were to disagree with her or dislike her for her opinions that she would be OK. She iterated that she was not always like that, for before she went for individual counseling, she would have been disturbed by disapproval but today, she feels secure in her opinion and in finding her voice. Today, she said she is comfortable in choosing to be compassionate over fundamentalism or conservatism. She emphatically affirmed that today "I embrace difference."

Her husband stated that "I am conservative and she leans towards liberal," and so we have differences of opinion on some issues. He said that he is open to other opinions but it will be hard for him to change that opinion based on his life's experiences, but he thinks that they can work that out.

Researcher: How much work has gone into understanding and acceptance of each other's worldview? "To keep an open mind about other person's opinion knowing that you love the other person." "Talking about issues without the stereotypes."

"We were one of the first American/Canadian couples. There are differences in worldviews. There is a resentment about the national laws which is much bigger than the couple themselves. For example, welfare in a capitalistic society, politics of universal health care. My views are viewed as bad—there is judgment. I didn't think that moving from Canada to America will be a different transition but it is very difficult. We make fun of each other and we don't relent. We try not to talk about issues."

Ways Culture has Changed Their Value System

"I have seen many relationships broken between family members for things that seem unclear, insignificant, or due to a misunderstanding—makes me focus and realize what is important in life is the small, simple things and to not let materialistic things get in the way." "Appreciating culture has made me appreciate and be thankful for what I have. It's greatly affected my outlook on life. I often say I'm a glass-half-full person and I can always find something to be grateful about." "Deep respect and value for family and religion, Culture has instilled a strong work ethic and self-respect. Caring and respecting the elderly and the loving demeanor showed to children. Emphasis on education is also the key. The respect for people, everyday life, work hard, do your duty with honesty. My parents grew up in segregation, being the only minority in majority schools being positive, I have a bigger threshold for pain, more stability, support system for each other."

"Yes there was, but we viewed ourselves only as Catholic and not as intercultural. We did not see much difference between America and Canada. Values like moral, respect for parents, culture, religion, rigidity in following belief system, following rules and practices, understand ourselves, being one with God we are similar. The difference is in some doctrines, or how we give back to society, specific rules followed by the church or how a person perceives those rules." "Growing up in two different countries definitely contributed to our life, for example, trusting factor on the government, ours is more social and here it is more conservative. I feel I am more liberal and my spouse is not so much. Culture influences worldview and worldview influences personality. For example, recycling. As I reflected on both of us I realized that even though we have so many similarities we are so different. Both of us are western and eastern as well as even western is different."

"My father always wanted me to explore other possibilities. My father did not want me to go to Catholic school but wanted me to go to public school. My mother wanted the opposite and my father relented. He introduced us to different religions and different foods. I am more open-minded because of it. I come from Toronto which is a big city and very multicultural." "Some of my behaviors stem out of a cultural paradigm, for example my love for hospitality, my particular way of treating elders, the way I dress, the way I think of myself in the context of family are some things that are shaped by culture. Some of my choices of movies (I dislike violence) like romantic movies, like poetry and mushy songs– these are all a direct result of my own cultural shaping."

"In every way. I grew up here. I am a product of my culture. My religious subculture is the strongest influencer." "We do. Hospitality and entertaining at home is a cultural value that I bring and he shares that value. Care of an older parent. Raising kids and how much exposure to doing things independently is something we have discussed. We are a newlywed couple so at this stage it is not an area of conflict, but it could turn into that."

Ways Value System Plays Out in Their Relationship

"Yes, we value similar things." "The same value system is our common bond or common 'language.'" "Majority of the time yes but not always." "Both are honest, down to earth, believe in the goodness of the world, more giving, loyalty and being grounded in religion and faith vs. language and culture. It comes back to family of origin. I try to be independent and to accept responsibility for my wrongs. I try not to show-off or make excuses. I think all these are American traits as well as southern traits and values, and this is how I was brought up."

"Yes, but our values cohere along most lines, so it's not a conflict. Instead they keep us together more than anything else, and include everything from our sense of humor to what we think of as good morals to how we like to spend our time." "Values will also play a role raising children. I'm not worried because we've already talked about our values and what matters to us, and what we want our children to know and to have from us as parents."

"Because of my culture, I value collaboration and have a strong sense of social responsibility, doing your part to contribute for the betterment of the group."

"Not really."

"Yes it does. I think the way I treat my husband comes directly from my cultural background, i.e., making warm meals, saw my mom do things that I have observed that I repeat in my relationship. Growing up in a pluralistic society gives me a broader and more tolerant perspective. (Share an example from the first conflict that arose in our marriage.)"

"Yes. I am not as communal in my orientation." "Because I am introverted I don't communicate as much as my spouse would like."

Being an Intercultural Couple a Help or Hindrance

"If there is a conflict in my family, everyone jumps in together to find a way out. There is ownership and relational thing attached to it and that is nice but it also gives rise to expectation. When issues come up I rely on my family. Team work and collaboration is valued. That's the way I grew up and it comes up naturally to me. Friends matter. Helping is important. It is not like the American way to volunteer, etc., but to take care of friends and those who know me well. Example: For our wedding, his mom told him to inform the guests how much it will cost for the wedding and so that they will come prepared. My father was not willing to ask people to pay for food particularly when they are our guest."

"It is great to be an intercultural couple because you open your world to new ideas, possibilities and ways of life and truly can become a more diverse, open minded individual." "I feel as though because of being an intercultural couple we think more openly and focus on the bigger picture instead of getting stuck with small details." "It is amazing to see their friends and their families blend."

"It is also challenging—people don't always support us, or don't think we are 'good people' and we have a lot of negative energy directed towards us." "People from one's native culture or faith sometimes feel we have 'sold ourselves out' and are therefore not always accepting or kind towards us." "There is a sense of concern in that we are navigating waters that are unchartered or less chartered and therefore may not know what we are faced with in the future."

"Each individual does compromise a bit of their background or religion in the process of combining with someone else of a different background, i.e., my partner doesn't speak the same language so for my children, it will take extra effort to teach them and have them learn (however, we have seen it done so it's not impossible)." "My partner is from Canada and I think they are much more accepting there so he has helped me to see instances where I could be more culturally accepting and I am working on that."

"Help: we learn things from each other; Hindrance: I don't have anything in mind." "Yes. The world is gradually changing but we still get stares and curious looks, even in cities like New York. It's a pressure from society as well as family and friends."

Cultural Attitudes That Attracted Them to Their Partner

One of the male Caucasian participants reported about his partner of African descent that at first he was physically attracted to her but the more he got to know her the more he liked her and the fact that she is hardworking attracted him to her. He added that she was easy to talk to and I felt that she was a genuine person and stated that, "It is hard to find all these qualities in one person." He also said that people from her country are hard workers, generous, they care for family. He said "Some are arrogant, but my wife is humble and dislikes loudmouths and braggarts. She also shares my sense of humor, which I think she gets from her parents." She in turn reported that "he was respectful and did not seem to indicate that he was entitled." "I love his egalitarian approach, which I could not have gotten had I married a man from my own culture. His appreciation for me is heightened because I am different which is good for me as a woman. He loves my clothes, my food." She added that "I did date a man from my culture in which men generally do not show affection in the way that I needed—being romantic or show affection in public. But I liked the way the man I am dating now showed affection and tenderness. We are affectionate in public as well. Therefore, culture did play a role in selecting my partner."

Another female participant of Indian descent said about her African American partner, "My partner is kind, loving and loyal. He has a strong sense of family and never lets me down. He is always on my team and always supportive of me and encouraging. He believes in me probably more than I believe in myself." She added that, "My partner is a person of strong, solid character and his value system is one that I respect and admire. Culture did not play a role in us getting together, as far as I think." He in turn said that, "She was extremely caring, thoughtful, and calm. I've had many friends throughout school, who were from a similar culture as she is. I think she liked the idea that I loved the food and knew quite a bit about her culture." She practices Hindu faith and he practices Christianity. He said that, "Initially, I did not foresee any relationship issues due to cultural differences. I truly feel that although we are different in culture and faith, we have very similar values and beliefs and align with one another in all other aspects of life. We both respect God, in whichever form, and feel the same way when it comes to treating others, treating ourselves, and our ultimate goals in life." "However," he added, "The cultural differences were highlighted more when my family made it clear they are not accepting." "I was attracted to her mainly because of her kindness and generosity. Yes, I did foresee major relationship issues due to religious differences but she was pretty persistent in showing me that a relationship could work. We had many discussions about culture, race, and religious differences before we started dating.

A female participant, who is from the same ethnic background as her husband but grew up in a different country than him, said "I was attracted to him because of his personality, that he was handsome and was from similar ethnic and religious background as me, Malayalee, Catholic, and we clicked." "I loved his sense of humor and we understood each other. I did not foresee any issues due to Canadian/US differences." She added, "Culture played a huge role. I was looking only for a mate from my own ethnic and religious group namely Malayalee Catholic. He in turn added, "I was attracted to her because of her prettiness, slim figure, intelligence, and good conversation." He further stated that, "My partner was easy to be with and that was the first thing. It was young love, we spent every day with each other for years. And in spite of the arguments it was always good. At the time I didn't foresee any problems because I didn't look into the future. It was one day at a time for many years."

A male Caucasian participant said this about his Indian bride: "Physical attraction was what was at the start but later I discovered that I related well to her. She was easy to talk to. I had a good vibe. The more I got to know her the more I realized we shared the same values, and in that sense culture played some role." The Indian bride stated that "I was attracted to him because he is sweet, tender, quiet but confident, he is also handsome and very good hearted. From the start of our relationship, he always made me feel accepted." "Culture did not play a big role in us getting together." She added, "His American egalitarian values were definitely very attractive to me. His value system was similar to me that made me feel safe. His similar work ethic makes me full of hope for the future. I was attracted to him because of his love of God and love of people in general. What attracted me to him was his kind, caring nature, his strong sense of family and his overall demeanor. He has a strong value system, is loyal and trustworthy and has principles that he always abides by."

"Being humble and finding good in other people, being fair, open mindedness, what motivates people and the fact that nobody is perfect. These are not necessarily that I had, I was quick to judge and I have learned a lot from her. Though I always had these core values but I have become more open and accepting. I was brought up as a Republican and so was less forgiving of other people's faults. I am better at it now. This leads to more acceptance of each other." "Being less anxious."

Cultural Issues Brought up in the Relationship

One of the male participants mentioned that "my partner brings it up because of her family dynamic and her family's lack of acceptance of our relationship." Another participant said that it was their therapist that brought up cultural issues. One of the female participants from Ghana expressed that she feels embarrassed being in social situations when they are together and that she is "not entirely comfortable around large groups and don't like being the center of attention, so it can be trying when we go to places we know people will stare." However, she said that "our therapist taught us to talk about these situations and rely on each other during such times."

Another Caucasian male participant said that "our counselor brought some cultural things to our attention and that led us to conversations about our cultural differences, fears, etc."

Cultural Issues that Lead to Discord in Relationship

"I have written about "White Privilege" where White people tend not to really spend time with any other culture, don't necessarily talk about it and think about it, that it really exists. I have realized that it actually does exist."

"White people don't particularly see the cultural aspect. For example, we were watching an episode of *Law & Order* and a White policeman walks into a Black neighborhood and wants to question a Black woman. The Black woman does not want to talk to the policeman and asks him to leave. He was perplexed as to why she would not talk to the policeman? I explained that maybe because she is not very trusting of the White policeman. I am more sensitive to race issues but he doesn't seem to get it. It does impact him because I find him more tuned in to those issues."

"The acceptance of my partner and treatment of my partner due to cultural differences is the biggest issue we deal with. My culture is somewhat closed off and does not tolerate or easily accept my partner and for this reason, we often feel isolated and excluded." "Addressing these issues and concerns is a problem, because there is no good solution but to keep trying and hope for change." "I think I have always been respectful towards other cultures but being with my partner has further made me understand how everyone truly can be the same person despite differences in color, race and, faith. My partner's family is very similar to my own (but a different faith) and the way we spend each day is actually quite similar. They, however, may not realize that." "Yes, I've always been respectful of other cultures because many times I've been the minority."

"My partner has helped to broaden my view by providing her opinion or hearing her describe a situation in each we both were present but had different interpretations and reactions." "Being newly married, we have had very few issues but when they come, I have tried to be very open and clear about my stances. The way kids are to be raised has been one issue. The care of an older mother-in-law is another issue. The judgment towards divorced people is another issue." "Yes, we try to be aware of our different ideas, opinions, and reactions to life. When we discuss issues, it's important to identify which ones are cultural versus which ones are just our own individual quirks or preferences."

"Gender issues." "Language and living in India." "We have a lot of issues with time. I tend to be more relaxed and think of time in a relative sense, while he is very punctual. Initially, we fought a lot over this because we lacked understanding of the cultural differences but in recent years, and through therapy we have become more aware and understanding of each other and have tried to compromise and accommodate each other."

"For example working on time or being punctual. He would think that I had a personality defect. When he was with my family, he learned how laid back we are. Earlier he thought that I was being rude and disrespectful of him. Now, I have learned to adapt and be on time and he has learned not to get offended. I am influenced by my culture about how to relate to people of the opposite sex. He is more accepting now and does not judge me."

Discussing/Resolving Issues of Discord

One participant acknowledges that it is easier to work with issues with a third party rather than trying to work at it by themselves as a couple. Another participant admits that after premarital counseling they have made much progress with communication. Yet another realizes that it is a work in progress and that he is intentional about solving conflict. For one participant communication was not successful at times because there was more irrationality, but now she is learning to give up on always trying to be "right" and focusing on what is good for both. One responded by saying that for a long time she believed that the way her husband communicated with her was more a personality trait rather than learned behavior but after seeing the changes in the pattern of communication she feels that it is possible to solve conflicts. Another said that one partner had a very difficult father and the other had a very difficult mother and so a behavior pattern got passed on but now with premarital counseling they were able to recognize that and effectively address it. One of the participants indicated that they are making much progress because they now have the tools of conflict resolution as well as changed pattern of communication. Another said that earlier they just avoided those issues but now are able to work towards a satisfactory resolution. One participant said that they try different things, at times they procrastinate and sometimes the conflict doesn't get addressed or resolved but most of the time they are able to sit together and resolve amicably. One husband noted that his newly wedded wife has strong opinions about parenting and sibling position, that he is open to her input but ultimately he will make the choice with his son from his first marriage. He said that mostly he understands his wife's point of view but that he may get there from a different way. The participant husband said that we don't think the same way and her insights were often very foreign to him, even challenging, for example, once she told him that "I want to be real than proper." He responded that if am in her place I would rather be proper than real.

"Because we talked about culture we were able to understand the differences and how they play an important role in our relationship. Now we have a better understanding of our situation and thus a better perspective. Earlier, there were some issues that were causing conflicts but we really could not put our finger on it. Our therapist helped us tap into it and now as we go through these questions together we are able to figure out where we stand."

Researcher: How will you work through mutual respect for both cultures? "Spend time with each other's families." "By experiencing both cultures equally. I want it to be balanced and I know it is not going to be easy."

Cultural Issues Most Effective in Premarital Counseling

One of the participants stated the following: "couple decision-making process, financial honesty, having someone understand my culture and then be able to explain it to my partner—it was effective to relate these issues to our situation and apply it." Another said that "we wanted to get married and so really wanted to explore whether we could make the lifelong commitment necessary for marriage. Another participant said, "understand better ways to communicate with each other based on how partner's own cultural "language." One male Caucasian participant, who attended individual therapy, and talked about premarital issues but not necessarily cultural issues said, "We didn't really touch on cultural issues." Another female participant from Africa married to a Caucasian male participant said that "It helped me to learn about my partner's culture because I used to get offended when he would tell me to be quiet and to be less loud, but in talking about how he grew up, being a quiet personality, I was able to take it less personal and able to understand that his culture was generally more subdued and calm."

Cultural Issues Least Effective in Premarital Counseling

All the participants were in agreement in saying, "none." Were they aware of their cultural differences while in premarital counseling?

"We were aware of some cultural differences but not all." "We chose to do counseling for differences in faith more than culture." "We needed someone to guide us through our differences and find common ground." "With all of the external pressure, we started to lose sight of what had brought us together in the first place and we needed someone to help re-align this." "I realized that in India everything is relational and barter and negotiating, whereas I don't do that. It requires more emotional energy to accomplish a task." "Yes. I'd say we went to premarital counseling more for communication and arguing, though." "There has been cultural divide between my spouse's family and mine. Some of it is because of the different places where our parents are from with respect to religion and exposure."

Foreseeing Any Cultural Issues While Dating

"Culturally, most Indian women take care of their house. I have been a single woman and been very independent. Since I am a working woman I feel that I am not being a good wife. He does cleaning and laundry. I like cooking and so I cook. These are cultural things and I bring it to bear on me." "I feel a little uncomfortable when I am in the Indian Church setting but otherwise nothing much. We are just people. She feels bad that she is not being 'house-wifey'. I am fine with that." "I think most of my expectations stem from what I need in a partner and my values. I don't expect her to be girlish because I wouldn't be attracted to her if she was. So the rest is mostly to be good, kind, understanding, diligent—that sort of thing."

"Probably the only thing that was conditioned for me to expect from my wife is to be clean. My mother was very clean, and I'm not sure I'd be all right with her not keeping the house fairly clean. But she does, so it's no issue."

"I don't know . . . have not thought about it." "None, since he is not from my own culture, however, his egalitarian approach warms my heart, however not being able to share a beautiful piece of poetry with him has been sad. A lot of joy of watching movies is lost in cultural translation." "Submit to my leadership." "To respect me."

Experience of Premarital Counseling

"In the Catholic Church it is very organized, they go through various topics, theological, finance, conflict resolution, contact survey, one-on-one with the priest, comments from priest. The group activity was good but we missed the one on one with the priest and feel that we missed out on something."

Researcher: Initially you both did not come for premarital counseling but more because of a crisis in the relationship and for discernment whether this will work for both of you.

"During the course of two and a half years we did work on some issues to work towards preparation for marriage in terms of premarital counseling. One of the main things that we had conflict was about competiveness or 'you' vs. 'me.' The biggest thing that I learned was it is never you vs. me but you and me. The commitment piece that there is no escape route in marriage and buying into it helped changed my approach."

Reasons for Choosing Premarital Counseling

"Talking to someone else helps when we are in that crazy emotional state, especially talking to a therapist. It doesn't help to try and work things out just by ourselves." "We sought counseling because we faced religious differences that are cultural in our case. We participated in premarital counseling for about two years before marrying." "I was aware in a subconscious way but did not really have discussions about it. Culture was not the reason we participated in counseling."

Married couple who did not have premarital counseling together said, "I am very aware of the differences and we keep addressing them as they come up, however, it may be a good thing to have a therapist lead us into a deeper understanding and find out potential problems that may occur."

"I certainly was aware of many of them. I chose to embrace our similar subculture." "Needed an outside opinion from someone who is neutral to help us negotiate some of our issues." "To have a third person go through potential areas of concern or trouble we may have in the future, to lay it out for us so we can discuss now instead of later, and so we are prepared for it at least a little bit." "We were finding that we were overwhelmed and needed to air our voices and concerns" "We needed to do some damage control. We were in bad shape coming back from a long break. I was a mess. We needed someone to help show us how to love each other again." "To help us move through a tough time in our relation (did not know if we wanted to be together)." "We also needed a lot of help to communicate with each other."

Helpfulness of Premarital Counseling

"It was a very worthwhile experience. We were exposed to differences as well as similarities and were able to discuss these in an open manner." "We had discussed some issues on our own but did not make much progress until we had a neutral third party." "It is something I would recommend to anyone, even if same-race or same-faith." "It allowed us to see each other's perspectives better."

"It helped us build a strong bond by offering a forum to discuss things with a moderator. Our counselor was also a translator at times, able to get the point also in terms more easily understood by the other person." "Very minor—we met with the priest briefly and attended a weekend long Pre-Cana retreat."[2] "It was required by the Church.""Pre-Cana retreat was enlightening and bonding experience. We opened up quite a bit to each other through journal entries (writing)."

"Not sure if we took full advantage. We did the couple Catholic retreat and that was very good. It was for three days and we reviewed a lot of material and were given the chance to practice a lot of communication techniques." "We did not properly do the couple survey and did not work with a priest as we were supposed to."

---

2. Pre-Cana is a course or consultation for couples preparing to be married in a Catholic church. The name is derived from John 2:1–12, the wedding feast at Cana in Galilee, where Jesus performed the miracle of turning water into wine. https://en.wikipedia.org/wiki/Pre-Cana.

"I did not realize cultural differences until after we were married. This was nuclear family differences." "Really pulling and working on the issues between us versus the impact of other people in our lives."

"Therapy is good, to address issues, to expect to know what will come up. My friends cannot find a therapist who can understand all cultures. It will be good to have a data base of mixed couples. After you go through animosity and hate it is hard to trust anyone. You cannot go to your church or faith resources because you know they will not be on your side." "I realized that we were making progress. Therapy brought about issues that were not just skin deep. Our individual sessions were just as important as couple and those were good."

"Culture is very important. After we move forward from our honeymoon phase it begins to surface. Taking the time to talk about premarital counseling is a fantastic idea. We view marriage as a covenant and the church does all they can to see that marriage work. The premarital counseling worked exceptionally well for us but it is not the case with every couple. For many it is a drag. After the weekend, it will be beneficial to have one or two one on one sessions. It is good to become aware and then continue to work on issues."

"We were in a road to progress and we would have benefitted more if we had stayed longer. Couples should be mandated by law to be in marital counseling. Because of the taboo on counseling it is so difficult to opt for counseling. People think that you must be in dire strait to go for counseling and not just for fine tuning."

Aspects of Premarital Counseling That Were Most Helpful

"Having the reinforcement from a third party on our ideas and approach." "Having a third person help navigate some issues." "Having confidence instilled in me." "Seeing things in a new light." "So the emphasis on complimenting each other was helpful. It brought in commitment and ownership." "Just started to act on it. I realized that I have only one choice and how do I make it work rather than hope it works." "Without the counseling we would not have made it. She gave us the tools that showed us how to work together and communicate." "Learning about the impact our differing backgrounds and culture has on our relationship." "Learning how to express needs in ways the other can hear." "Learning about myself."

"Helpful to identify what issues may come up." "Helpful to 'name' things as I felt it." "Helpful to get an 'outside' perspective so that I saw things from the outside rather than how I felt subjectively." "To know what to expect and to know that way that I should respond." "We found it helpful because it was a systematic approach." "Each issue was addressed and given potential solutions." "If there is an issue that has no good solution, we were at least given some type of coping mechanism." "Sometimes there is no good answer to something but we still felt like we had discussed it enough to feel better about it."

Aspects of Premarital Counseling That Were Least Helpful

"Anything abstract where I could not find a place for it in my life." "Any concept that was ambiguous or too wide a topic." "We took a required pre-marriage test and priest forgot to give us results but told us after we were married that there were significant discrepancies in our results and that we should meet with counselor to go over them but he never provided them." "I didn't get much out of at-home exercises." "Least helpful was giving the options for what we would like to talk about versus approaching all problems in a systematic manner." "Talking about day-to-day issues that are top of mind." "Can't think of any." "Can't think of anything right now."

Tools in Premarital Counseling to Enter into Marriage

"In our case things were tenuous for a long time. We absolutely needed it. I personally had to do a lot of work in my own personal life in general to even participate being in a relationship. We had reached an impasse in our life and I don't know if we could have figured it out on our own. It would not have worked out if we had not had counseling. We got tools and the time a third party who could look, most importantly at reality check and not so much in trying to understand her but understand myself and to see when I was improving and when I was declining."

"Life seems less flighty and more secure and because we had done premarital counseling, even when we are faced with difficult situations we know how to handle it." "It was a question of whether we want to move forward or not. We had some trust issues. I had to honestly answer the question "Is it really worth moving forward with this person?"

Researcher: What kept you going?

"I saw glimpses of what he can be. We were really good partners. I could see the end goal. Our families were supportive. I took their advice and that also influenced. There were times when I wanted to give up but it was a combination of that he is worthwhile, I loved him, and that I had support. My faith and religion helped me." "Religious difference, when you do the questions in the beginning that you will be able to find out what the focus of each person. My main focus was raising kids, so good to have a questionnaire just for this. A person who has done mixed couple is more helpful."

Reasons for Choosing that Particular Therapist

A particular participant's reason for getting into counseling was because of an ultimatum given by his partner saying that he needed to be counseled. Participants had varied responses to the question about the choice of a particular therapist. For one of them, it didn't matter who the counselor would be. Another preferred someone older than self. A third one preferred a therapist married for a long time. The need for feeling connected with therapist was yet another preference. One participant mentioned that culture of the therapist was not an issue. The fact that a particular therapist was assigned by the counseling center to this participant made the participant feel right about it. Non-judgmental and patient approach of the therapist was important to one of the participants. Demonstration of good insights was a trait that a participant looked for. To one of the participant the ability of the therapist in helping to deal with anger issues and moving past the marital conflicts was important. Similar cultural and faith background of the therapist was important to another participant as this would help the therapist understand particular issues that the participants faced.

One of the participants stayed with his therapist for two years and said he would continue onwards indefinitely if given the opportunity. Another felt the therapist really understood the couple's issues and was able to relate to them well. This participant was with this therapist for roughly three years and the reason for choosing this therapist was because of similar ethnic and religious background. Another participant said that they continued to stay in therapy because they found it effective for gaining greater insights into one another and the therapist helped them navigate very difficult times related to family issues. Another participant accepted the therapist chosen by the spouse. They worked with the therapist for a little over two years. The couple stayed in therapy because they felt that the therapist understood them and they felt that they made progress through the therapy.

Helpful Characteristics in Their Therapist

"I was able to relate to her because she was of the same religion and I felt comfortable. We were looking for a translator, so that both can understand each other's 'language'. I feel even though religion may be different but culturally you can be close. I separate religion and culture. Religion is more difficult to work through. My therapist helped me to work through issues and name them. It made both of us to think and even change our mind in some ways, to think and work out for ourselves. She was afraid that if she went to a pastor for counseling he/she may judge her because of her faith and may want to convert her. However even though my therapist's religion was different from her's she was comfortable to work with the therapist because my therapist was from her culture."

"We both felt the therapist was like a big sister or mom that made us feel comfortable." "Every culture is different but I am more used to the nurturing type and so my therapist's personality helped me." "Non-judgmental approach of the therapist helped us a lot—forcing us to examine ourselves and our own actions, and reminding us we love each other." "Empathetic, caring, great listening skills." "Able to identify with my faith or culture or both. Not taking sides." "Having the ability to explain and advise without having any personal biases, being nonjudgmental."

"I suppose someone who was married and had been married for a long time. Someone older than my wife and me, too." "Someone who is fair, a good listener, nurturing." "Fair, non-judgmental, open and willing to see different perspectives.""Being a woman, an immigrant, coming from a collectivist culture herself she was very tuned in to my cultural experience."

"My time with her was very transformational. I continue to dip into the wisdom I gained from her. We want to go back to therapy together. He was overwhelmed by the love and affection he got. He got a better idea of my life and who I am and also why I am the way I am. Part of the joy of coming to United States was to live my life with freedom as a single woman. Thinking through the questionnaire helped me to understand how culture impacts my marriage. It was an awareness-generating tool for me." "I could relate to my therapist because she too was from another culture."

"For White people in general it is a serious thing that you keep time. This was my problem with her. I thought that she does understand but that she doesn't care. My therapist helped me understand the cultural piece in time and I began to calm down and not get offended." "I now believe that the importance of punctuality is culturally conditioned. I did not understand anything about White privilege and so did not see it but my therapist helped me to see it."

Recommending Their Therapist to Another Couple

"Yes." "Attentive, caring and neutral." "Has a strong understanding of humanity and the importance of forming a set of values." "Very empathetic." "It's important that the therapist has strong cultural tie/similarity that both individuals receiving counseling can identify." "I think the Pre-Cana retreat is very beneficial, but I think one-on-one counseling by a trained priest for more than five sessions is key." "Trust is important, whenever you asked us to do something we did it." "Trust was built because we saw the therapy work." "Yes." "Yes, in fact my wife has. Our therapist's personality is well-suited to counseling, she's been married for a long period of time, she was born and raised in a separate culture and so understands." "Also her techniques seemed to work, she was consistent and persistent in getting us to try them and stick with it, and she never gave up or showed signs of frustration in spite of the fact we spun our wheels at times." "Yes. Her cultural sensitivity." "Being totally objective will be helpful. Understanding the nuances of the cultures will be helpful." "Yes! I would recommend my therapist to any Indian that is married in an intercultural setting."

Themes in Premarital Counseling

When asked what themes would they suggest in premarital counseling, one of them suggested that "themes help the couple to be more grounded in reality rather than be on cloud nine."

"Communication, parenting, having a first child, recycling, personality issues, understanding in-laws, governing attitudes vs. romantic attitudes, body image, sibling-order." "Psycho education—take-home material is helpful to know that a topic is coming up." "Communication, achieving goals, finance, career, salary, parenting and raising biracial child (ren)." "Keeping up the romance, practices in accepting the differences and to feel loved and valued in the relationship, roles and responsibilities, expectations changing with regard to cooking and house work and the need to be equal partners, finance—as to how we will support a family, about parenting, gender roles, raising biracial children, better communication."

"It was good to have my therapist help me understand the need to ask for help from my partner. I started doing this and my partner would help if I asked him to. The same was true when it came to asking to get engaged or get married. When my therapist helped me to name the issue or the problem then I was able to proceed in finding the solutions."

"Because of my travels I am more open to diversity whereas he is not as open. To talk about how we can be different yet together. How we can share our opinions openly without feeling threatened, to be comfortable with the fact that I am different. Another area is in the area of bringing up children. I want them to be exposed to different people and situations. He thinks I am more liberal than he expected me to be and I think he is far more conservative than what I expected him to be. I wish we had talked about it before. I feel that I did the work in therapy that I am good and I don't need his approval always. He says that he wants to change and that he lives life vicariously through me. We had a discussion about being 'proper' than being 'genuine or authentic.'"

"Aging parents, where will we live, religious differences, raising kids, and how we expect to navigate through all these. When we started dating we didn't talk about it. But now we do because we want to make sure we are on the same page and counseling helped us to bring that out and helped us find truthful answers."

Process of Therapy

"Sometimes I felt fairly stuck and no movement because my partner was stuck and we had to repeat some issues. But once my partner was able to resolve those we were able to move forward. I don't think about the past but I found my partner to be very nostalgic." "I felt good that things were coming out in the open. I did feel challenged but happy that it needed to happen."

Duration of Premarital Counseling

Of the eight participants, one said that she attended individual weekly sessions for two years that included sessions of premarital counseling. Her husband too attended forty individual sessions that included six to eight sessions on premarital counseling. Another participant couple said that they attended about fifteen sessions together. Yet another participant couple said that they attended more than fifty sessions over a period of two years. One other participant married couple attended about four to six sessions in premarital counseling.

"Focus on the issue and guide them through it, twelve to sixteen sessions 25 percent individual and 75 percent tandem." "It is hard to generalize. Each couple is different."

Dealing with Matters of Finance

"Money is both a cultural and a personal issue. I have to pay to belong to my family. I don't expect him to pay." "As an only child I am not in a family where I have to take care of siblings." "I like to give gifts but it is not something in her culture. They have a family fund, because she supports the whole community. My father will never ask for money. Old people are expected to take care of themselves in my family. In her family there is an expectation to take care of the whole family." "I think we just assumed they were the same since on paper we were the same. Probably it would have been wise to discuss it at more length."

Support from Family of Origin

"Both parents and immediate family of this couple have been extremely supportive. And even at the college (Georgia State) at which they studied, where the student body was culturally mixed and progressive, they found a lot of support." "We were faced with huge geographic hurdles whether to move to United States or Canada." "We had very different views on patriarchal nature of our culture with my husband's side placing much greater emphasis on it and my side finding that somewhat insulting."

"My family has been extremely supportive. My wife's family has been extremely supportive too. We broke up for a while, and before getting back together I spoke with her mother a number of times trying to figure things out (as well as speaking to my mother a couple of times a week). And everyone all around has always been in favor of us marrying and starting our family." "We have been very lucky with support from both sides of the family and friends. We have not had any conflicts thus far." "My family has been very supportive and encouraging. Our community has been very helpful and supportive as well." "Grandma gave me a long talk about raising kids according to God's will. They were upset that I did not agree with everything. I felt frustrated and angry."

In-Laws and Hardships in Intercultural Marriage

"It was a shock to my grandmother, however, both families have tended to be supportive. The extended family knows about it and they don't express shock or surprise." "My side of the family, both immediate and extended, does not support or tolerate my relationship with the exception of my brother and his wife (who are also an intercultural couple but initially also were not too supportive)."

"My parents, my mom especially, do not acknowledge the relationship nor do they 'tolerate it' (in their words) and feel as though I will never fit into my partners' family. They feel as though I am failing in life. They are in denial and will not discuss the relationship with their friends or extended family as they feel embarrassed. These hurdles ultimately have been challenging but counseling has been helpful in dealing with them. The majority of my family and friends have been extremely supportive. The main hurdle was choosing to marry someone of a different faith. I was pleasantly surprised by some of my friends who were way more supportive than expected."

"My partner's family on the other hand has been anything but supportive, which has contributed to a lot of hurt feelings and anger with respect to my family. This has been very difficult to navigate but again my family and friends have taken things in stride as best expected."

Negotiating Different Faith Practices

"Religiously we are different but ultimately believe in God and the idea of a supreme-being who takes care of us, whether he or she is Jesus, Allah, Krishna, etc. Having this common belief shapes how we act, how we live and how we treat one another as well as those around us." "We both believe in mutual respect and fairness, which comes from our different faiths. Although we are different religiously, we share many of the same spiritual and core values."

"Strong part—view marriage as a spiritual commitment that is a covenant with God and not breakable even when times are tough." "We have differences in day-to-day style following two different Scriptures–Bible and *Bhagavad Gita* (Hindu Scriptures), hymns and chants. The concept is the same but how it is communicated is different, figurine, sweets at the temple, honesty, trust, transparency." "All along growing up I have been very accommodating. Initially, I wanted her to convert but she was unwilling and so we sought help but soon I realized through counseling that I need to value her for who she is rather than be concerned about her faith."

"Differences are good but it should work for us. How do we understand challenges together? We are not willing to change if we believe in something very strongly. Though we call ourselves Catholic how we view religion is very different. The daily practice can be so different." "I've been very involved in the past in the Catholic faith but not as much as I would like at the present. My husband and I have similar faith (both Christians) but we have not consistently attended church and have talked about finding one together."

"My faith and my spirituality is central to my life and hence I was keen to meet someone with a similar background. Having met my husband and finding that his values are shaped by same faith and spirituality, makes decision-making easier. It is also plays an important role in setting joint goals. (For example: tithing, paying back creditors, hospitality.) Our faith has a strongest influence on us." "Yes, we have different faiths. We have decided to respect both faiths and allow for both to be practiced in our home. We will teach our kids both and ultimately allow them to choose which they follow as they got older. We will celebrate festivals associated with both." "We may not both participate in some traditions, for example I will not tithe and my partner will not contribute financially to my faith."

"We've discussed it many times and hope to raise children with both faiths and let them decide which faith is more suited for them." "We belong to the same tradition but we have differences in emphasis and in viewing how important religion is. Again, on paper—we are the same. Greater discussion would have been helpful in flagging issues that continue to come up now." "She's Catholic and I'm Presbyterian, but neither of us are regular churchgoers. When we have children we'll start going to church and at that point we'll have to decide which denomination to join."

"We respect these denominational differences and do not usually have major conflicts. If there is a certain event, festival, etc., we will both take part but one person is usually more involved and will lead the way." "We both respect other differences, like not eating certain foods (beef). We practice our own faiths but participate in each other's events."

"Religious is the main difference but it's so integral to my worldview and how I react to the normal struggles that everyone faces in life. Initially, I wanted her to convert so that we could share the same faith. Ultimately, that approach didn't work and now we try to share the same religious principals and look at them spiritually and focus on applying to life situation rather than think of it as a principal of one religion."

"Yes, I did foresee major relationship issues due to religious differences but she was pretty persistent in showing me that a relationship could work. We had many discussions about culture, race, and religious differences before we started dating." "Having figurines and posters around the house. We have a life-size statue of Buddha in our living room."

"Tithing is a difficult concept to accept. Since he is not comfortable with it so I won't do it. Once his family knew whose statue it is they wanted it out. We decided to see a counselor to discuss these differences and it's still a work in progress."

Suggestions for Future Intercultural Couples

"Talk about the issues you face, acknowledge your differences, avail yourself counseling, maybe with a person of a different culture. Therapist from a majority culture would not be able to tap through sensitive issues."

Researcher: Most intercultural couples that do come in for counseling do not necessarily come for premarital counseling? What is your response?

"Though we had differences we never recognized it as cultural and thought of it more as a personal characteristic. Understanding culture makes you more accepting, less judgmental, less angry. Seeing other members of the family helps in getting better insight into why she behaves as she does." "I felt each session was challenging and sometimes it forced me to think about unpleasant situations or those I rather avoid, but in the end, I have a sense of peace and I feel more safe."

"The turmoil inside has been addressed and I feel that although there is still a fair amount of uncertainty, there is also some security in knowing how we both feel and that we have a coping mechanism." "I know it was helpful because when we had tried to discuss some issues on our own, we got nowhere. But with counseling, we made progress." "We always felt better after leaving counseling even if the session was tense. It really encouraged us to think longer and deeper about whatever came up during our sessions and work through things we probably wouldn't have addressed or discussed otherwise." "Pre-Cana and meeting with priest was required to get married. This was part of the Church's requirement."

"We were having relationship problems, which really turned out to be life problems, at least in my case. I wasn't convinced it would work, but I was willing to try. My life was in shambles at the time." "My personal therapy journey was extremely helpful and hence we are both very keen to explore marriage counseling." "For the moment we have a great understanding of each other and we have spent a lot of time and energy asking the hard questions and addressing each other's concerns and fears as we move forward in our relationship."

"It helped us communicate better." "Maybe to lead them in that direction. It is very helpful to have a third opinion. After being in counseling I have become a big fan of it and want to suggest it to everybody."

What is the contribution of partner in acceptance and understanding?

"Yeah, I guess it feels a lot because I had to move to a different country. I want to make my mother happy. There are some dreams that you have to compromise and give in. Overtime it adds up and differences arise." "My partner has taught me a lot about a lot of things. I can't say it even has to do only with Africa, her home country. She has taught me about people in general and about myself. What many of us don't understand, what I didn't understand, was how cultural diversity is one-way people are different, but that people are people. She taught me about understanding people."

Other Suggestions

"Counseling is valuable and important for anyone in a relationship." "We need to communicate and be open in order to succeed and have a long relationship." "Sometimes we hear advice or suggestions that we may not always like but ultimately it is for the best and is beneficial in the long-term, whether or not we see it." "I enjoyed having individual sessions as well as sessions together. I learned how to really communicate something troubling me that I wasn't quite sure how to discuss or bring up with my partner." "I know they have a fantastic setup and yet I feel that somehow I was not aware of it. I did not see a checklist. Even though there is a three-day retreat, it needs more time and needs more one-on-one time with the priest."

Summary

The participants were able to take a good look at their own understanding of culture and how they relate to people from other cultures. They realized that understanding and accepting others are two different things. They were able to express their views about premarital counseling and how it has helped them and areas of interest for other couples seeking premarital counseling. I felt they were candid in their expression and I was very satisfied by their answers on various questions pertaining to culture, cultural values, differences, discords, resolutions, and a will to go and to make the relationship work. They also made suggestions on what worked in therapy and what can be improved, themes to be discussed in therapy, and the like. One of the participants remarked about working on intercultural relationship, "Hard work doesn't hurt if you know that you are in it for the right reasons."

CHAPTER VI

Interpreting the Findings of the Research for Intercultural Premarital Couple Counseling

Introduction

IT WAS INDEED A meaningful experience working at something that I enjoy. Counseling couples in general and intercultural couples in particular has been a challenging yet satisfying task. Working with intercultural premarital couples has given me more exposure and insight. The participant couples that I researched with were all wonderful people, very cooperative and willing to learn. Even though 50 percent of the participants were of South Asian origin, I was able to experience the cultural diversity of different backgrounds. There was a lot of diversity even within the South Asian participants as two of them had grown up in Canada one from the East and the other from West. Both of them belonged to two different families of origin, both were born and brought up in the West so they were second-generation immigrants (or as some sociologists would say second-generation Americans), one's parents were from South India and the other from North India. Then the third and the fourth South Asian participants also came from very different backgrounds. One came to the United States as an adult and was a first-generation immigrant from Central India and the other was a second-generation American born and bred in Atlanta, Georgia. I, as a researcher, came to the United States as an adult and am a first-generation immigrant from North India but from a very different part of North India than the parents of one of the participants from North India. We all spoke different languages and so there was no common language between us. The South Asian couple participants were equally different in their upbringing. Even though their parents came from the same State in India and spoke the same language and both were first-generation immigrants the participant couple grew up in different countries, namely Canada and the United States. The male participant grew up in a household of three boys and the female participant grew up in a household of three girls.

Then there was a participant from Ghana in Africa who came to the United States as an eleven years old, so closer to the 1.75 generation, who was born in Africa but lived most of her adult life in America. There were two native-born Caucasian male participants. Even though they were Caucasian they had a different upbringing, one was from North Georgia and the other grew up in Florida. One came from a conservative Republican background and the other grew up Reformed Presbyterian. The family of one of them was more open to diversity whereas the family of the other was not. They perhaps had heard the term "White privilege" but failed to see its implications for their partners until it was pointed out to them. It was interesting to note the contribution that their culturally and racially diverse partner made in their life by exposing them to diversity and to the cultural nuances that they were oblivious to.

Thus, there was both cultural and religious diversity in the sampling which addresses the concerns of this research on intercultural premarital couples counseling more meaningfully. The cultures represented include African, African American, Caucasian, and South Asian (North and South India). Faiths represented were Protestant, Catholic and Hindu.

In the section below I present an interpretation of the findings of the research on intercultural premarital couples counseling. For the purpose of clarity and meaningful discussion I have sought to divide the material into four major sections.

The first section deals with the participant's understanding of culture and culture vs. personality and ways culture has shaped their value system, their understanding of racial divide in our society and negotiating cultural divide/racism, their openness to diversity and being culturally sensitive and ways culture has shaped their value system, their exposure to other intercultural couples and learning experiences from their intercultural exposure, their cultural expectations (both their expectations of themselves and that of their partner) that are culturally conditioned, and cultural aspects participants appreciate and or do not appreciate in their respective cultures.

The second section deals with cultural attitudes that attracted them to their partner, contribution of partner in acceptance and understanding, and their identity as an intercultural couple, being an intercultural couple—a help or hindrance, cultural issues that arise in their relationship, discussing/resolving issues of discord, raising biracial child(ren), negotiating different faith practices and significance of support from family of origin.

The third section deals with participant's experience of intercultural premarital couples counseling, their reasons for choosing intercultural premarital counseling, helpfulness of intercultural premarital couples counseling, cultural issues most and least effective in intercultural premarital couples counseling, their awareness of their cultural differences while in intercultural premarital couples counseling, their reasons for choosing that particular therapist, their experience of helpful characteristics they found in their intercultural therapist and would they recommend that therapist to another couple and themes in intercultural premarital couples counseling, process of intercultural premarital couples counseling, and duration of intercultural premarital couples counseling,

The fourth and the last section looks into their suggestions for future intercultural couples, aspects of intercultural couples counseling most and least helpful, and their suggestions for therapists engaged in intercultural premarital couples counseling.

Section A

Understanding of Culture and Ways Culture Has Shaped Their Value System

The understanding that a particular culture is integrally and dynamically related to a specific group of people was pointed out by all the participants in one way or the other. Culture is what gives one a sense of belonging and of connectedness with one another. The values, traditions, beliefs, attitudes, and rituals in one's culture give a sense of identity to the group and to the individual. Culture shapes us and partially forms who we are. The view is summed up well in the words of one of the participants where C113 said, "Culture is a set of rituals, customs, traditions and shared patterns and behaviors and values that help to define and shape a group of people." E115 added, "Culture is what makes a person belong to a group. This includes language, behavior, food, music, manners of talking, things that matter." The uniqueness of each culture can also be seen in the fine arts such as music, dance, poetry, and other creative expressions of the specific group of people. Culture shapes the way people interact with those around them based on social norms. Such an understanding brings its own dynamics into intercultural marriage where it is not just the two individuals who are seeking to relate to one another but to a whole group of people represented by each individual. Therefore, it is important to understand how the individual is viewed and treated by the cultural group of the partner and how that impacts the couple's relationship with one another. This is a question that needs to be addressed in order for therapy to be more effective.

There are aspects of culture that needs to be viewed critically. For example, a culture that upholds patriarchy can tend to subdue women, propagate sex stereotypes, promote dowry system. When speaking about "White privilege" one often wonders how it is possible for Whites not to see color? Hardy and Laszloffy suggest, "One of the reasons it is difficult to acknowledge seeing color is that it will automatically be equating with discriminating against another on the basis of color. Many people, Whites especially, live with the fear that they will be accused of being a racist."[1]

E115, a male Caucasian participant, stated that "I didn't really know people from other cultures except for African American. I got a job in the kitchen and I began to come across people from other cultures. They were interesting because they had something to offer to me. In Atlanta I met people from all backgrounds and ethnicities. I learned how to relate to other people. I have always been interested in other people. I had a strong value system that whoever they are they are human beings. That is why I want to live in the city and not in the suburbs." He also stated that "White privilege is something that White people don't really spend time with any other culture, don't necessarily talk about it and think about it that it really exists but I have realized that it actually does exist." The same participant earlier to his exposure to people from other cultures found it difficult to understand people from other cultures for he himself recognized that "I sometimes hold ignorant views" and had a preconceived notion that the "majority of people are taking advantage like people on welfare." He felt that, "if people made better choices they would not be poor." This stereotypical view was unhelpful to him in accepting and

---

1. Hardy and Laszloffy, "Dynamics of a Pro-Racist Ideology," 10.

appreciating people from other cultures. In talking with their respective partners they were able to have a wider view of others and to understand deeper cultural factors that they were unable to see on their own. Earlier it seems that they were more "reactive" to difference and now they are more "reflective." Hardy and Laszloffy confirm the participants view when they observe that "White privilege is usually exercised outside the conscious awareness of White people."[2]

We do live in an age of cultural diversity. While on the one hand this diversity brings about a good feeling of identity, warmth and acceptance on the other hand the same diversity can cause difficulty and resistance. We also live in a chaotic world of violence, hatred and anxiety. People are stressed about various things and often lack social support to navigate through those stressors. In his writings existentialist Rollo May focused on practical and spiritual matters. His intent was to promote the worth of the individual in order to contribute to the potential of human beings and thereby to their development. May was of the opinion that alienation and anxiety in individuals was primarily a result of a kind of chaos in culture and society rather than the result of individual psychological problems.[3] One of the main emotions that most couples bring to counseling in general and intercultural counseling in particular is anxiety. They are very anxious because of the turmoil they are experiencing be it the differences, the daily misunderstandings between them, fights, arguments and often parental or family disapproval and distancing. The goal of psychotherapy is to convert anxiety and guilt to normal anxiety and guilt; to help the client actualize his/her potentialities. What is the client trying to express by the presenting problems? This understanding helps the client find meaning in circumstances he/she would otherwise find meaningless or hopeless. Therapy should be an encounter between two selves coming together and sharing their existence. Empathy for the client is a key ingredient.

The focus on 'interculture' often brings us to the themes of alienation and anxiety. Oftentimes individuals are caught between what is temperamental or cultural or the "result of personality disorder." Maybe there is a combination of all of these and other things but they are unable to sift all of the matter to begin to address it and find resolution. That is when they throw up their arms in despair and distress and begin to find

---

2. Hardy and Laszloffy, "Dynamics of a Pro-Racist Ideology," 10.
3. May, *Meaning of Anxiety*.

a way out of the relationship. Research participants did seem to have difficulty distinguishing what aspects of behavior are culturally conditioned and what aspects are part of one's personality disorder. Some individual characteristics such as stubbornness and arrogance were viewed as being part of one's personality disorder. One of the participants viewed a trait in his partner of "not being very punctual consistently for an appointment or meeting" was as part of her personality disorder. However, as a result of engaging in counseling the discovery was made that not being very punctual was part of cultural upbringing and not an individualized behavioral issue. As a result of intercultural therapy partners will be able to better accept and appreciate each other if they are able to recognize traits in the mate which are culturally conditioned instead of labeling them as personality issues or personality disorders. It was also recognized that personality is shaped by culture and therefore it is not always easy to decide what perspective to take on certain issues. There could be a combination of culture and personality being played out in a particular behavior but that needs to be taken out of the purview of a disorder.

Culture impacts each of us in different ways and helps shape our value system. Participants shared their views on how culture has impacted their worldview in the past and how it continues to play a significant role in their lives today in the following ways:

Developing a deep respect and value for family and religion, in instilling a strong work ethic and self-respect, in teaching the importance of caring for and respecting the elderly, the children and the vulnerable, in emphasizing the role of education in one's progress and growth, in being positive, a bigger threshold for pain, more stability, in developing respect for one's religion. A111 said, "What is important in life is the small, simple things. One should not let materialistic things get in the way of living together happily."

In one of his greatest works, May traces the problem of love in modern society, arguing that "love and will are interdependent and belong together. . . . Will without love becomes manipulation (and) love without will becomes sentimental and experimental."[4] Most of the couples that decide to go for premarital counseling find themselves in love with their partner, however, what they also need to sustain the relationship is a will to make it work. There is a need to develop the ability to recognize the positive aspects of the partner's culture and affirm the same, as this will

---

4. May, *Love and Will*, 9.

not only help the partner in being more appreciative of his/her culture but also have an impact for good on how the partner thinks of herself/himself.

Understanding of the Racial/Ethnic Divide in Society and Negotiating Cultural Divide/Racism

Until recently race was largely defined as a biological concept, often constructed on the basis of physical and or genetic or color of one's skin characteristics. However now with the advancement in the field of psychotherapy and sociology, the term has grown to include sociopolitical factors, economic or trade considerations, values and belief systems, and even psychological considerations. Professor of Psychology and Religion Robert Carter defines race as a "visible sociopolitical variable that one individual or group uses to assign worth to another individual or group based on racial group membership. Additionally a person can use this sociopolitical variable to determine his or her own self-worth."[5] The concept of ethnicity includes one's nationality, religion, or spirituality, language, and cultural background, one's ancestry or lineage. Ethnicity can be transmitted to people through families and communities.

Participants indicated the fact that they have witnessed and experienced racism in school, neighborhood, and family. People of certain races can have an attitude of indifference, where they feel a sense of superiority but not necessarily hate towards other races. But there are also people in certain cultures who tend to hate and despise other groups or races. It is the latter that becomes a matter of greater challenge. Rastogi and Thomas, citing American sociologist Kimmel, states that he compares having a privileged identity to walking with a strong wind at your back, rather than having to face it and fight it with every step.[6] The authors quote Kimmel saying, "You do not feel the wind; it feels you. . . . Only when you turn around and face that wind do you realize its strength."[7]

An awareness and sensitivity to other cultures is made possible when one is exposed to people of different cultures. As an immigrant, a person can experience the racial cultural difference in a real way. It can happen in the workplace or school where the immigrant may have to struggle with culturally different people. One has to negotiate a lot and

---

5. Carter, *Influence of Race and Racial Identity*, 225.
6. Kimmel, "Toward a Pedagogy of the Oppressor," 1–10.
7. Rastogi et al., *Multicultural Couples Therapy*, 11.

learn to be tolerant in such situations. When one is curious about other cultures and takes interest in people who are different from him/her, one can learn and grow. And when there is mutual respect between people of different cultures, there is an atmosphere of acceptance and trust. A partner who has grown up in a pluralistic setting is often in an advantageous situation over those who have been confined to one culture because he or she would tend to be better equipped, mentally and emotionally, to make the needed adjustments. However, this does not in any way guarantee that one is free of holding any prejudice or stereotypes. An intercultural couple can become aware of the prejudices and stereotypes that might be present in each other. It is possible that there could be diverse attitudes and outlooks within the members of a family of one's origin. This is because of the different circumstances and experiences they have gone through while growing up. One needs to keep this in mind and be understanding. The practice of respecting people of other races and cultures could be part of the culture or family upbringing.

The experience of an intercultural couple treated as being odd or unusual and consequently being discriminated against by the people of each of the partner's culture was reported by some of the participants. Being the objects of scrutiny or discrimination can be an experience in public places like shopping malls, theaters, etc., though there may not be any bad intentions. It is a reminder that they are unusual couples. The immediate family of the couple could also have a negative attitude and be intolerant of the relationship which could in turn create stress in the couple's life. A111, who is in an interfaith relationship, observed, "We are mostly struggling to have my family accept us and involve us in their lives, and this is ultimately related to culture." How a partner is accepted and treated in the face of cultural differences can be one of the central issues in intercultural marriage. This is particularly a difficult issue if a culture is inward-looking and does not tolerate or easily accept a partner. A couple can often feel isolated and excluded. The stress that results from such an experience is summed up by A111 who said, "I often fall into bouts of sadness that also then affects my relationship with my mate as well." Another issue is where the majority culture takes the minority culture for granted and is not respectful or sensitive to the minority culture—expecting the partner from a minority culture to adjust to the majority culture and thus fail to allow the mutual and meaningful intermingling of their respective cultures. Participants indicated that it requires a lot of patient interaction between the couples to understand each other's cultural perspectives and make the needed compromise. E115 noted, "As time passes I think about her position, or she mine. Some of these issues we've revisited multiple times over the years and I've been able to watch mine and her position change (or not change sometimes). But mostly we are in tune on the significant issues." The support received from their parents and immediate family as well as the immediate community in which they live is greatly valued by intercultural couples. The support one finds in places like school, college, etc., can also play a very encouraging role.

There is a need for those in the dominant culture to move beyond the state of living out their privileged status and acknowledge the existence of other minority cultures and be willing to intermingle with other cultures. In an intercultural marriage the partner from the dominant culture needs to embody this sensitivity to the partner from the minority culture. This point is well illustrated by one of the participants who comes from an African culture and is in a relationship with a Caucasian male (F116): "White people don't particularly see the cultural aspect. For example, we were watching an episode of *Law & Order* and a White policeman walks into a Black neighborhood and wants to question a Black woman. The Black woman does not want to talk to the policeman and asks him to leave. He was perplexed as to why she would not talk to the policeman? I explained that maybe because she is not very trusting of the White policeman. I am more sensitive to race issues but he doesn't seem to get it."

Having a respectful attitude towards other cultures is seen by participants as an important ingredient in intercultural marriage. Interacting with one's partner over a period of time does help in developing this respect and the ability to transcend the barriers of race, color, and faith. It also helps to acknowledge the similarities in values and practices. Each of the partners can play vital roles in broadening the others views by expressing their opinions about issues affecting them and listening to each other, and by discussing issues such as how raising kids, caring for an older mother/father, and how divorce is viewed and how divorced couples are treated have cultural perspectives and differences. It requires a willingness to be very open and clear about ones stance on issues and not apologetic or downplay them. One may have had to negotiate racial divisions acknowledging the reality of racism that is present and the fact that one cannot easily change the beliefs of someone who has lived with that attitude for a long time. There is also the challenge of profiling where people make conclusions based on looks or appearances or the skin color and find it difficult to see the person as he or she really is.

Openness to Diversity and Being Culturally Sensitive

Exposure to other cultures often results in cultural sensitivity and a willingness to find a balance between the differences. It helped participants to recognize that certain behavior, which was initially thought to be a personality issue, was actually a cultural trait. For example, how one generally tends to speak–loudly or softly. Certain practices such as paying children's educational bills, giving gifts to postman, baby shower thank you notes, packing food in yogurt containers for family to take back could be part of the way a person has been used to living in his/her native community. One could be culturally silenced while being immersed in a foreign culture that is dominant. This was illustrated by an exchange between a couple where one of the partners said that the other partner does not notice any cultural differences or issues between them. The other partner responded by saying that it is because she is planted in this dominant foreign culture and so there is a tendency to over-adapt to the dominant culture while silently suffering the pain of having one's own culture being subdued.

Fifty percent of the participants expressed openness to learning about diversity which was demonstrated by their willingness to make friends of people from other cultures, to attend social or cultural events, to be free from making judgments based on stereotypes, to help people from other cultures, to learn a foreign language, etc. They expressed the fact that as a result of this intercultural relationship they have begun to give thought to their own personal cultural beliefs and to change their worldview and their stand on diversity. They expressed that they have become increasingly aware and sensitive to the cultural, racial, and ethnic diversity in their surrounding and have begun to respect diversity. They expressed the fact they are now opening up to the idea of celebrating cultural diversity rather than questioning it. Only half of them grew up in a family environment that tolerated diversity. The other half said that they get very conscious of themselves when they are in the presence of people who are different from them. This is a work in progress and requires tolerance and mutual respect.

Exposure to Other Interracial Couples and Learning Experiences from Intercultural Exposure

One hundred percent of the participants indicated that they knew and interacted with other interracial couples. This experience was helpful in several ways. As one African American participant (B112) pointed out, "Many of our friends are intercultural couples and it's very encouraging to see them happy and prospering." He also pointed out that "There are a few intercultural couples in my family but they do seem more isolated and don't attend family events as much." Another participant (A111) observed, "Many of our friends are in mixed relationships and we interact with them regularly. My brother is in a mixed marriage as well. However, the remainder of my extended family is homogeneous and this concept is foreign to them. Having friends in a similar situation has been helpful because it does not make us feel like we are doing something completely crazy. Our friends have kids and some have been married for ten years plus. It is helpful to have them as role models and to go to for questions. It is also helpful to have them to use to see what does and doesn't work, for example, how we would do something and how we wouldn't? One set of friends has emphasized language (French and Chinese) for their kids and we think this works well. Another set has completely disregarded the Indian aspect of their relationship and we have seen how this upsets the Indian in-laws and why this doesn't work."

Participants were aware of the inherent biases against people of other cultures—some have stronger biases than others which can be hard to change. Formal education and material progress is not a guarantee that biases are no longer present. There may be an external expression of acceptance and approval but on the inside there may be resistance and disapproval. One Caucasian participant (E115) said, "I have also learned that people in my generation are still racist and have double standards and even those I had considered to be open minded and accepting are not necessarily so." This gives rise to the question of how one can be fully trusting of people's intentions and build healthy relationships with them. Intercultural exposure helped participants to understand certain 'unacceptable' behaviors of individuals and be tolerant to them. There is a need for a calm and rational approach where one is willing to engage in conversation and interaction.

Couples can learn tolerance when exposed to each other's cultures. One learns from being in the minority culture at certain times and also from being in the majority culture at other times. It enables one to have greater insight into how actions or words maybe perceived or misunderstood. The experience of racial divide may not exist in any extreme form but there is a general awareness of its presence. This awareness can turn into an acute sense of self-consciousness for the partner when he or she is the only person of a particular race or culture in a particular social setting. A particular participant indicated how she had assimilated certain values into her native culture from the current culture in which she had been living for some time and had formed her own version of culture. This is a phenomenon that does seem to happen to individuals as they are exposed to other cultures over a period of time.

Cultural Expectations of Themselves and Those of Their Partner That Are Culturally Conditioned

Culture does give rise to expectations or beliefs about what is acceptable, good, or preferable, for example, housekeeping, food habits, punctuality. These expectations come to the forefront when one has to actively engage with people of other cultures. Familiarity with what is expected culturally could be a great help in how couples relate to one another.

The various roles at home are culturally conditioned as observed by G117: "Culturally, most Indian women take care of their house. I have been a single woman and been very independent. Since I am a working woman I feel that I am not being a good wife. He does cleaning and laundry. I like cooking and so I cook. These are cultural things and I bring it to bear on me." A mate may impose on himself/herself the expectations that have been ingrained in his/her culture—for example the tendency to wait for the approval of others before making any major decisions, the belief that the male should always play the dominant role in the family, the belief that women should be submissive and should be good homemakers, rigid gender stereotypes, etc. One could be conditioned by various ideals such as always be an "obedient and good girl," always please those in the community even if it does not please oneself, always try to "look good" and save one's face in the society.

A partner can be culturally conditioned to expect some of the following behavior from the mate: participate in all activities and programs of the extended family, be able to treat others like family and extend hospitality to strangers, be willing to financially support children's college education, be more emotionally tuned in and nurturing, husband should be a leader who is very caring and responsible, wife should ensure the house is kept clean.

Cultural Aspects They Do or Do Not Appreciate in Their Own Culture

A partner needs help especially in understanding and appreciating what is important in the other partner's native culture—for example the importance of family and of community, the strong sense of pride and belonging, a sense of extended family involvement while at the same time respecting individual freedom, hospitality—where even strangers are treated as family, being polite. As pointed out by F116, "I appreciate the way people in my culture are constantly giving and there is never anything they wouldn't do. Even strangers are family." Some cultures may exhibit a strong will to live beyond just getting by and getting through. This could be a strength that couples can tap into in making their marriage richer and more resilient. The history of a particular culture could be very enlightening and create a sense of appreciation about upholding moral and ethical values such as liberty, responsibility, modesty, respect for neighbor, tolerance, forbearance, hard work, etc.

A mate also needs help in overcoming those aspects of his/her native culture which is not appreciated and is a hindrance in the marital relationship—for example, double standards, interference of extended family in a couple's decision-making process, the tendency to be enmeshed in relationships, lack of individual freedom, rigid beliefs and expectations, the role of women, materialism, feelings of superiority over other cultures or communities, rigid or narrow ways of looking at life which takes on expressions such as, the best profession one's child must pursue is being a medical doctor or an engineer; there is no support for you unless you do what society thinks is appropriate; you cannot be different.

The status and role of a woman and the class inequality espoused in a culture is a matter of concern as observed by G117 who said, "I struggled with the place of women in my culture and struggled to live in India as a single woman. I did not like that the communal aspect of my cultural background forced me to do things that I did not really have to do. Families tend to be enmeshed in my country. I have also struggled with inequality of class in my country."

There is the challenge of a culture holding on to the past and celebrating past events or happenings that are not necessarily what the rest of the world would celebrate and be proud of. They may be entrenched in a state of conservatism and not be willing to move on and be open to changes and to the progressive ideas in the larger society. Such a mindset is a hindrance in a healthy relationship across cultures.

The emphasis on financial success and accumulating material wealth is often at the cost of building genuine relationships and leaves one feeling empty. People can tend to look at relationships from the point of view of what they can gain out of that relationship rather than building deep meaningful relationships. Such a culture leads to a lack of trust in others and questioning of the motives of others.

Identity as an Intercultural Couple

From their answers it was evident that most of the couples have not begun to see themselves as a unit. They are very much individualized and have not necessarily learned to name themselves as of a mixed couple. One of the couples stated themselves as a "mixed" couple. This is one area where a trained and sensitive therapist can help them integrate as a "mixed" couple who are in this together. This calls for an acceptance and celebration of themselves as a unit because inasmuch as they join together it will be that much easier for their children to accept their identity as bicultural or biracial.

Section B

Cultural Attitudes that Attracted Them to Their Partner, Contribution of Partner in Acceptance and Understanding, and Their Identity as an Intercultural Couple

It was interesting to note that, predominantly, it was not any particular aspect or aspects of culture that played a prominent role in drawing them to their partner but it was the virtues or basic human values that they saw in their partner. Virtues or values such as integrity, humility, fairness, willingness to work hard, ability to be kind, loving, and loyal, dependable, have a strong sense of family, willing to trust, willing to encourage and be supportive were considered as being very important. There were also certain cultural traits that were attractive that were mentioned such as, the ability to show affection and tenderness in public and not be shy or reserved, the ability to interact and communicate easily. One female participant pointed out how men in her native culture did not know how to be romantic and to show affection to their mates publicly. This was something she did not like or accept. She was attracted to a man from her same culture, who shied away from public display of affection. Thus culture did play a role in her choosing her partner. Another participant observed how he had some understanding and appreciation of his partner's culture before he got to know her and this made a big impression on his partner. In general, it could be said that there is attraction between the partners when the values promoted by the cultures they represent tend to resonate and they find a connection and sense of meaning.

E115 affirmed that his partner has taught him a lot about many things and that she had taught him about people in general and about himself. He began to understand that people thought differently and how people are culturally diverse. He learned to value people for who they are and his partner had a lot to do in helping him come to this understanding. Living with an intercultural partner, whether second generation or even 1.5 generation, has its own challenges regardless if it is just one partner or both partners. Thus it is imperative to pay attention to the cultural upbringing of each other, to take time to listen to each other and to talk about one's own culture and traditions and way of life. It is important to educate your partner about your worldview and nuances in culture that matter to you, and then to be able to find a middle ground or a win-win situation for both. I liked what one of the participants (E115) said, "Talking about issues without the stereotypes."

D114 had to struggle with the embedded idea that he had about patriarchy with the male being the dominant figure. When asked to elaborate he replied, "the way my father and my brothers behave with their wives and the reaction of their wives." I guess he feels that other wives are more empathic and maybe even submissive to their husbands whereas his wife is not. So there is a judgment that his wife was non-compliant. He disregarded the fact that his wife is a modern educated woman of the twenty-first century. She is a lawyer and knows about standing up and speaking up for herself. Ironically, that is what attracted him to her in the first place. When asked, "Who is more rigid, you or her?" he stopped to think for a while. "Hmmm! There is rigidity on both sides. Our parents' generation has a different culture and today it seems to be in contradiction with our value system." This response showed much work that was done in marital counseling of helping them to complement each other rather than get competitive. Patience is everything and learning to be patient and accepting of each other is a great virtue, as the saying goes, "where there's a will there's a way." Therapy is about one's self awareness and not about trying to change your partner. No one can change the other. One can only be the change one wants to see in the other. Sometimes we can get so righteous about our own way of life and put down the other. That attitude may be unhelpful in moving forward. It is important to listen to the other's viewpoint and be respecting of their cultural journey.

In response to how their partner contributes in gaining better insight into cultural acceptability G117 stated that "culturally, most Indian women take care of their house. I have been a single woman and been very independent. Since I am a working woman I feel that I am not being a good wife. He does cleaning and laundry. I like cooking and so I cook." She struggled with the idea that she as a working woman was unable to find time for keeping the house clean and tidy. In her life back in India, husbands or fathers did not do laundry or cleaning and so she was feeling guilty about not fulfilling her responsibility at home. Her husband who is a Caucasian was brought up with egalitarian values and so he does not think it is a big deal to clean house or do the dishes or do laundry. He helped her not to feel bad but to do whatever she can. She enjoys cooking and he enjoys eating so that makes it a win-win.

Only 2 percent of the participants answered the question about their identity as a blended or mixed couple. One of them said that as a couple, they describe their identity just as "mixed" or "blended." The other participant explained that even though they were from the same ethnic background, they don't' see eye to eye when discussing their own racial/ethnic/cultural issues. To my mind most intercultural couples are not fully able to verbalize their mixed cultural identity. They often live in their own separate worlds and cultural identities. It takes some work on their part to begin to assimilate and integrate into each other's cultures as well as into each other.

Being an Intercultural Couple—A Help or a Hindrance

Thirty percent of the participants were more verbal about this topic. They felt that it was both a help and a hindrance to be a multicultural couple. This attitude is helpful in reality. Multicultural parents can help bring up children who are better equipped to relate to people of other cultures/races. In one couple's experience it seemed that biracial children usually hailed from good, educated families and they seem to have the advantage of greater exposure to opportunities to learn and grow than other children. There is the privilege of experiencing what is good and excellent in two different cultures which makes a person to be more diverse and open-minded. It helps in bringing very different attributes and perspectives to the relationship. Each of the couple brings different strengths to each other and that helps in making them a stronger unit together.

A111 observed, "It is great because you open your world to new ideas, possibilities and ways of life and truly can become a more diverse, open minded individual. I feel as though because of it, we think more openly and focus on the bigger picture instead of getting stuck with small details. It is amazing to see people blend and their friends blend." This is a very positive way of looking at the reality. However, it may not always be true for all mixed families. For example, F116 observed that "If there is a conflict in my family, everyone jumps in together to find a way out, there is ownership and relational thing attached to it and that is nice but it also gives rise to expectation. When things come up I rely on my family, teamwork and collaboration is valued. That's the way I grew up and it comes up naturally to me. Friends matter, helping is important." For example, she elaborated, "For our wedding his mom just said inform people that it will cost so much and they will come prepared. My father was not willing to ask people to pay for food particularly when they are our guest." This is more of an example of a hindrance where two cultures collide. They are unable to reconcile with the cultural differences. What matters most to one family is matter of fact for the other family. F116 further observed that "Each individual does lose a little bit of their background or religion in the process of combining with someone else of a different background, i.e., my partner doesn't speak the same language so for my children, it will take extra effort to teach them and have them learn (however, we have seen it done so it's not impossible)." C113 stated that "my husband is from Canada and I think they are much more accepting there so he has helped me to see instances where I could be more culturally accepting and I am working on that." C113 was speaking about the how this exposure has helped her to broaden her own attitude about the "other."

An observation was made to the effect that there are difficulties already present in any marriage because of the differences present and intercultural marriages add to the differences and makes things harder. A strong relationship is needed between intercultural couples to make the marriage work. Living out one's life as an intercultural couple in a social setting is not as easy as being with a person of the same skin color or culture. A111 stated that "It is also challenging for people don't always support us, or don't think we are "good people" and we have a lot of negative energy directed towards us. People of the same culture of faith sometimes feel we have "sold out" and are therefore not always accepting or kind towards us. There is a sense of concern in that we are navigating waters that are unchartered or less chartered and therefore may not know what faces us in the future.

Cultural Issues Arising in Their Intercultural Relationship

A hundred percent of the couples shared some cultural dimensions or differences that arise in their relationship that they struggle with. Very soon in their relationship they are able to recognize the differences and they try to work to resolve them. Sometimes it works but mostly it does not. Gradually the differences begin to snowball and that is when they seek help. Often those who do not have a wider network of intercultural friends or family find themselves struggling alone. D114 observed that they were one of the first American/Canadian couples in their community. Their worldviews were very different. There was resentment about the national laws which are much bigger than the couple themselves. For example, welfare in a capitalistic society and universal health care. Sometimes he felt that his views were bad, and he felt judged by her and her family. He states that before marriage he did not think that moving from Canada to American would be a different transition but he found it very difficult. They often ended up ridiculing each other and each other's country of birth which brought discord and distancing, so much so that they began to shy away from talking about issues. He said that sometimes the differences are overwhelming because he had to move to a different country. But now he wants to make his mother who lives in Canada happy and he wants to move back to Canada. He glumly stated, "There are some dreams that you have to compromise and give in. Over time it adds up and differences arise." Ten years after marriage they are still working on this one.

Looking back at how they viewed cultural issues and difference before they were married one partner, D114 stated, "I think we just assumed they were the same since on paper we were the same. Probably would have been wise to discuss it more at length." There can be any number of things that one is sensitive about and once they become defensive then that leads to ridicule and dissension. They needed help and so they sought marital counseling.

B112 talked about struggling with hard questions. When asked to elaborate on those hard questions, he stated, "aging parents, where will we live, religious differences, raising kids, and how do we expect to navigate through that. When we started dating we did not necessarily talk about it. But soon we did because we wanted to make sure we are on the same page and counseling helped us to bring that out and helped us find truthful answers." Counseling helped them to become objective about issues and drop taking everything personal that was not working for them.

Talking about financial matters F116 stated, "Money is both a cultural and a personal issue. I have to pay to belong to my family." What she meant was that she takes her cultural financial responsibilities of supporting her parents seriously. All of her siblings contribute towards the maintenance of the parents. However, her husband, as the only child of Caucasian parents, does not have any such responsibility or obligation and thus is at a loss to understand why she has to support her family. Money can become an issue of contention because different cultures view money differently, for some money can be an individual asset but for others it can be a community asset. Money is to be shared and the needs of the family or elders in the family or even situations in the family call for shared responsibility. His wife (E115) confirmed that. F116 went on to say, "I like to have the pleasure of giving gifts to family members but in her culture they have a family fund to which she contributes and which serves to provide for the whole family. My father will never ask for money. Old people are expected to take care of themselves in my family. In her family there is an expectation to take care of the whole family."

Giving another example of where differences crop up F116 stated that, "Once in a while, when a story in the media comes up or I read something with racial or cultural themes, we will have discussions and even arguments about it. Sometimes we differ in our perspectives. I feel like I am more tuned in to cultural and racial factors in certain situations where he does not consider it as much." This was continuing for them even after almost eight years of being together. Finally, after coming for therapy they were able to resolve some of these cultural differences and eventually developed a style of communication that helped resolve these differences.

B112, who is a Christian in relationship with a Hindu girl, stated, "Religious is the main difference but it's so integral to my worldview and how I react to the normal struggles that everyone faces in life. Initially, I really wanted her to convert so that we could share the same faith. Ultimately, that approach didn't work and now we try to share the same religious values and principles but consider them as spiritual and life focused rather than religious." B112 was being real candid as to his expectation from this relationship. He probably approached religious issues with the thinking that his religion was better or that he being a male had the right to expect his female partner to comply. Of course, he did not necessarily come up with this thinking on his own. It was just a given to which he had been socialized. In the initial stages of the relationship she agreed to the idea of converting to his religion but very soon she turned back and said no. Their therapist was able to help them value not only each other's culture but also to accept and respect each other's religion. As a result, they were able to find balance and peace.

B112 on addressing cultural issues that arise in their relationship stated, "Because we talked about culture it was nice to talk about the differences and how they play around. Now we have a better understanding of our situation and thus a better perspective. At an earlier period in our relationship there were some issues that were causing some conflicts but we really could not put our finger on it. Our therapist helped us tap into it and now going through these hard questions together helped us to figure out where we stand." On enquiring, "What are some hard things culturally to accept?" He responded, "Religious figurines and posters around the house. We have a life-size statue of Buddha in our living room." His girlfriend (A111) responded "tithing." She also stated that since he is not comfortable with figurines in the house she won't do it. She says, "Once his family knew whose statue it is they wanted it out." They both agreed that, as an interfaith couple, religious differences is a very big issue. "We decided to see a counselor to discuss these differences and it's still a work in progress."

F116 talking about dealing with cultural issues in their relationship stated, "We had a lot of issues about how we understand time. However, as time passed, I tended to be more relaxed and think of time in a relative sense, while he is very punctual. Initially, we fought a lot over this because we lacked understanding of the cultural differences but in recent years and with the help of therapy we have become more aware and we are more understanding of each other and have tried to comprise and be accommodative to each other. For example, working on time or punctuality, he would think that something was wrong with me like personality defect. When he was with my family, he learned how laid back we are. Earlier for him, I was being rude and being disrespectful of him. Now, I have learned to adjust to it and be on time and he has learned not to get offended. It is the way we are brought up, even when it comes to how we relate to one another and how we deal with people of the opposite sex. Now he is more accepting and does not judge me."

In response to cultural issues that arise in their relationship H118 stated, "family interaction, parents who need to be taken care of (she wants my mom to move in with us whereas I would prefer to place her in a nursing home), financial planning, decision-making, religious differences, patriarchy, women's empowerment, conflict resolution, language, food, education, being in public around people who have not met us as a couple. We try to talk about it in advance if we know we are visiting a place where we will be uncomfortable and sometimes we talk about it after. Mostly we try to rely on each other while we're in those situations." G117 stated, "Hospitality and entertaining at home is a cultural value that I bring and he shares that value. Care of an older parent, raising kids, and how much exposure to doing things independently is something we have discussed. It is not an area of conflict at this stage of our life together since we are a newlywed couple. It could turn into conflict later."

E115 stated, "It has to do with decision-making process. We try and learn from each other the positive aspects of each other's approach to solving problems. In the end I have learned that these discussions will not get us anywhere and it has not helped us or worked for us. Now that I've been with her these years I've softened my views on some issues of civil rights and equality (e.g., education subsidies) although I still identify as Republican. These sorts of interactions generally take this form: F116 or I will mention some hot-button issue. One of us will disagree, and at times we have heated argument. Usually each of us are sure our individual position is correct. Time will pass and I'll think about her position, or she mine. Later we'll happen to bring it up (not purposefully) and see where we stand. Some of these issues we've revisited multiple times over the years and I've been able to watch mine and F116's position change (or not, sometimes). But mostly we are in tune on the significant issues."

Discussing/Resolving Issues of Discord in Intercultural Relationship

One couple indicated that they discussed racial/ethnic/cultural issues without reservation and did see areas where they disagreed with each other. For another couple the discussion about culture was needed when a certain action or behavior of one of the partners made sense or meaning from a cultural point of view. A couple brought up the discussion about cultural issues in order to help their children to better deal with them.

Discussion about culture for yet another couple was initiated as a result of one of the partners being anxious or concerned about certain issues while the other partner seemed less anxious or concerned. H118 said, "We don't talk about politics. I am conservative and she leans towards liberal. It's a core belief deep in my soul that we have differences of opinion on some issues. I am open to other opinions but it will be hard to change that opinion based on my life experiences. I think we can work that out." B112 stated that his partner brought up cultural issues, "because of her family dynamic and her family's lack of acceptance of our relationship." F116 stated that it was the therapist who guided them through the cultural issues. "She touched on issues about experiencing embarrassment while being in social situations. I'm not entirely comfortable around large groups and don't like being the center of attention. Therefore, it can be trying when we go to places where we know people will stare at us. Our therapist taught us to talk about these situations and rely on each other during them." E115 joined her and said, "Our counselor brought some things to our attention and that led us to conversations about our cultural differences, fears, etc."

Majority of the participants accepted the fact that not everyone has all the tools of communication. Often they are irrational about their communication and obviously it does not yield good result. They even expressed that perhaps discord or the inability to communicate effectively is a personality trait that is difficult to handle and can be very stressful. One of them stated that when they are unable to make progress they just avoid discussing such topics altogether. Others stated that they try different things, including procrastination, and that most of the time the issue of discord doesn't get addressed or resolved. So they felt that it is good to take it to a therapist who can help them resolve conflict. For example, H118 who is in a second marriage and has young adult children stated that, "She has strong opinion about parenting and sibling position. I am open to her input but ultimately I will make my choice with my son. I want to accomplish what you are saying but I may get there on a different way. We don't think the same way and her opinions were very foreign to me, even challenging. Like once she told me that 'I want to be real than proper.' If I am in her place, I would rather be proper than real. So she was forthright and we ended the discussion there." Another stated that they argue sometimes but find it difficult to resolve and so they mostly compromise. They prefer to work this out with a counselor who helped them see things differently.

Raising Biracial Child(ren) in Future

Participants tended to have mixed attitudes towards possibility of raising biracial children. The positive outlook was displayed by noting that the children of intercultural couples tend to be in an advantageous situation as they are exposed to diversity and they get the best of two different worlds. They grow up to be more open-minded. As one participant pointed out that intercultural couples "bring very different attributes and perspectives to their relationship." Biracial children will be in better position to handle the issue of race as they will be learning from two different cultures.

McGoldrick and Hardy[8] rationalize that children need more than one or even two adults to raise them and adults need more than one or two close relationships to get them through life and thus as family therapists we need to encourage our clients to go beyond the dominant culture's definition of family to pay close attention to relationships with siblings, nieces and nephews, grandchildren, aunts and uncles, and even further to include community context of health, safety, school, social life in which families live. We need to be mindful of the roles of housekeepers, maids, nannies, as well as godparents, grandparents, teachers, and other mentors, in the rearing of children.

There were certain concerns and anxieties expressed. There was the concern about biracial children not being accepted and treated well by others. There was also concern about biracial children growing up with an identity crisis as they may not be sure which culture they belong to. They may not be strongly grounded in any culture. The possibility of biracial children favoring one parent over the other and rejecting the parent they don't favor was also expressed. A111 said, "Sometimes these cultural issues are related to us having children and how they will be raised and our expectations of them. The expectations of our kids are different because in Indian families, parents do a lot for their kids in the early years but maintain that type of mentality throughout life. If the worst thing that I will do to my child is to have them biracial but healthy then I will take it. They will get the best of both worlds. They will have different worldviews and they can make their choice."

On asking F116 if she wants her children to learn her language and will E115 support her? F116 replied, "I don't speak the language but I would like them to be around my sisters and parents so that they will

---

8. McGoldrick and Hardy, "Re-Visioning Family Therapy," 3–24.

learn. F115 joined her and said, "I will support her. Her culture is important and I would like for her to teach them about food, values etc." He also added, "Our children will be mixed, which is an odd idea, but it will not matter." The mixed-race couples stated that one of their concerns was the acceptance of our kids by others and they were worried about people treating them poorly. They also expressed concern about being nervous about them not having any identity and not feeling like they belong to either partner's community.

E115 further stated that he has two concerns, firstly, that he wonders how he will be able to help his children on issues of racism, and secondly, he wonders that perhaps his child will one day identify more with one race than the other, and push one parent out. He was unsure how common this is. He stated that he did not have significant fears but that he did think about how to provide an environment that is diverse. He wanted to make sure that his children are exposed to both cultures and races equally. He stated that biracial children get the benefit of parents who are open and exposed to different cultures and raise their child by teaching them that all people are good. He wants to make sure they are loved and accepted and take a strong positive place in life.

Another major hurdle is in the area of raising biracial children. The two participating couples who were in the midst of doing that had both positive views about it as well as some challenges. They were happy about the fact that the child will receive the best of both worlds, will be open to exposure of different ways of life, of mores and traditions that bring about stability and growth. However, they were aware that these children could have some identity issues because of being biracial. They expressed concern whether the children will face acceptance issues, will be discriminated against, and the like. Yes, all this is possible. But the mutual respect and even admiration that each partner or parent shows for the other will play a major role in helping the child to come to terms with their own identity. It is imperative to be positive about the other's culture and upbringing and give out positive feedback to the child so the child grows up loving and respecting that part of the culture in himself/herself.

It is helpful to have friends who are also intercultural couples. They have navigated a lot of intercultural territory themselves and so in many respects can serve as a role model for new intercultural couples. This will help them feel normal about their status as interracial couple. They can also provide the insights on how raise biracial children.

Negotiating Different Faith Practices in Interfaith Couples' Relationship

There was only one interfaith couple among the participants. It was an emotionally distressing journey for them as they faced resentment and anger from their parents from the very moment they shared about their relationship. It seemed an uphill task to convince the parents that it will all work out. They were experiencing two levels of disapproval: one had to do with race and the other with faith. There were a lot of differences that they were encountering and they felt very stressful. Gradually, with counseling they were able to experience some calm and begin to take on a new and different perspective on the issue. They believed that even though they have different religious beliefs they have similar spiritual core values. Ultimately what mattered was that they both believe in God and the idea of a supreme-being who takes care of them, whether he or she is Jesus, Allah, Krishna, etc. Having this common belief shapes how they act, how they live and how they treat one another as well as those around them. They both believe in respect and fairness, which comes from their faiths although in different ways. They both viewed marriage as a spiritual commitment, a covenant with God and not breakable even when times are tough. They believed that even though they had two different sacred books, namely the Bible and *Bhagavad Gita*, and different styles of hymns or chants, that the concept (of worship) is the same. The only difference to them was how religion is expressed, for example the Hindu use of figurines, and distributing sweets at the temple. B112 stated that even though initially he wanted his girlfriend to convert but she was unwilling and so they sought therapeutic help and soon he realized that he needs to value her for who she is rather than be concerned about her faith. He said that differences are good but it should work for them. A111 stated that they have decided to respect both faiths and allow for both to be practiced in their home. They were of the opinion that as their children grow older they will teach their children both faiths and ultimately allow them to choose whichever they want to follow and that they will celebrate festivals associated with both religions. If there is a certain event, festival for example, they will both take part but one partner will usually be more involved and will lead the way. In terms of other differences, like food (for example, not eating beef), they both respect each other. They practice their own faiths but participate in each other's events.

G117, who belongs to the same denomination as her husband but is of a different race, stated that her faith and her spirituality were central to her life and hence she was keen to meet someone with a similar background. Having met H118 and finding that his values are shaped by the same faith and spirituality, made decision making very easy for her. The similarity in faith is also an important aspect in setting joint goals in tithing, paying back creditors, hospitality and the like.

One of the biggest challenges for the interfaith couple, even if one was to navigate all other issues, is the issue of the other faith dynamic, which can be huge and can become cumbersome. It does not just remain cultural but moves into dimension of religion and theology. Depending on what one's upbringing has been, at some point one or both partners begin to feel uneasy about navigating through the faith differences. The biggest obstacle seems to be in the area of deciding what religious symbols or practices are allowed in the house such as sacred literature, figurines or doing *puja* (worship) or doing *namaaz* (prayers) or doing rosary, or burning of incense. Dealing with theological differences is a big part of interfaith marriages. What is familiar and natural to one partner can be totally offensive to the other. How do they work through this in that neither one has to give up one's faith or things associated with one's faith. Again as in other matters, imposition of one's agenda on the other will not work. Talk about what is most important to you and how it can be respectfully carried out without causing moral injury to the other. There is great power in dialogue. Ask your therapist to suggest a pastor or faith leader who demonstrates an openness to diverse faiths and is progressive in his/her views on theology and who will help you look at these issues more closely and objectively. Work on the value system that you both enjoy. Another related challenge is that of raising children with two religions. Some of the questions that often bother couples are: whose religion will the child follow? If I give in will she/he try to bring up the child in one partner's faith tradition? How can I see my child worship another deity or follow faith traditions that are difficult for me to accept? These are questions to discuss both with your partner as well as your therapist.

Significance of Support from Family of Origin

Waldegrave[9] states that it is very essential to pay attention to family structure in counseling intercultural couples. To ignore or be ignorant of cultural perspectives is to devalue ethnic and ethical guidelines. It amounts to offending the family and her individual members. To be insensitive to

---

9. Waldegrave, "Cultural, Gender," 10.

the original issue at hand is to be indifferent to the problem that brought the couple to therapy.

Except for one percent of the participants, most of them agreed that their family has been extremely supportive, that all their friends and family and community alike have been in favor of them getting married and starting their own family. They counted themselves lucky to find such support and it certainly meant a lot to them. E115 expressed that "It was a shock to my grandmother but for most part both families have been supportive. The extended family knows about it and they don't express shock or surprise." A111 stated that, "My side of the family, both immediate and extended, does not support or tolerate my relationship with the exception of my brother and his wife who are also an intercultural couple but initially also were not too supportive." Her parents of Indian origin were supportive of their son who was marrying a Caucasian girl but were against her marrying an African American man. It clearly has a lot to do with racial acceptance because in the brother's case his wife is also a Christian. What made it worse was them telling her that they feel as though she is failing in life. "They are in denial and will not discuss the relationship with their friends or extended family as they are embarrassed." These hurdles were very challenging for her but premarital counseling helped her to address these conflicts and to individuate and take a stand for herself. Her boyfriend (B112) stated that the majority of his family and friends were extremely supportive even though he wanted to marry a girl from another faith. The support he received was more than he expected. This helped tremendously as he was able to care for her better. Both of them were able to work this out by allowing "time to play its course and not be aggressive." They said that, "Forcing the matter has not helped and or trying to have discussions to explain things or discuss the issues." A111 stated that her family has been unwilling to listen and instead puts both of us down even if he is not present and she found this to be emotionally damaging. "The recovery from this type of emotional blackmail/burden is difficult for me and I often fall into bouts of sadness that also then affects my relationship as well." During the phase of premarital counseling she often found herself swinging from one position to the other—from going ahead with the relationship and sometimes holding back and not wanting to move forward. They did eventually get married and had two weddings, one a Hindu wedding and the other a Christian wedding. Incidentally, both sets of parents participated in the wedding and gave them their blessing. Navigating through the extended family or even the immediate in-laws can be another area of work especially if one partner has experienced disrespect and or avoidance and rejection. One way that some couples deal with it is to stay away and maintain distance. It is possible to do that but it may result in a breakdown of relationship between the partner and his/her parents/in-laws. This may produce unnecessary burden on that partner and even guilt and remorse. For the most part, breakups in relationships are not healthy for the overall growth of the individual and so it will be helpful to be mindful of that and talk about it in the therapy session and learn new ways of reconciling. Being angry and or not consenting to the other partner mixing with his/her parents may amount to punishment that the partner does not deserve. The objective is to lessen the gap between the other partner and the in-laws. This is something that can be worked on patiently and that can be navigated gradually.

Shibusawa states that it is important to consider the possibility that no matter how acculturated clients are, it is most likely that their worldviews contain constructions that differ from those of Westerners. It is also important to note that in most Asian cultures marriage has traditionally been viewed as a union of two families or households rather than two individuals. Also, the goals and needs of the family take precedence over the needs and desires of individual members. Western notions of selfhood and ego development—that individuals need to develop the ability to make their own decisions—may not be aptly suited to the Asian couple/partner. To consider the impact that immigration had on the particular partner and the hardships that the partner and his/her parents had to go through should not be minimized.[10]

Section C

Awareness of Cultural Differences While in Intercultural Premarital Couples Counseling and Experience of Intercultural Premarital Couples Counseling

Forty percent of the couples were aware of some but not all cultural differences. Twenty percent of them chose to do counseling for differences in faith more than culture. With all of the external pressure around

---

10. Shibusawa, "Interracial Asian Couples," 383.

them, they started to lose sight of what had brought them together in the first place and they needed someone to help re-align them. A hundred percent of the participants agreed that they needed someone to guide them through other differences and find common ground. Forty percent felt that they went for premarital counseling to learn to communicate better with each other and not engage in hurtful and unhelpful arguments.

C113 stated that in the Catholic Church premarital counseling is very organized and also mandatory. They go through various topics such as theology, finance, conflict resolution, contact survey, one-on-one with the priest and with comments from priest. She and her partner found the group activities very helpful. When asked to elaborate why she replied that it made them feel one with the group, she said that they did not feel the spotlight on them. They were unable to have the one on one session with the priest and she felt that they missed out on something.

Couple E115 and F116 did not come specifically seeking premarital counseling but to address a crisis in their relationship and for discernment whether this relationship will work for them. E115 stated that during the course of their two and a half years of couples counseling they did work on some issues to work towards preparation for marriage in terms of premarital counseling. She elaborated that, "One of the main things that we had conflict was about competitiveness or "you vs. me." The biggest thing that I learned was it is never you vs. me but you and me. I took seriously the commitment piece, that there is no escape route in marriage. Buying into it helped changed my approach." Continue to focus on what traits attracted you to your partner. What are the similarities you cherish, what differences make you unique and attractive. Know that you are in this for love and you can make it work. I also admired the participant's openness and awareness of themselves when one of them remarked, "Yes, we try to be aware of our different ideas, opinions, and reactions to life. When we discuss issues, it's important to identify which ones are cultural versus which ones are just our own individual quirks or preferences." It is always good to be aware of what is coming between them. When asked how they will work through two cultures, one of the participants remarked, "By experiencing both cultures equally. I want it to be balanced and I know it is not going to be easy." I think this is very helpful, to know that it is not easy but we will work on it.

Reasons for Choosing Intercultural Premarital Couples Counseling

Couples in general and intercultural couples in particular may choose counseling for various reasons. It can be communication issues, financial issues, in-law issues, and or intimacy issues. B112 and A111 came for counseling because even though everything else was working smooth for them they were unable to tide over the religious differences. B112 said that "We sought counseling for religious differences, which is cultural in our case. We participated in it for about two years before marrying. I was aware in a subconscious way but did not really have discussions about it. Culture was not the reason we participated in counseling." His answer seems to imply that religion is not part of culture. Religion is a big part of culture and affects many different areas of one's life. It is so because for some religions it is a way of life rather than following some rituals once a week. B112 said that during their courtship he was certainly aware of many of the issues however he chose to embrace their similar subculture, meaning their value system.

H118, a Caucasian male, observed that soon after his divorce he went for individual counseling. In the meantime he fell in love with a South Asian girl from his church. So the intent of counseling was not premarital. He also said that, even though he did inform his Caucasian therapist about his new love interest, the therapist did not bring up the subject of intercultural concerns.

E115 and F1116 stated that they were unable to really pinpoint their struggles, they felt overwhelmed and "needed to air our voices and concerns." Their immediate concern was "damage control." Their relationship had gotten so bad that they had actually separated for a year but decided to get back together. This phase of coming back into the relationship was not working out for them. E115 said, "We were in bad shape coming back from a long break. I was a mess. We needed someone to help show us how to love each other again." His partner F116 joined him in saying that the reason they came for counseling was "To help us move through a tough time in our relation for we did not know if we wanted to be together. We also needed a lot of help to communicate with each other."

G117, the newly wedded bride in the intercultural partnership, stated that she was very aware of the cultural differences and that they keep addressing the issues as they come up. However, she felt that instead of handling those differences alone, that it may be a good thing to have a therapist lead them into a deeper understanding and find out potential problems that may occur in future. She recommended it to her partner as she felt that they needed an outside opinion and someone who is neutral to help us negotiate some of their issues. She felt it advisable to have a "third person go through potential areas of concern or trouble" that they may have in the future to lay it out for them so that they "can discuss now instead of later so that they are prepared for it at least a little bit." That was good foresight. They took their time to address some of these cultural issues that could come up and had a good discussion and even expressed emotions connected to those issues. This enabled them to move forward in their relationship with confidence and preparedness. G117 had gone in for individual counseling. She stated that "My personal therapy journey was extremely helpful and hence we are both very keen to explore marriage counseling."

Helpfulness of Intercultural Premarital Couples Counseling

E115 stated that for them premarital counseling was a very worthwhile experience. In therapy they "were exposed to differences as well as similarities and were able to discuss these in an open manner." H118 stated that counseling is very helpful and it is good to have a third opinion. "After being in counseling I have become a big fan of it and want to suggest it to everybody."

A111 stated that they had discussed some situations on their own but "did not make much progress until we had a neutral third party." Premarital counseling, she said, is something "I would recommend to anyone, even if same-race or same-faith." She added that, "I felt each session was challenging and sometimes forced me to think about unpleasant situations or those I rather avoid, but in the end, I have a sense of peace and I feel safe. The turmoil inside has been addressed and I feel that although there is still a fair amount of uncertainty, there is also some security in knowing how we both feel and the fact that we have a coping mechanism. I also know it was helpful because when we had tried to discuss some issues on our own, we got nowhere—but with counseling, we made progress." For A111 "Counseling is valuable and important for anyone in a relationship. We need to communicate and be open in order to succeed and have a long relationship. Sometimes we hear advice or suggestions that we may not always like but ultimately it is for the best and is beneficial in the long term, whether or not we see it."

Her partner B112 stated that "It allowed us to see each other's perspectives better. It helped us build a strong bond by offering a forum to discuss things with a moderator. Our counselor was also a translator at times, able to get the point in terms more easily understood by the other person." He added that "I realized that we were making progress. Therapy brought about issues that were not just skin deep. Our individual sessions were just as important as couple and those were good." He further added, "We always felt better after leaving counseling, even if the session was tense. It really encouraged us to think longer and deeper about whatever came up during our sessions. We were able to work through things we probably wouldn't have addressed or discussed otherwise." He stated that he understood that people always change "but for the moment we have a great understanding of each other and we have spent a lot of time and energy asking the hard questions and addressing each other's concerns and fears moving forward in our relationship."

One of the Catholic couple participants, C113, stated that the "Pre-Cana retreat was enlightening and bonding experience. We opened up quite a bit to each other through writing journal entries. C113 and D114 came to counseling many years after their marriage. They stayed in marital counseling for a while and then discontinued. Talking about her experience she observed, "We were on a road to progress and we would have benefitted more if we had stayed longer. Couples should be mandated by law to be in marital counseling. Because of the taboo on counseling it is so difficult to opt for counseling. People think that you must be in dire straits to go for counseling and not just for fine-tuning." Her husband D114 added that they did not properly do the couple survey and did not work with a priest as they were supposed to. In the three days they reviewed a lot of material and were given the chance to practice a lot of communication techniques. He said, "I did not realize cultural differences until after we were married. This was nuclear family differences." He felt that counseling helped him to really work on the issues between them versus the impact of other people in their lives. What D114 was referring to was how in-laws on both sides impacted their relationship because of expectations and nuclear family issues.

On asking E115 if he thought that premarital counseling was hard work for intercultural couples, he responded, "Probably a little but if you are in it for the right reasons then it is not." I asked him if premarital counseling gave them sufficient tools to enter into marriage. Do you think you will need marital counseling? He replied, "In our case things were tenuous for a long time. We absolutely needed it. I personally had to do a lot of work in my own personal life in general to even participate in being in a relationship. We were having relationship problems, which really turned out to be life problems, at least in my case. I wasn't convinced it would work but I was willing to try. My life was a shambles at the time. We had reached an impasse in our life and I didn't know if we could have figured it out on our own. It would not have worked out if we had not had counseling. We got the tools and a third party who could help most importantly at reality check—not so much in trying to understand her but understanding myself and seeing when I was improving and when I was declining." His partner F116 said, "Life seems less flighty and more secure. Because we had done premarital counseling we know how to handle situations when they come up. It was a question of whether we want to move forward or not. We had some trust issues. I had to answer the question if this person was worth moving forward with." On being asked, "What kept you going?" she responded, "I saw glimpses of what he can be. We were really good partners. I could see the end goal. Our families were supportive. I took their advice and that also influenced. There were times when I wanted to give up but it was a combination of that he is worthwhile, I loved him, and that I had support." She further added that "though we had differences we never recognized it as cultural and thought of it more as personal characteristic. Understanding culture makes you more accepting, less judgmental, and less angry. Knowing other members of the partner's family helps to get better insight into why he behaves like he does." She stated that premarital counseling helped them to communicate better, to think about issues that they had failed to name as cultural.

Aspects of Counseling Most and Least Helpful in Intercultural Premarital Couples Counseling

Most couple participants found it very helpful to have some form of "reinforcement from a third party on our ideas and approach and to help them navigate some issues. Often under stress they felt their confidence shake. Their therapist helped to instill confidence in them. Counseling also helped them to see things in a new light. They began to shun their ignorance and or insistence that they are right. They were willing to accommodate other perspectives. What worked for one participant was the emphasis on complimenting each other. This aspect helped him bring in commitment and ownership in the relationship. E115 stated that he just started to act on it for he realized that he has only one choice and so he needs to make it work rather than hope it works. He stated that without counseling they would not have made it. He said that their therapist gave them the tools that showed them how to work together and communicate. For most of them, intercultural counseling was an eye-opener for it helped them learn about the impact their differing backgrounds and culture has on their relationship. They learned how to express needs in ways the other can hear. Most of all they learned about themselves. The couple learned that counseling is about self-awareness and not about shifting the blame on to their partner but to owning responsibility for their own actions. Counseling also helped them get foresight into what to expect in future and to be able to identify issues and concerns that one or both partners may have. They also learned to "name" things as they felt it so as to be able to better and more effectively address those issues.

For most of the participants it was helpful to get an "outside" perspective so that they could begin to see things objectively rather than how they felt subjectively. One of the participants, F116, stated that "When we would revisit arguments we had at home in the counseling session, it helped to have someone there to go through the process of listening and expressing to each other that made us both feel valued. It was also very helpful to do activities practicing active listening skills. It helped to have a counselor with cultural awareness. It made both of us more comfortable and trusting of her." A111 observed that she thought it was most helpful to clearly talk about real-life situations and not abstract situations. "For example, I liked when our counselor discussed situations like "Will you go to church on Sunday?" or "Will you have Indian (Hindu) idols in your home?" instead of saying "Will you allow Christianity in your life?" This approach made it real and more practical to her and to them both. For one of the participants it was to know what to expect and to know the way that she should respond. Several of them found counseling helpful because it was a systematic approach, as each issue was addressed and given potential solutions. Even if there was an issue that did not have an immediate solution, they were given some type of coping mechanism to work with the issue. "Sometimes there is no good answer to something but we still felt like we had discussed it enough to feel better about it."

Aspects of counseling that were not helpful were anything abstract where they could not find a place for it in their life or any concept that was ambiguous or too wide. In the case of the Catholic couple they stated that they took a required pre-marriage test and their priest forgot to give them the results but told them after they were married that there were significant discrepancies in the results and that they should meet with a counselor to go over them. But he never provided them the result. This was unhelpful in addressing issues that were significant and became contentious later in their marriage. One of the participants stated that he did not get much out of take-home exercises/reading material. He also stated that he did not like the idea of giving the options to him to talk about versus approaching all problems in a systematic manner. He also did not like the idea of talking about day-to-day issues from the top of his head as opposed to the therapist working with issues and concerns that were listed and agreed upon.

Cultural Issues Most and Least Effective in Intercultural Premarital Couples Counseling

The couples found the following as most helpful themes in counseling: couple decision-making process, financial honesty, having someone understand my culture and then be able to explain it to my partner, to relate cultural issues to our situation and apply it, they only want to get married once and really explore whether they could make the lifelong commitment necessary for marriage, better understanding ways to communicate with each other based on partner's own cultural "language."

None of the couples mentioned any topic that was ineffective in premarital counseling.

Reasons for Choosing Intercultural Premarital Counseling Therapist

E115 stated that he was given an ultimatum that he needed to be in counseling. It didn't matter to him who his counselor will be. All he was looking for was a person who would be older than him and also married for a long time. He felt a connection with his therapist in terms of her personality. He said that he chose their therapist randomly and they stayed because they clicked. As time passed, her counseling worked. Since he was not thinking about differences as cultural differences, he did not think of finding a culturally sensitive therapist. "I didn't think too much about culture." He felt that the therapist that was assigned to him felt right. He did not ever feel judged by his therapist and he found her to be very patient with good insights. He said that, "We went in angry for almost a year and their therapist had a way about moving them past the fights." F116 joined with her boyfriend in saying, "My husband found our counselor. We worked with her for a little over two years. We stayed because we felt that she understood both of us and we made progress through the therapy."

Being a second-generation South Asian immigrant, A111 was looking for someone with an Indian background as well as the Christian faith mix. Her boyfriend was Christian. So they needed a balance. She said that, "We needed this so someone can understand the issues we face as the Indian background has particular difficulties." They stayed in counseling for three years and would have continued to stay on indefinitely. She stated that both of them felt that their therapist was able to really understand them and the issues they faced.

B112 stated that they were with their therapist for roughly three years and they chose her because of ethnic and religious background. They continued to stay in therapy because "they found it effective for gaining greater insight into one another and our therapists helped us navigate very difficult times related to family issues."

Every culture is different and so the expectation from the therapist is different; some prefer the therapist to be their mentor or guide while others to relate well as a mother, or an aunt or a big sister. This is where a good understanding of transference and countertransference is important for the therapist and also to know what works with a particular culture and what does not. They want someone who understands the nuances of the cultures present in the room. It is important that the therapist has strong cultural tie/similarity that both individuals receiving counseling can identify with.

Characteristics Helpful In Intercultural Therapist

B112 stated that he was able to relate to his therapist because she was of the same religion and he felt comfortable. He said that they were "looking for a translator so that both could understand each other's 'language'. It was my belief that even though religiously they may be different but culturally you can be close. I separate religion and culture. Religion is more difficult to work through. My therapist helped me to work through issues and name them. It made both of us to think and even change our mind in some ways, to think and work out for ourselves. She was afraid that if she went to a pastor for counseling he/she may judge her because of her faith and may want to convert her. He further stated that "However even though my therapist's religion was different from her, she was comfortable to work with the therapist because my therapist was from her culture."

One of the participants stated that for both of them their therapist felt like a big sister or mom and that made them feel comfortable. Another said that "every culture is different but I am more used to the nurturing type and so my therapist's personality helped me." Another found theirs to be non-judgmental. Another appreciated the idea that their therapist helped them "to examine ourselves and our own actions, and reminded us that we love each other." Another liked the fact that she was "very empathetic." Another said "caring." One of them said that she had "great listening skills." Yet another stated that she was "able to identify either with my faith or culture or both without taking sides." Another participant stated that he liked that she had the ability to explain and advise without having any personal biases. Another added that his therapist was fair, a good listener, nurturing, nonjudgmental, open, and willing to see different perspectives and that she was very effective in her communication style. One of them said that she was very tuned in to my cultural experience of being a woman, an immigrant, because she also came from a collectivist culture herself. Still another added that she was attentive, caring, and neutral. That she had a strong understanding of humanity and the importance of forming a set of values. One of them felt that it is important that the therapist has strong cultural ties/similarities that both individuals receiving counseling can identify with. Another added that trust is important; whenever their therapist asked them to do something (homework) they did it. He said that trust in her was built because they saw the effectiveness of the therapy work. One of them said that their therapist's personality is well-suited to counseling because she has been married for a long period of time, she was born and raised in a separate culture and recognizes that this culture as well as has lived here for many years, so understands this culture as well. One of them said "that her techniques seemed to work, she was consistent and persistent in getting us to try them and stick with it and she never gave up or showed signs of frustration in spite of the fact we spun our wheels at times."

The participants recommended that it will be helpful for the intercultural couple therapist to be patient, demonstrate good insights, to help deal with anger issues, to understand the couple's issues and to relate to them well, to help the clients to work through issues and name them, to make them think for themselves, to be very empathetic, caring, and possess great listening skills, to be attentive, to identify with their faith or culture or both, and to not take sides. In other words, they must both feel that the therapist is objective and be able to explain and advice without any personal bias or prejudice. Several of the participants mentioned that he/she should be fair, nonjudgmental, open, and willing to see different perspectives. I guess there is always a fear that the therapist will align more with a particular partner because he/she is of the same ethnicity or faith tradition or nationality. One mentioned that they want their therapist to have a strong understanding of humanity and the importance of forming a set of values. A couple of participants were also looking for someone who has been married for some time and someone older than them so that he/she understands conflict and has some personal experience of conflict resolution. One of the participants wanted to be given a questionnaire in the beginning that will help the therapist to know what the focus of each partner is.

The participants like the fact that they could be themselves and know that they are accepted. This is a good model for them to see in their relationship with their therapist that they are accepted regardless of their background and for them to emulate in their own relationship with difference and disagreement. Thus they reiterated the need for a therapeutic alliance to move the therapy forward. Therapeutic alliance or a therapeutic relationship is observed between a therapist and his/her individual client or couple. It is a significant means by which a therapist and a client communicate or engage with each other which then helps to foster movement and desired change. Psychologists agree that good therapeutic alliance aids in predicting treatment, adherence to objective/goals in treatment plan and or counseling outcome.

Section D

Suggestions for Future Intercultural Premarital Couples

Underscoring the value and importance of counseling for intercultural couples, the point was made that counseling helps in better communication and openness. One learns to communicate one's deepest feelings and thoughts that otherwise remained suppressed and where one did not know how to bring them out in the open with one's partner. Individual sessions are seen as beneficial along with joint sessions with one's partner.

They said that many things that are talked about in the session may not make sense immediately but in the course of time proves beneficial. They also iterated that resources available at the Care & Counseling Center are excellent and people need to be made aware of it.

The Catholic couple stated that even though there is a three-day retreat, it needs more time and needs more one-on-one time with the priest. Another added that when couples who have the intention of getting married come for counseling in order to resolve conflicts they can be led in the direction of availing themselves of premarital counseling. F115 suggested that intercultural couples who acknowledge their cultural differences and discuss these differences seem to prefer a person of different culture as their counselor. He clarified saying that "a therapist from a majority culture would not be able to tap through sensitive issues."

A111 stated that "Therapy is good to address issues and to expect to know what will come up. My friends cannot find a therapist who can understand all cultures. It will be good to have a data base of mixed couples. After you go through animosity and hate, it is hard to trust anyone. You cannot go to your church or faith community because you know they will not be on your side." A111 was stressing the fact in interfaith relationships they will find it hard to get a listening ear from their clergy or faith leader. No therapist can be well versed in all cultures; however, a therapist who has some experience of another culture most of the time can be a good fit to listen and understand a person from an ethnic culture or a different culture. What I hear them saying is that intercultural couples are seeking out intercultural therapists on the internet but they are not always able to find one in their location.

Suggestions for Therapists Engaged In Intercultural Premarital Couple Counseling

All the participants agreed that it will be helpful if the therapist is totally objective. They want the therapist to understand the nuances of the cultures. C113 stated that "Culture is very important. After we move forward from our honeymoon phase it begins to surface. Taking the time to talk about premarital counseling is a fantastic idea. We view marriage as a covenant and the church does all they can to see that marriage works." This Catholic participant suggested that after the weekend, it will be beneficial to have one or two one-on-one sessions with the priest. She had gone for marital counseling and had experienced one or two one-on-one sessions with her therapist and found it helpful.

A111 suggested that there should be a questionnaire for interfaith couples, so that when they work on the questionnaire in the beginning itself that they will be able to find out what the focus of each person is. Another said that her main focus was raising biracial kids, and so she thought that it will be good to have a questionnaire just for this. B112 stated that he enjoyed having individual sessions as well as sessions together. He felt that he could really communicate something that was troubling him that he was not quite sure how to discuss or bring up with his partner. Most of the participants found the one-on-one sessions built into the couples counseling beneficial. They were able to be non-defensive and free of judgment as they sat with the therapist. This helped them to be objective as well and to be open for self-reflection and change in their own selves.

Suggestions for Themes to Be Used in Intercultural Premarital Couple Counseling

All the participants were very engaging and offered some useful suggestions in terms of themes in premarital counseling. Based on their experience of counseling they were able to offer these suggestions listed here not in any given order of importance:

Communication, parenting, having a first child, raising biracial child(ren), recycling, personality issues, understanding in-laws, governing attitudes vs. romantic attitudes, body image, sibling order, psycho education take-home material (helpful to know that a topic is coming up), achieving goals and time frame, finance (how to support a family), career, salary, keeping the romance alive (practicing different things to feel loved and valued in the relationship), roles and responsibilities (cooking and housework and being equal partners), and time frame of getting engaged or married. Life together for an intercultural couple can get hard. It often seems like an uphill task and often the overwhelming feeling is to quit. It seems too hard to navigate through the many different and seemingly difficult curves and steep climbs to move forward. Yes, it is hard to navigate this journey because there is a possibility that there may be many things that have to be navigated such as food, clothing, entertainment, literature, family of origin issues, in-laws, extended family, worldview, political ideology, decision-making process, financial honesty, power dynamics, roles and responsibilities, conflict resolution, habits, attitudes, stereotypes, and just speed at which one lives one's life, expectations changing with regard to cooking and housework and the need to be equal partners, finance—as to how they will support a family, better communication, aging parents, where they will live, religious differences, and how to expect to navigate through all these. This is quite a long list and it would take several sessions to go over all of these. Therefore, it will be helpful to let the clients decide what themes are important to them and what would they like to focus on. However, one needs to keep in mind that when couples first come for counseling they need not be coming for premarital counseling but only for conflict resolution and that itself can take weeks. Premarital counseling can happen only when the couples are in a more stable place and able to focus on some of these issues. But once you begin this journey, take time to breathe and enjoy the scenery around you. Be surprised, get curious, and most of all live without judgment, then it will all work out good for both. The beauty of the intercultural journey lies in acceptance and respect for the other and all that the other brings to the table. When asked if intercultural couples have to work harder, one participant responded, "Probably it is a little hard but if you are in it for the right reasons then it is not."

Suggestions for the Process of Intercultural Premarital Couple Therapy

It is often possible that sometimes one partner has to work more on certain issues than the other partner and while this work is ongoing the other partner feels fairly stuck with no movement in the therapy session. Sometimes the issues are recurring and need to be addressed several times over. This can be a frustrating experience for the other partner. So partners develop patience and listening skills. As they observe their partner bring up issues with the therapist that in their mind they have already resolved they begin to see an example of how an issue needs to be addressed over and over again until it feels resolved in the mind of their partner. This way they learn new communication techniques. Another participant stated that talking to someone else helps when they are in that crazy emotional state and are trying things out just by themselves. Believing in the process of therapy can be a very liberating experience where they know that they have help and they do not have to struggle alone. While in the process it is not always easy to become vulnerable and open up your inhibitions and your prejudices. It is often said that therapy is not for the fainthearted. Therapy is hard work. One of the participants remarked, "I felt good that things were coming out in the open. I did not feel challenged but happy that it needed to happen." This was one courageous participant who was willing to be vulnerable and uncomfortable only because he/she knew that at the end it would yield good result for them both. This is a good example of openness and transparency.

Suggestions for the Duration of Intercultural Premarital Couple Counseling

One of the participants stated that since every couple is different, it is hard to generalize how many sessions would be required. Each of the partners come from so many different places in their lives. Everything goes to contribute a little to where they find themselves in the counseling session. It could be their gender or age or their upbringing or life transition or divorce or second relationship, issue of commitment, or lack of trust. Thus each couple takes different time to ease out of their current stress. One of them said that it will be helpful to focus on one particular issue at a time and guide them through it. Another participant suggested having twelve to sixteen sessions, 25 percent individual and 75 percent tandem. That is a good estimate but again each case is different. A lot also depends on the amount of work that each is willing to do at home in the relationship. They cannot expect to get good results if they are unwilling or de-motivated to put some things into practice.

CHAPTER VII

Conclusion and Recommendations for Intercultural Premarital Couple Counseling

Conclusion

THIS STUDY SET OUT to investigate how integrated approaches can assist in determining ways that different cultural aspects can be addressed within intercultural premarital counseling. In fulfilling this purpose, an empirical research was conducted to gather data on how couples understand culture, how they understand the dynamics of culture, how they respond to the possibility of learning and incorporating certain values and belief systems of their partner, what is the place for negotiation and how they go about it, how they respond in the face of conflicts and disagreements, how they communicate in the context of cultural differences. The research questions that I set out to explore were in the area of their understanding of culture and race, their belief and value system, what brings about conflict in their relationship and how they resolve conflict, their present and future concerns as an intercultural couple, their therapeutic experience and their suggestions to other intercultural couples and intercultural therapists that are helpful in intercultural couples counseling. The goal was to discover what has been effective in the life of the intercultural couple participants, what works for them and what does not.

I believe that psychotherapeutic techniques have a place in giving us structure and movement. However, I also agree that we need to emphasize other aspects and approaches around us that aid in granting us healing and wholeness, which we often overlook and pass by. Rollo May was an existentialist psychologist and he pointed out that a major resistance of mainstream psychology to other psychotherapeutic approaches particularly in the United States is "the tendency to be preoccupied with technique and to be impatient with endeavors to search below such considerations to find the foundations upon which all techniques must be based."[1] He was pointing to something that was beyond techniques or even theories and perhaps to one's existential reality, to the here and now. Thus, one of the main objectives of this research on intercultural premarital couples counseling was to discover effective and sustaining approaches to intercultural premarital couples counseling.

An important aspect of this research on intercultural premarital couples counseling was to discover the kind of understanding and exposure that partners have of cultures, race, and racial identity, the assumption being that their level of exposure and cultural awareness will help or hinder their relationship together. What has been their experience in their upbringing of race and culture? If they have an exposure of other intercultural couples and how this impacts their life, their value system, their acceptance and respect of the other? And what is the impact of it all on their identity as an intercultural couple as well as an intercultural couple raising biracial children? What external sources if any help them to stay connected and to sustain their relationship? Another important area of this research on intercultural premarital couple counseling was to ascertain what experience they have of premarital counseling with an intercultural therapist and how that impacted or influenced their therapy. Lastly, this research sought to articulate their input for intercultural couples as well as for intercultural therapists.

Participants pointed out the subtle aspects of race that they experience in their everyday life. Those participants belonging to ethnic minority cultures seemed to be more aware of the racial divide in society than the Caucasian participants. The two male Caucasian participants (E115 and H118) in this research on intercultural premarital couples counseling talked about the fact that for a long time they were unable to figure out race as a problem in their relationship. For them the fact of White privilege did not appear. They were good people trying to woo Black or Brown partners but never realized that them being White had a very definite

---

1. May et al., *Existence*, 9.

significance. Lee[2] explains how White people may see instances of difference but fail to understand their connection to Whiteness and its inherent privileges. Therefore, in the words of Lee, "White privilege acts on us, and on our cross-cultural clients, confounding our search for mutual understanding while preventing us from realizing or acknowledging that it is doing so." This concept of "White Privilege" is not just relevant for the couple partners but also for the therapists. Lee[3] in his article on race as a construct in therapy talks about the subtle ways in which race shows up in the therapy room. Lee also talks about the fact that as therapists we are all trained and taught to be mindful of our own biases, also known as countertransference. This awareness is significant in therapy in order that "we do no harm" to our clients in the clinical context. Lee states that, very early in his work with intercultural couples, he realized the importance of building a foundation around parallels and points of connection around each of their experience of oppression. He believes that the use of oppression/racism narratives can provide a powerful bridge to understanding and reconciliation in couple therapy. It became evident in this research that both partners were often not on the same page. An interesting instance was reported by one of the White male participants (H118) in this research who was doing individual counseling with a White therapist. The fact that this White male participant was seeking to marry a South Asian woman (G117) was known to his therapist but the therapist totally overlooked any cultural issues that needed to be addressed. It seems to me that his therapist lacked awareness that cultural difference can impact the relationship in negative ways. Also that there is a need to create awareness about cultural concerns and help couples handle them effectively.

It has been observed that "Interventions help improve our understanding of the interactions of the couple that can influence both the quality and the stability of the premarital or marital relationship."[4] This was evident by the remark of a couple participant (E115) how counseling helped improve the way they interacted with each other and the interventions that the therapist engaged in. "During the course of two and a half years we did work on some issues to work towards preparation for marriage in terms of premarital counseling. One of the main things that we

---

2. Lee, "Unspoken Power of Racial Context," 77–102.
3. Lee, "Unspoken Power of Racial Context," 77–102.
4. Holman et al., "Assumptions and Methods," 29–45.

had conflict was about competiveness or 'you' vs. 'me'. The biggest thing that I learned was it is never you vs. me but you and me. The commitment piece that there is no escape route in marriage and buying into it helped changed my approach." Bradbury and Kamey state that "most marriage and family therapists strive to help clients create and maintain healthy premarital and marital relationships."[5] In affirming the positive impact of counseling on their life a participant (A111) noted, "Life seems less flighty and more secure and because we had done premarital counseling, even when we are faced with difficult situations we know how to handle it." To one participant (B112) counseling was very important because it enabled "learning about the impact our differing backgrounds and culture has on our relationship."

Ting-Toomey states that "to sustain the relationships of intercultural couples it is important to work towards cultural adjustment that helps foster positive relationship outcomes."[6] As a result of being in counseling, one of the couple participants (F116) acknowledged how as intercultural couples they became aware of the need to complement each other culturally and which enabled them to deepen their commitment to each other. In their own words, "So the emphasis on complimenting each other was helpful. It brought in commitment and ownership."

Crippen and Brew noted that they find much less research evidence on positive traits and behaviors or actions that bring about an opportunity for transformation.[7] This research brought up several characteristics that the couples found helpful and enjoyed in each other. Complimenting his wife, E115 said, "At first I was physically attracted to her but the more I got to know her, the more I liked her and the fact that she is hard working attracted me to her." He added that "she was easy to talk to and I felt that she was a genuine person. It is hard to find all these qualities in one person." He also said that "people from her country are hard workers, generous, they care for family." In turn his wife, F116, added that "he was respectful and did not seem to indicate that he was entitled," and that she loved his egalitarian approach. G117 said, "My partner is kind, loving and loyal. He has a strong sense of family and never lets me down. He is always on my team and always supportive of me and encouraging. He believes in me probably more than I believe in myself." She added that

5. Bradbury and Karney, "Understanding and Altering," 862–79.
6. Ting-Toomey, *Communicating Across Cultures*, 246.
7. Crippen and Brew, "Intercultural Parenting," 107–15.

"My partner is a person of strong, solid character and his value system is one that I respect and admire." Her husband H118 stated, "She was extremely caring, thoughtful, and calm," and that "I was attracted to her mainly because of her kindness and generosity." C113 said, "I loved his sense of humor and we understood each other." Her husband (D114) in turn said, "I was attracted to her because of her prettiness, slim figure, intelligence, and good conversation." He further stated that "My partner was easy to be with and that was the first thing." These are sufficient to point out that there are these great positive humanistic qualities in each other that partners find attractive and endearing.

Crippen and Brew also noted that intercultural couples are on the rise, that intercultural couples may struggle more in decision-making, problem-solving, and child-rearing and suggest that intercultural couples must acknowledge the impact of their own cultural background on themselves and on their partner in order to decrease conflict.[8] E115 spoke candidly about his intolerance of some people: "I sometimes held ignorant views that majority of people are taking advantage like people on welfare. I felt that if people made better choices they would not be poor. She brought understanding about why people make these choices. Now we do not get heated about issues." With the awareness created in the therapeutic sessions he was able to let go of his own stereotypes and be more accepting of others. Another interesting piece was given by G117 regarding the example of her conversation with her husband: "We had an interesting conversation as we were driving down here. He said that I don't notice any cultural differences or issues between us and I replied that that's because I am planted in your culture. Just imagine if you were planted in my culture and he agreed that I was right."

Crippen and Brew also state that "when each partner's values regarding aspects of the blueprint do not coincide, or are not understood by the partner, greater levels of conflict and lower relationship satisfaction occur."[9] G117 stated that "We have a similar value system. Practicing similar traditions is helpful. However, what comes up for me from my culture is my self-esteem issues about the color of my skin, physical appearance, and keeping the house clean; different food habits is also an issue. I have to work through the different expectations." E115 stated, "We had difficulty in understanding the different ways each of (our) cultures

---

8. Crippen and Brew, "Intercultural Parenting," 107–15.
9. Crippen and Brew, "Intercultural Parenting," 107–15.

handled the issue of punctuality. It was easy accepting that not being very punctual is culturally conditioned. I have changed a lot of things now. I am late to more things now (laughs)." There can be any number of issues emerging out of cultural differences and once you begin to see that it is cultural and not personality then it gets easier for both to change and accept each other.

I have given careful consideration to participants' stories that emerge through the use of an integrated paradigm of looking at the data. Through stories of cultural background, immigration, transition to marriage, parenting, communication, and bicultural issues I was able to further explain emerging themes. This study can inform other providers and caregivers that are working with the intercultural couple's population and introduce topics to discuss in intercultural premarital counseling with intercultural couples. It also seeks to give guidelines to intercultural couples who are looking for guidance to navigate their relationship in a meaningful way.

Quantitative literature has shown that healthy communication[10] among intimate partners is a strong predictor of relationship and marital satisfaction.[11] Healthy communication is defined by one's openness with his/her partner, the ability to discuss particular issues and behaviors that bother him/her and request changes without being negative or critical.[12] A participant (E115) observed that "Without the counseling we would not have made it. The counselor gave us the tools that showed us how to work together and communicate. We learned how to express needs in ways the other can hear."

We are in the process of gaining a better understanding of our "neighbors" and "others." We still have a long journey ahead of us and we can succeed if we continue to work on genuine acceptance, empathetic understanding, and non-judgmental attitude. There is a great need to be curious about our differences rather than be critical. Many people in different fields of life are working to bridge the gap. There has been a steady growth in the area of pastoral counseling and pastoral psychotherapy. In this research I realized that the family of origin is of paramount importance as it helps to answer the question of race, religion, value system and acceptance. It also became evident that an intersubjective or

---

10. Gottman, *What Predicts Divorce?*, 131.
11. Gottman et al., "Predicting Marital Happiness," 5–22.
12. Nichols, *Family Therapy*, 70.

interdependence and relational paradigm between the therapist and the client are equally engaged in making a difference. In this way, pastoral counseling, particularly intercultural counseling, is moving towards an integrated approach.

Ethnic therapists are often confronted with the dilemma of who is teaching them and what. It is hard to be oneself when you are constantly bombarded with stuff that this is the right way of doing therapy and everything else is either codependency or enmeshment or so on. How do we balance our therapeutic stance?

It becomes increasingly clear that it is imperative to have a clear understanding of culture. Culture can be broadly defined as a human characteristic that encompasses language, social mores, customs and traditions, religion, religious rituals and beliefs, festivals and observances, ways of being in the world, a way of life, decision-making, problem-solving, familial bonds and ties, music, arts, literature, dress, food habits, and many other things. In recent years, culture has been viewed as a way of accepting a person and his/her worldview. In our day and age, America has become a melting pot of cultures and all of life is influenced by the variety and the diversity of life. Thus, an important cultural consideration today is that culture and cultural beliefs are fluid and can change over time.[13] Additionally, it is important to consider the uniqueness of each culture.

It is imperative to acknowledge and understand the cultural richness and complexity of the immigrant generation, especially those cultures that embody values which are in many ways different from the dominant European American values. McGoldrick and Hardy[14] offer us the possibility for re-visioning who we are and who we can be. There is a need to move past the fear of diversity to making it our strength. It is our fear of other cultures that makes us exclude others and dehumanize those who are different from us. I did discover this with the couple participants, who moved gradually from mistrust of and stereotyping others to a more empathic understanding of the other. Their ethnic partner as well as their ethnic therapist enabled them do this.

This research about intercultural couples recognizes that the couples and each partner within that couple-hood can be so very different.

---

13. Laird, "Theorizing Culture: Narrative Ideas," 29.
14. McGoldrick and Hardy, "Re-Visioning Family Therapy," 4.

Therefore, nothing can really be taken for granted. Each of them can be at a different stage of growth and acceptance of difference.

Many therapists do not tie themselves to any one approach. Instead, they blend elements from different approaches and tailor their treatment according to each client's needs. An integrated approach is a method or approach that is composed of elements drawn from various sources.[15] Through the interview process, when asked to name any of the different approaches that their respective therapists would have used, what became clear to me was that most of the participants were unable to name any of the theories or approaches apart from family systems therapy. I think what matters is that an integrated mix of therapies is helpful in counseling intercultural couples. However, each case is different and needs to be analyzed on its own merit. I think that what worked best was the overall approach of the therapist who was nonjudgmental and curious, and they felt that he/she provided them a container and held them safe. In the midst of feeling insecure and rejected by the family or others, they felt upheld by their therapist. The important fact that emerged was that they were able to share their difficulties even without knowing or recognizing that it was a cultural nuance and that their therapist was able to name it for them and make it look like they could deal with it.

My aim through this research was not only to gain insight into the cultural background of each individual participant but also to delve deeper into their "thick" narrative and flesh out needs and concerns that often get overlooked. One of the concerns in which this became more evident was in the area of raising biracial children. While there was much optimism expressed in the sense that (A111) "Biracial children are positively impacted because you have not made race as a big deal, though you live in two cultures." "They will get the best of both worlds. They will have different worldviews and they can make their choice." But on the other hand, one of the participants E115 expressed his concern, "I am concerned about the acceptance of our kids by others and people treating them poorly." "I am nervous about them having no identity and not feeling like they belong to either mine or my partner's community." "I am concerned about them not having a childhood rich of culture, in whatever form or tradition, or learning our languages." "I wonder and hope that if we have children they will be able to associate to both our cultures and not be too one-sided." He added, "I have two concerns: One,

---

15. http://www.merriam-webster.com/dictionary/eclectic.

I wonder how I will be able to help my children with issues of racism. But I don't think it will be that much of an issue. Two, I wonder that perhaps my child will one day identify more with one race than the other, and push one parent out. I don't know how common this is." These words were coming from a very deep place inside him that perhaps he was voicing for the first time.

In order to address the impact that cultural issues can have on varying aspects of mental health and the services provided in a therapeutic setting, this study sought to explore ways culture can be addressed within intercultural premarital counseling. When talking with the participants several of them observed that this study helped them to delve deeper into their own understanding of culture, their spoken and unspoken concerns about race, raising biracial children, the role of the extended family, and how they can offer support or cut off the relationship and how deeply it affects them. Several of them were not necessarily concerned about culture as they all considered themselves American first, and their ethnic identities took a backseat. However, through therapy they were able to recognize the part that culture has played all along and had taken them to therapy. This is not to say that all issues of discord were cultural, but that they had not brought culture to the forefront and to take a good look at it to see if culture was a bane or blessing in their relationship and what it had to do with their own upbringing and how by recognizing and working through it, that they were able to minimize the damage.

Reflections on the Contributions of this Research

I have been passionate about the topic of this research and the journey I have undertaken in doing this research has been very satisfying as well as challenging. In my clinical work I had discovered that the use of existing theories and or approaches to address the issues and concerns faced by intercultural couples was inadequate. Therefore, I decided to research and come up with understanding that would serve to be more effective therapy for intercultural couples.

Culture is a vast topic that encompasses a complexity of diversity and differences. In and through this research, I owned my own subjectivity as well as the subjectivity of my participants by giving them a voice and making their unique experience credible. I learned from the couples that they feel happy that they are in this for the right reason. However, they also feel isolated by their own families, society, and the clergy. They feel misunderstood and rejected and turn to a therapist for support and validation. They are more than willing to work on their differences so that they can live peacefully and happily but are in need of some direction and empathy.

Helping them to come out of their web of discord between personality and culture is crucial for their well-being so that they can begin to celebrate diversity and difference. What is also significant is to enable them to begin to develop a new identity as an intercultural couple so that they begin to feel one as a unit. Another important area would be to help them realize that conflict arising out of difference is not a bad thing. Resolution of conflict together leads to greater intimacy and potential enrichment. Yet another area of guidance and support is to enable them to "welcome the stranger" not only in their partner but also in themselves. Some of them have dual or even triple identities that they do not know how to live with. This is not to happen at the negation of another but to work towards an integrated self-identity that is all encompassing and self-liberating.

Though the participants did not say much about the failure of clergy in accepting interfaith couples, there was a hint that clergy tend not to understand or promote their union. This is where I feel the need for the faith community leaders to develop a theological stance that is open and accepting of mixed faith partners where no one feels rejected or shunned because of their faith. There is such a huge need for caregivers and faith leaders to work towards curiosity over critique. I believe that organizing support groups or "holding space" for intercultural or interfaith couples in therapy centers or places of worship will go a long way in them feeling held.

As a result of my research, I propose an integrated psychotherapeutic approach that brings together selected theories or approaches of psychotherapy. This approach incorporates a theoretical base and standards of practice alongside gleanings from selected techniques that are relevant to intercultural couples. The attempt is different from an eclectic approach. It is not merely borrowing ideas from here and there and throwing them together for each couple but more as a standard model that can be utilized for most clients by different practitioners. The guidelines that the research sets forth to therapists and para-professionals will enable them to do their work with greater sensitivity and effectiveness. Intercultural couples are looking for support and encouragement and this research provides them a friend who understands them and their particular experience.

Recommendations for Intercultural Couples in Premarital Therapy:

Valuing Each Other

Value each other and each other's faith practices: B112, "value her for who she is rather than be concerned about her faith"; A111, "believe in mutual respect and fairness, which comes from our different faiths. Although we are different religiously, we share many of the same spiritual and core values."

Communication

Premarital counseling is important: F116, "Talk about the issues you face, acknowledge your differences and avail yourself of counseling, maybe with a person of a different culture. Therapist from a majority culture would not be able to tap through sensitive issues"; E115, "Counseling . . . really encouraged us to think longer and deeper about whatever came up during our sessions and work through things we probably wouldn't have addressed or discussed otherwise."

Get Informed About Each Other's Culture

Understanding of culture and cultural nuances is important: E115, "Though we had differences we never recognized it as cultural and thought of it more as a personal characteristic. Understanding culture makes you more accepting, less judgmental, less angry. Getting to know other members of the family helps in getting better insight into why she behaves as she does"; F116, "By experiencing both cultures equally. I want it to be balanced and I know it is not going to be easy"; C113, "Culture is very important. After we move forward from our honeymoon phase it begins to surface. Taking the time to talk about premarital counseling is a fantastic idea."

Recommendations for Therapists Engaged In Intercultural Couples Counseling

Intercultural Information

Introduce the intercultural couple to the dynamics of culture: E115, "It helped us communicate better." "Maybe to lead them in that direction. It is very helpful to have a third opinion. After being in counseling I have become a big fan of it and want to suggest it to everybody."

Premarital Counseling as a Prerequisite

Effective premarital counseling will open the door for marital counseling: G117, "My personal therapy journey was extremely helpful and hence we are both very keen to explore marriage counseling."

Data Base of Ethnic Therapists

Work on a database of local and or national intercultural therapists and make it available as a resource: A111, "My friends cannot find a therapist who can understand all cultures. It will be good to have a data base of mixed couples."

Individual and Tandem Sessions

Individual sessions are as important as tandem sessions: B112, "I enjoyed having individual sessions as well as sessions together. I learned how to really communicate something troubling me that I wasn't quite sure how to discuss or bring up with my partner"; C113, "After the weekend, it will be beneficial to have one or two one-on-one sessions with the priest."

Intake Questionnaire about Cultural Awareness

Have a built-in intake questionnaire for intercultural concerns: A111, "There should be a questionnaire for interfaith couples so that when they work on the questionnaire in the beginning itself that they will be able to find out what the focus of each person is"; F116, "My main focus is raising biracial kids, so it will be good to have a questionnaire just for this."

Themes to Discuss in Therapy

Helpful themes to discuss in therapy (listed not in any given order of importance): E115 and F116, communication; C113 and D114, parenting, having a first child; A111 and B112, raising biracial child(ren); D114, recycling; C113, personality issues, understanding in-laws; C113, governing attitudes vs. romantic attitudes, body image, sibling-order; B112, psycho education take-home material (helpful to know that a topic is coming up); E115, achieving goals and time frame, finance (how to support a family), career, salary, keeping the romance alive (practicing different things to feel loved and valued in the relationship); C113, roles and responsibilities (cooking and housework and to be equal partners); F116, time frame of getting engaged or married.

Time Frame for Therapy

Set up a time frame for therapy: A111 suggested, "have twelve to sixteen sessions, 25 percent individual and 75 percent tandem." This can be a good number for intercultural premarital couples who are coming in for a brief overview of themes in their relationship with a goal of marriage.

Personality of the Therapist

The personality of the therapist and her belief in a particular theoretical base is important: B112, "Every culture is different but I am more used to the nurturing type and so my therapist's personality helped me." A111, "nonjudgmental." E115, "Therapist helped us to examine ourselves and our own actions, and reminded us that we love each other." G117, "she was very empathetic." D114, "caring." G117, "great listening skills." A111, "was able to identify either with my faith or culture or both without taking sides." "She had the ability to explain and advice without having any personal biases." B112, "therapist was fair, a good listener, nurturing, non-judgmental, open and willing to see different perspectives and she was very effective in her communication style." F116, "she was very tuned in to my cultural experience of being a woman, an immigrant, because she also came from a collectivist culture herself." E115, "she was attentive, caring and neutral and she had a strong understanding of humanity and the importance of forming a set of values." B112, "she had strong cultural ties/similarity that both individuals receiving counseling can identify with." D114, "trust is important, whenever my therapist asked me to do something (homework) I did it. He said that trust in her was built because they saw the effectiveness of the therapy work." E115, "their therapist's personality is well-suited to counseling because she has been married for a long period of time, she was born and raised in a separate culture and so understands both that culture as well as has lived here for many years so understands this culture as well." E115, "her techniques seemed to work, she was consistent and persistent in getting us to try them and stick with it, and she never gave up or showed signs of frustration in spite of the fact we spun our wheels at times."

Recommendations for Future Research

Issues in Raising Biracial Children

There is a need to interview interracial couples who are raising children in order to understand better what issues and challenges they face in raising their biracial children, and what are the implications for counseling. None of the couples interviewed in the present research were actively involved in raising biracial children. The present research did attempt to address the issue of raising biracial children but it was done from the point of view of what concerns the couples have about raising biracial children in the future.

Parents/Families/In-Laws of Intercultural Couples

An enquiry into the perspectives and concerns of the parents/families of intercultural couples will enrich the counseling process. It will help the couples to better understand how to relate to the parents/families and it will also provide better insights to the therapists in the counseling process. There is also a need to provide counseling to families either before or after marriage of intercultural couples. The support of family is an important factor as they in turn can become a positive support system for this couple. It will be helpful to investigate what kind of support will be helpful and why.

Intercultural Couples In the Premarital Stage

There is a need to interview more couples who are in the premarital stage as this will provide a deeper and more holistic idea of the issues that need to be addressed as they go through the discernment process and help them be better prepared to take the important step of marriage.

Therapists Working with Intercultural Couples

The input from therapists who have counseled intercultural couples is a much-needed component. The varied experience of therapists in this important works needs to be documented and made available.

LGBT Intercultural Couples Concerns

There is a definite need to study the therapeutic needs of intercultural LGBT couples. What is their voice on this concern and what help are they seeking?

The Influence of Clergy/ Priest On Intercultural Couples

There is also a need to study the influence of clergy of all faith practices on intercultural relationships in general and interfaith couples in particular. Their role is crucial in interfaith couples feeling at ease in approaching them for guidance and support.

Premarital couples with particular ethnic background (e.g., Caucasian married to Indian) needs to be studied.

Intercultural couples in alternate relational patterns or "live-in" relationship needs to be researched.

Appendix A

Participant Recruitment: Letter to Therapists

Dear Therapist,
My name is Sunita Noronha and I am a doctoral candidate at Candler School of Theology, Emory University and am residing in Decatur, Georgia. I am currently working on recruiting participants for my qualitative research on 'Doing Therapy with Intercultural Couples: A pastoral theological study of psychodynamic approaches to premarital counseling.' I am seeking participants who are English-speaking and have participated in premarital counseling together within the last five years from a marriage and family therapist. I am calling on therapists to assist me in recruiting participants by speaking with current or past clients about being a part of my study. I have attached a flyer that you can provide to participants or feel free to provide them with my contact information listed below.

If you have any questions regarding my study or recruitment of participants please feel free to contact me via phone at (404)--- ---- or via email at s------@emory.edu.

    Contact Information:
    Sunita Noronha M.Th., Th.M., Th.D. Candidate
    Candler School of Theology, Emory University
    Phone Number: (404)--- ----
    Email: s----@emory.edu.

Appendix B

Emory University Advertisement

I am a doctoral candidate at Candler School of Theology, Emory University residing in Decatur, GA and am doing my doctoral dissertation on the topic, "Doing Therapy with Intercultural Couples: A pastoral theological study of psychodynamic approaches to premarital counseling." I wish to gain knowledge of intercultural couple's experiences in premarital counseling through my dissertation. The purpose of the study is to provide participants who have participated in premarital counseling with the opportunity to share their experiences and insights in order to improve and strengthen counseling of intercultural premarital counseling. This is an Institutional Review Board approved study that is seeking participants where one or both members of the couple considers themselves intercultural, speak English fluently, and have participated in premarital counseling within the last five years from a therapist. Your involvement would require to meet individually and then as a couple for two interviews, lasting an hour each, regarding your experiences.

Additional contact may be needed with the researcher in order to confirm the findings of the study. There is a brief screening process. Participant's identities will be kept confidential. If you believe you qualify or know someone who would qualify for this study please contact Sunita Noronha by phone at (404)--- ---- or via email at s----@emory.edu.

Appendix C

Research Participants Wanted

Do you feel that you have insights regarding
Intercultural marriages that can assist counselors?
Do you describe yourself as an intercultural couple?

Would you like the opportunity to provide therapists and researchers with insights about intercultural premarital counseling and your culture?

Please Contact:
Sunita Noronha at (404)--- ---- or
s----@emory.edu.

Potential participants will go through a screening process, and if selected will be expected to participate as a couple in two interviews lasting one hour each.

Appendix D

Interview Packet

Tentative Interview Questions

1. What is your understanding of culture?
2. What things do you appreciate in your culture?
3. What things you do not appreciate in your culture?
4. In what ways has culture shaped your value system?
5. Does your value system play out in your relationship with your partner?
6. What part does religion/faith/beliefs/spirituality play in your relationship?
7. What expectations do you have of yourself that are culturally conditioned?
8. What expectations do you have of your partner that are culturally conditioned?
9. What is your experience of your premarital counseling?
10. Were you aware of your cultural differences? Is that why you chose to go for premarital counseling?
11. What aspects of counseling were most helpful to you?
12. What aspects of counseling were least helpful to you?
13. What cultural aspects did you change in yourself to benefit your relationship?

14. Was your therapist culturally inclined and sensitive to both of your cultures?
15. Did you experience any prejudices or stereotypes in her/his attitude?
16. Were you satisfied with her/his cultural understanding in your therapy?
17. Did you feel that s/he was taking sides?
18. Did you feel that s/he was culturally relevant in her approach?
19. Did s/he inform you of any particular or integrated approach that s/he used in premarital therapy that was culturally relevant?
20. Were you aware of any therapeutic approach in counseling? If yes, name them?
21. What suggestions would you give for therapists engaged in intercultural premarital counseling?
22. What aspects of counseling, interpersonal relationship, techniques or structure were most beneficial to you?
23. What aspects of counseling, interpersonal relationship, techniques or structure were least beneficial to you?
24. Would you recommend this therapist to other intercultural couples seeking premarital counseling and why?
25. Is there anything you would like to add that has not been addressed above?

Appendix E

Emory University

Description of Research and Consent to be a Research Subject

Title of Study

"Doing Therapy with Intercultural Couples: A pastoral theological study of psychodynamic approaches to premarital counseling."

Principal Investigator: Sunita Noronha

Introduction

You are being invited to participate in this research study because either you are a therapist who works with intercultural couples and can provide insight regarding premarital counseling or are an intercultural couple either in the process of discerning about intercultural marriage in premarital counseling or already married having received premarital couples counseling. It is entirely your choice. If you decide to take part, you can change your mind later on and withdraw from the research study. You can skip any questions that you do not wish to answer. You will be asked to fill out a survey to determine if you and your partner are eligible for this study.

Before making your decision:
Please carefully read this form or have it read to you
Please ask questions about anything that is not clear

You can take a copy of this consent form, to keep. Feel free to take your time thinking about whether you would like to participate. By signing this form you will not give up any legal rights.

Study Overview

The purpose of this study is to explore intercultural couples' and therapists insights and ideas in ways that premarital counseling can address intercultural marriage. It is hoped that the information gained from this study will provide clinicians and researchers with information about how and what to address regarding the topic of culture within premarital counseling. The objective is for the researcher and therapists to discover the effectiveness of current therapeutic approaches and choose the ones that are best suited for an intercultural premarital couples counseling. The hypothesis is that an approach to an intercultural premarital couples counseling is multiple and varied and shows up in different forms in the therapeutic process. These approaches are different from the theory and need to be documented for practice and further research.

Description of Procedures: For Intercultural Therapists

If you agree to be a part of the research study your participation will last for up to four months. You will be given a study number and this study number will be used to present the findings of the study and keep your identity confidential.

Description of Procedures: For Intercultural Couples

If you agree and are selected to participate in this study, your participation will last for up to four months. Prior to completing any paperwork you will be given a study number that you will use to fill out the demographic and screening question, this study number will also be used to present the findings of this study and keep your identity confidential.

During the Study You May Expect the Following Study Procedures to Be Followed

First, you will complete a form describing your demographic information and an initial screening survey to determine your appropriateness for the study. You will also be emailed or mailed a set of tentative interview questions.

Second, you will be contacted within one week of the screening by the primary researcher via phone or in person to let you know if you have been selected for the study. If you have been selected for the study the researcher will set up a time and place for the individual interviews with both partners.

Third, approximately one week prior to the interview you will receive the interview questions via email or via mail. You are invited to look over the questions, reflect on potential answers.

Fourth, the interview will consist of individual partners present for an hour each time, to talk on the topics of culture, premarital counseling, and marriage.

Fifth, after the individual interview correspondence about findings, researcher interpretations and presentation of findings will occur on an as-needed basis either in person, via telephone, or via email. The researcher may ask you a few short questions in order to confirm or clarify interpretations from the interview. Interviews will be recorded using a digital audio recorder. The recordings will be stored in a locked office cabinet at the Care and Counseling Center of Georgia and will be destroyed after transcription.

Sixth, a second couple interview will be scheduled for an hour and both members will be present to answer questions and discuss.

Seventh, after the couple interview correspondence about findings, the researcher interpretations and presentation of findings will occur as needed basis either in person, via telephone, or via email. The researcher may ask you a few short questions in order to confirm or clarify interpretations from the interview. Interviews will be recorded using a digital audio recorder. The recordings will be stored in the locked office cabinet at the Care and Counseling Center of Georgia and will be destroyed after transcription.

Eighth, you may skip any question throughout the interview or demographic information that you do not wish to answer or that makes you feel uncomfortable.

Risks and Discomfort

While participating in this study you may experience the following risks: emotional conflict may arise among participants. If this does occur and you feel you need additional counseling, you may contact Carol Pitts at CCCG at (404)--- ----. You will pay for it out of pocket or through your own personal insurance. There may also be a breach of confidentiality.

New Information

It is possible that the researcher will learn something new during the study about the risks of being in it. If this happens, she will tell you about it. Then you can decide if you want to continue to be in this research study or not. If you decided to stay in the study you may be asked to sign a new informed consent form that includes the new information.

Benefits

This study is not designed to benefit you directly. It is hoped that the information gained in this study will benefit others in the future, such as the therapeutic community (researcher and therapists) by providing information about how one's culture affects the premarital counseling process and ways premarital counseling can be improved by addressing cultural aspects and approaches.

Costs and Compensation

This is your contribution to research and to many other intercultural couples who will benefit from this. You are contributing your valuable time and gas money to participate in this research. You will not be offered payment or compensation in any form for participating in this research study.

Confidentiality

To ensure confidentiality to the extent permitted by law, the following measures will be taken: records identifying participants will be kept confidential to the extent permitted by applicable laws and regulations and will not be made publicly available. The study number assignment sheet and the audio digital recordings are the only two pieces of evidence that will contain your actual identity. Certain offices and people other than the researcher may look at this research study records. These offices include the Office for Human Research Protections, the Emory Institutional Review Board, and the Emory Office of Research Compliance. Emory will keep any research records we create private to the extent we are required to do so by law. Wherever necessary, a study number rather than your name will be used on research study records. Your name and other records that might point to you will not appear when we present this study or publish its results. We will do everything we can to keep others from learning about your participation in this research study. All paper documents and audio conversation recordings will be destroyed after transcription.

Voluntary Participation and Withdrawal from the Research Study

Your participation in this study is completely voluntary and you may refuse to participate or leave the study at any time. If you decide to not participate in the study or leave the study early, it will not result in any penalty.

The researcher also has the right to stop your participation in this study without your consent if:

She believes it is in your best interest

If you feel you have a research-related injury, or

If you have questions, concerns, or complaints about the research

If you were to object to any further changes that may be made in the study plan

Or for any other reason.

Questions or Problems: Contact Information

You are encouraged to ask questions at any time during this study.
For further information about the study contact _____ at
    (404)--- ---- or via email s----@emory.edu.
Or the Research Advisor _____ (404)--- ----
If you have any questions about this study or your part in it,

If you feel you have had a research-related injury, or
If you have questions, concerns, or complaints about the research
Contact the Emory Institutional Review Board:

If you have any questions about the rights of research subjects or research-related injury, please contact the Emory Institutional Review Board at 1599 Clifton Road, 5th Floor Atlanta GA 30322 or phone (404)-712-0720 or 877-503-9797 or irb@emory.edu. You may also let the IRB know about your experience as a research participant through our Research Participant Survey at http://www.surveymonkey.com/s6ZDMW75.

Please, print your name and sign below if you agree to be in this study. By signing this consent form, you will not give up any of your legal rights. We will give you a copy of the signed consent to keep.

_____   _____

Name of Subject   Date

_____   _____

Signature of Subject   Date

_____

Signature of Person Conducting Informed-Consent Discussion

_____   _____

Date   Time

Appendix F

 Institutional Review Board

To: Sunita Noronha, M.TH., Th.M.
Principal Investigator
Theology School

DATE: November 24, 2014

RE: **Expedited Approval**
IRB00078391
DOING THERAPY WITH INTERCULTURAL COUPLES:
A pastoral theological study of psychodynamic approaches to premarital counseling

Thank you for submitting a new application for this protocol. This research is eligible for expedited review under 45 CFR.46.110 and/or 21 CFR 56.110 because it poses minimal risk and fits the regulatory category F[7] as set forth in the Federal Register. The Emory IRB reviewed it by expedited process on 11/24/2014 and granted approval effective from 11/24/2014 through 11/23/2015. Thereafter, continuation of human subjects research activities requires the submission of a renewal application, which must be reviewed and approved by the IRB prior to the expiration date noted above. Please note carefully the following items with respect to this approval:

- SN Dissertation Scientific Protocol Documentation.docx dtd. 11/14/2014
- SN Dissertation Questionnaire for participants.docx dtd. 11/14/2014
- SN Dissertation email to therapists.docx
- SN Dissertation Email to Emory students.docx
- SN Dissertation Flyers for recruiting participants.docx
- IRBICF Couples.doc dtd. 11/19/2014 Version 0.02

Any reportable events (e.g., unanticipated problems involving risk to subjects or others, noncompliance, breaches of confidentiality, HIPAA violations, protocol deviations) must be reported to the IRB according to our Policies & Procedures at www.irb.emory.edu, immediately, promptly, or periodically. Be sure to check the reporting guidance and contact us if you have questions. Terms and conditions of sponsors, if any, also apply to reporting.

Before implementing any change to this protocol (including but not limited to sample size, informed consent, study design, you must submit an amendment request and secure IRB approval.

In future correspondence about this matter, please refer to the IRB file ID, name of the Principal Investigator, and study title. Thank you

Will Smith, BA
Research Protocol Analyst
This letter has been digitally signed

CC: There are no items to display
There are no items to display

Emory University
1599 Clifton Road, 5th Floor - Atlanta, Georgia 30322
Tel: 404.712.0720 - Fax: 404.727.1358 - Email: irb@emory.edu - Web: http://www.irb.emory.edu/
An equal opportunity, affirmative action university

Institutional Review Board – Emory University

TO: Sunita Noronha
Principal Investigator
Theology School

DATE: October 23, 2015
RE: Continuing Review Expedited Approval
CR1_IRB00078391
IRB00078391

DOING THERAPY WITH INTERCULTURAL COUPLES:
A pastoral theological study of psychodynamic approaches to premarital counseling

Thank you for submitting a renewal application for this protocol. The Emory IRB reviewed it by the expedited process on 10/23/2015, per 45 CFR 46.110, the Federal Register expeditable category [F (7)], and/or 21 CFR 56.110. This reapproval is effective from 10/24/2015 through 10/23/2016. Thereafter, continuation of human subjects research activities requires the submission of another renewal application, which must be reviewed and approved by the IRB prior to the expiration date noted above. Please note carefully the following items with respect to this reapproval:

- SN Dissertation Scientific Protocol Documentation.docx (11/14/2014)

Any reportable events (e.g., unanticipated problems involving risk to subjects or others, noncompliance, breaches of confidentiality, HIPAA violations, protocol deviations) must be reported to the IRB according to our Policies & Procedures at www.irb.emory.edu, immediately, promptly, or periodically. Be sure to check the reporting guidance and contact us if you have questions. Terms and conditions of sponsors, if any, also apply to reporting.

Before implementing any change to this protocol (including but not limited to sample size, informed consent, and study design), you must submit an amendment request and secure IRB approval.

In future correspondence about this matter, please refer to the IRB file ID, name of the Principal Investigator, and study title. Thank you.

Sincerely,
Will Smith, MPH
Research Protocol Analyst
This letter has been digitally signed

Emory University
1599 Clifton Road, 5th Floor - Atlanta, Georgia 30322
Tel: 404.712.0720 - Fax: 404.727.1358 - Email: irb@emory.edu - Web: http://www.irb.emory.edu/
An equal opportunity, affirmative action university

Appendix G

Demographic Questionnaire (Please print)

1. Name: _____ Middle _____
   Surname _____

2. Date of Birth (DD/MM/YYYY): _____/_____/_____
   Age: _____

3. Place of Birth: city _____ state _____
   country _____

4. Gender (check one):   Female   Male   Other

5. Relationship Status (check one):

   Single   Widowed   Married   Divorced
   Separated   Live-In

   Remarried   Other _____

DEMOGRAPHIC QUESTIONNAIRE (PLEASE PRINT)

6. Race (please check all that apply):

   White / Black / African American / Native American / Aleutian Islander / Eskimo / Asian or Pacific Islander / Hispanic or Latino / Other (please specify): _____

7. What language(s) do you speak? _____
   _____

8. What language(s) do you prefer to speak? _____
   _____

9. If single, how long have you known your partner? _____
   _____

10. Name of partner   spouse _____

11. If married, how long were you in this relationship before getting married? _____
    _____

12. Do you live with your (please check all that apply):

    parents   sibling   grandparents   spouse
    partner   friend   children - how many? _____
    alone

    other (please specify): _____

DEMOGRAPHIC QUESTIONNAIRE (PLEASE PRINT)

13. Occupation: _____

14. Highest level of education completed: _____

15. Income: _____

16. Years/months since married _____

17. Age at marriage: _____

18. If married, years since you had premarital counseling:
    _____

19. How many sessions of premarital counseling did you have?
    _____

20. If single, are you currently in premarital counseling? _____

21. How many sessions of premarital counseling have you had?
    _____

22. Mailing Address: _____
    _____

23. Email _____

24. Contact Phone number _____

25. Skype ID _____

Appendix H

	Cultural Diversity Screening Questions I:	Almost Never (1)	Sometimes (2)	Often (3)
a.	I am open to learning more about diversity			
b.	I like to make friends with people from other cultures			
c.	I like to attend social or cultural functions from other cultures			
d.	I do not make judgment of other people based on stereotypes			
e.	I like to help people in my neighborhood who are from other cultures			
f.	I like to look up cultural history of people on websites or books			
g.	I like to volunteer at refugee centers or after-school programs for culturally diverse children			
h.	I like to learn foreign language			
i.	I correct people when I see disregard for diversity			
j.	I like to talk about diversity with my family and friends			
	Total			

APPENDIX H 193

	Cultural Diversity Screening Questions II:	Agree (1)	Not yet (2)	Dis-agree (3)
a.	I am in the process of giving thought to my personal cultural beliefs, my worldview, and my stand on diversity			
b.	I am well aware of the cultural, racial, and ethnic diversity in my surrounding and have begun to respect diversity			
c.	I am opening up to the idea of celebrating cultural diversity rather than questioning it			
d.	I grew up in a family environment that tolerated diversity			
e.	I like to hang around with peers who make fun of other cultures			
f.	I get very conscious of myself when I am in the presence of people who are different from mine			
g.	I cannot tolerate the smell of food that is different from mine			
h.	I am attracted to people from other cultures			
i.	I have lived abroad for a period of time and enjoyed it			
j.	I am learning to respect all people and their cultural heritage			
	Total			

Appendix I

Research Questions to the Single Partner Participants

1. How do you describe your racial/cultural/ethnic identity? What aspects do you most/ least admire in your culture?

2. You are aware of the cultural/ethnic/racial divide in our society. Have you ever had to negotiate the same in your family of origin or at other places such as school, college, sports, shopping etc.? What did you learn from that experience?

3. In your relationship what cultural dimensions come to the forefront? In what ways do you take time to address those issues and concerns?

4. Were you always respectful of other cultures or how did you learn to accept diversity? What role (if any) did your partner play in broadening your worldview about diversity?

5. Do you have any exposure to intercultural couples in your family, or friends or neighborhood? Have you personally interacted with any of them?

6. What attributes attracted you to your mate/partner? What role did culture play in you both getting together?

7. Do you discuss cultural issues pertaining to your relationship and what are those?

8. Do you belong to different faith traditions? If yes, how do you negotiate the same in your relationship and in raising your child(ren) (if any)?

9. What convinced you personally that premarital counseling was helpful?
10. As an individual, what characteristics (if any) did you want to find in your premarital counselor?
11. Explain why being an intercultural couple is a help or hindrance?
12. What hurdles or support have you experienced from your family of origin / extended family / friends or others in your journey as an intercultural couple?

Appendix J

Research Questions to the Couple Participants

1. You are aware of the cultural/ethnic/racial divide in our society. As a couple have you ever had to negotiate the same in your family of origin or extended family or at other places such as school, college, sports, shopping, etc.? What did you learn from that experience?
2. What attracted you to your partner? At the time did you foresee any relationship issues due to cultural difference?
3. In your relationship what cultural dimension are you struggling the most to negotiate? What works best for you and why and what does not work and why?
4. How do you describe your identity as a couple? Do you discuss racial/cultural/ethnic issues in your current relationship? How does such an interaction play out?
5. If you are also an interfaith couple, how do you negotiate religious/faith/spirituality issues on a daily basis?
6. If you are a biracial couple then what fears and concerns, if any, do you have about raising biracial children of your own?
7. Why did you choose to go for premarital counseling?
8. Why did you choose this particular therapist for your premarital counseling, and how long did you stay? Why did you continue to stay in therapy with this particular therapist?
9. In your premarital counseling what cultural insights did you find most effective?

10. In your premarital counseling what cultural insights did you find least effective?
11. Who brought up the cultural issues the most—you, your partner, or the therapist?
12. In your experience did you find your therapist to be reflective of your cultural issues or was he/she totally disconnected?
13. In your experience in what ways did you find premarital counseling helpful?
14. What therapeutic approaches did you experience in your own therapy that yielded beneficial results (cognitive, behavioral, gestalt, object relations, solution focused, directive or non-directive, strategic, structural, family systems, relational, and others)?
15. What therapeutic approaches did you experience in your own therapy that did not yield beneficial results? (cognitive, behavioral, gestalt, object relations, solution focused, directive or non-directive, strategic, structural, family systems, relational and others)
16. What suggestions would you give to future intercultural couples in terms of improving their own intercultural marriage?
17. What suggestions would you give to future therapists in terms of improving their own intercultural premarital counseling services?

Appendix K

COLLABORATIVE INSTITUTIONAL TRAINING INITIATIVE (CITI)
BASIC/REFRESHER COURSE HUMAN SUBJECTS PROTECTION CURRICULUM COMPLETION REPORT
Printed on 11/03/2014

LEARNER	Sunita Noronha (ID: 4447301) 1052 N. Jamestown Rd. Apt D. Decatur Georgia 30033 United States
DEPARTMENT	Theology
PHONE	4047276324
EMAIL	snoronh@emory.edu
INSTITUTION	Emory University
EXPIRATION DATE	10/05/2016

GROUP 2. SOCIAL/BEHAVIORAL FOCUS: This course is suitable for Investigators and staff conducting SOCIAL / HUMANISTIC / BEHAVIORAL RESEARCH with human subjects. Social/Humanist/Behavioral research includes observational and survey research, population and/or epidemiological studies.

COURSE/STAGE:	Basic Course/1
PASSED ON:	10/06/2014
REFERENCE ID:	14243256

REQUIRED MODULES	DATE COMPLETED
Students in Research	10/06/14
History and Ethical Principles - SBE	10/06/14
Defining Research with Human Subjects - SBE	10/06/14
The Federal Regulations - SBE	10/06/14
Assessing Risk - SBE	10/06/14
Informed Consent - SBE	10/06/14
Privacy and Confidentiality - SBE	10/06/14
Research with Prisoners - SBE	10/06/14
Research with Children - SBE	10/06/14
Research in Public Elementary and Secondary Schools - SBE	10/06/14
International Research - SBE	10/06/14
Internet-Based Research - SBE	10/06/14
Research and HIPAA Privacy Protections	10/06/14
Vulnerable Subjects - Research Involving Workers/Employees	10/06/14
Conflicts of Interest in Research Involving Human Subjects	10/06/14

For this Completion Report to be valid, the learner listed above must be affiliated with a CITI Program participating institution or be a paid Independent Learner. Falsified information and unauthorized use of the CITI Program course site is unethical, and may be considered research misconduct by your institution.

Paul Braunschweiger Ph.D.
Professor, University of Miami
Director Office of Research Education
CITI Program Course Coordinator

Bibliography

Ali, Carroll A. Watkins. *Survival and Libration: Pastoral Theology in African American Context*. St. Louis: Chalice, 1999.

Almeida, Rhea V. "Couples in the *Desi* Community." In *Multicultural Couples Therapy*, edited by Mudita Rastogi and Volker Thomas. Los Angeles: Sage, 2009.

Anfara, V. A., et al. "Qualitative Analysis on Stage: Making the Research Process more Public." *Educational Researcher* 31 (2002) 28–36.

Asai, S. G., and D. H. Olson. "Culturally Sensitive Adaptation of Prepare with Japanese Premarital Couples." *Journal of Marital and Family Therapy* 30:4 (2004) 411–26.

Augsburger, David W. *Pastoral Counseling across Cultures*. Philadelphia: Westminster, 1986.

Basso, Keith H. *Wisdom Sits in Places: Landscapes and Language among the Western Apache*. Albuquerque, NM: University of New Mexico Press, 1996.

Berger, Peter L. *The Sacred Canopy: Elements of a Sociological Theory of Religion*. New York: Anchor, 1990.

Berry, John W. "Immigration, Acculturation and Adaptation." *Applied Psychology* 46:1 (1997) 5–34.

Berzoff, Joan, et al., eds. *Inside Out and Outside In: Psychodynamic Clinical Theory and Psychopathology in Contemporary Multicultural Contexts*. 3rd ed. New York: Rowman & Littlefield, 2011.

Bidwell, Duane R., and Joretta L. Marshall, eds. *Empowering Couples: A Narrative Approach to Spiritual Care*. Minneapolis: Fortress, 2013.

———. *The Formation of Pastoral Counselors: Challenges and Opportunities*. New York: Haworth Pastoral, 2006.

Biever, J. L., et al. "Therapy with Intercultural Couples: A Postmodern Approach." *Counseling Psychology* 1 (1998) 181–88.

Blagys, M. D., and M. J. Hilsenroth. "Distinctive Activities of Short-Term Psychodynamic-Interpersonal Psychotherapy: A Review of the Comparative Psychotherapy Process Literature." *Clinical Psychology: Science and Practice* 7 (2000) 167–88.

Blee, K. M., and V. Taylor. "Semi-Structured Interviewing in Social Movement Research." In *Methods of Social Movements Research*, edited by B. Klandermans and S. Staggenbord, 92–117. Minneapolis: University of Minnesota Press, 2002.

Bloomberg, L. D., and M. Volpe. *Completing Your Qualitative Dissertation: A Roadmap from Beginning to End*. Thousand Oaks, CA: Sage, 2008.

Bodenmann, G., and S. D. Shantinath. "The Couples Coping Enhancement Training (CCET): A New Approach to Prevention of Marital Distress Based Upon Stress and Coping." *Family Relations* 53 (2004) 477–84.
Bonheoffer, Dietrich. *The Cost of Discipleship*. New York: McMillian, 1949.
Bonilla-Silva, E., and M. Hovsepian. "If Two People Are in Love: Deconstructing Whites Views on Interracial Marriage with Blacks." *Southern Sociological Society* 30 (2000) 1–12.
Bons-Storm, Riet. *The Incredible Woman: Listening to Women's Silences in Pastoral Care and Counseling*. Nashville: Abingdon 1996.
Boyd-Franklin, Nancy. *Black Families in Therapy: Understanding the African American Experience*. 2nd ed. New York: Guildford, 2003.
Bradbury, T. N., and B. R. Karney. "Understanding and Altering the Longitudinal Course of Marriage." *Journal of Marriage and Family* 66 (2004) 862–79.
Bradley, J. "Methodological Issues and Practices in Qualitative Research." *Library Quarterly* 63 (1993) 431–49.
Bratter, J. L., and R. B. King. "'But Will It Last?': Marital Instability among Interracial and Same-Race Couples." *Family Relations* 57 (2008) 160–71.
Brotherson, S. E., and W. C. Duncan. "Rebinding the Ties That Bind: Government Efforts to Preserve and Promote Marriage." *Family Relations* 53 (2004) 459–68.
Browning, Don S. *Equality and the Family: A Fundamental Theology of Children, Mothers and Fathers in Modern Societies*. Grand Rapids: Eerdmans, 2007.
———. *A Fundamental Practical Theology: Descriptive and Strategic Proposals*. Minneapolis: Fortress, 1996.
———. "Pastoral Theology in a Pluralistic Age." In *The Blackwell Reader in Pastoral Theology*, edited by James Woodward and Stephen Pattison, 89–103. Malden: Blackwell, 2000.
Browning, Don S., and Terry D. Cooper. *Religious Thought and the Modern Psychologies*. 2nd ed. Minneapolis: Augsburg Fortress, 2004.
Browning, Don S., et al., eds. *From Culture Wars to Common Ground: Religion and the American Family Debate*. Louisville: Westminster John Knox, 2000.
———. *Sex, Marriage and Family in World Religions*. Columbia: Columbia University Press, 2009.
Busby, D. M., et al. "RELATE: Relationship Evaluation of the Individual, Family, Culture, and Couple Contexts." *Family Relations* 50 (2001) 308–16.
Campbell, K., and D. W. Wright. "Marriage Today: Exploring the Incongruence between Americans' Beliefs and Practices." *Journal of Comparative Family Studies* 41 (2010) 329–45.
Carter, Betty, and Monica McGoldrick, eds. *The Expanded Family Life Cycle: Individual, Family, and Social Perspectives*. 3rd ed. Boston: Allyn & Bacon, 1999.
Carter, Robert T. *The Influence of Race and Racial Identity in Psychotherapy: Toward a Racially Inclusive Mode*. New York: Wiley & Sons, 1990.
Cherlin, A. J. "The Deinstitutionalization of American Marriage." *Journal of Marriage and Family* 66 (2004) 848–61.
Clarke, S. *Social Theory, Psychoanalysis, and Racism*. New York: Palgrave Macmillian, 2003.
Comas-Diaz, Lillian, and Beverly Greene, eds. *Women of Color: Integrating Ethnic and Gender Identities in Psychotherapy*. New York: Guildford, 1994.

Coontz, Stephanie. *Marriage, A History: How Love Conquered Marriage*. New York: Penguin, 2005.
Coontz, Stephanie, et al., eds. *American Families: A Multicultural Reader*. 2nd ed. New York: Routledge, 1999.
Cooper-White, Pamela. *Many Voices: Pastoral Psychotherapy in Relational and Theological Perspective*. Minneapolis: Fortress, 2007.
———. *Shared Wisdom: Use of Self in Pastoral Care and Counseling*. Minneapolis: Fortress, 2004.
Cornell, S., and D. Hartmann. *Ethnicity and Race: Making Identities in a Changing World*. 2nd ed. Thousand Oaks, CA: Pine Forge, 2007.
Cottrell, A. B. "Cross-National Marriages: A Review of the Literature." *Journal of Comparative Family Studies* 21 (1990) 151–69.
Creswell, J. W. *Qualitative Inquiry and Research Design: Choosing Among Five Approaches*. Thousand Oaks, CA: Sage, 2009.
———. *Research Design: Qualitative, Quantitative, and Mixed Methods Approaches*. 3rd ed. Los Angeles: Sage, 2009.
Crippen, C., and L. Brew. "Intercultural Parenting and the Transcultural Family: A Literature Review." *The Family Journal* 15 (2007) 107–15.
Crohan, S. E., and J. Veroff. "Dimensions of Marital Well-Being among White and Black Newlyweds." *Journal of Marriage and the Family* 51 (1989) 373–83.
Crohn, Joel. "Intercultural Couples." In *Revisioning Family Therapy: Race, Culture, and Gender in Clinical Practice*, edited by Monica McGoldrick, 295–308. New York: Guilford, 1998.
———. *Mixed Matches: How to Create Successful Interracial, Interethnic, and Interfaith Relationships*. New York: Faucett Columbine, 1995.
Culbertson, Philip. *Caring for God's People: Counseling and Christian Wholeness*. Minneapolis: Fortress, 2000.
Cushman, Philip. *Constructing the Self, Constructing America: A Cultural History of Psychotherapy*. Garden City, NY: Da Capo, 1995.
Denzin, N. K., and Y. S. Lincoln. *Collecting and Interpreting Qualitative Materials*. Thousand Oaks, CA: Sage, 1998.
———. "Introduction: The Discipline and Practice of Qualitative Research." In *Handbook of Qualitative Research*, edited by N. K. Denzin and Y. S. Lincoln, 1–28. Thousand Oaks, CA: Sage, 2000.
Dykstra, Robert C. *Images of Pastoral Care*. St. Louis: Chalice, 2005.
Fadiman, Anne. *The Spirit Catches You and You Fall Down: A Hmong Child, Her American Doctors, and the Collision of Two Cultures*. New York: Farrar, Straus & Giroux, 1997.
Falicov, C. J. "Cross-Cultural Marriages." In *Clinical Handbook of Marital Therapy*, edited by N. S. Jacobson, and A. S. Gurman, 429–50. New York: Guilford, 1982.
———. "Immigrant Family Processes." In *Normal Family Processes*, edited by F. Walsh, 280–300. New York: Guilford, 2003.
Fontana, A., and J. H. Frey. "Interviewing: The Art of Science." In *Collecting and Interpreting Qualitative Materials*, edited by N. Denzin and Y. Lincoln, 47–78. Thousand Oaks, CA: Sage, 1998.
Fontes, Lisa Aronson. *Interviewing Clients across Cultures: A Practitioner's Guide*. New York: Guilford, 2008.

Frank, Jerome D., and Julia B. Frank. *Persuasion and Healing: A Comparative Study of Psychotherapy.* 3rd ed. Baltimore: John Hopkins University Press, 1991.

Furniss, George M. *The Social Context of Pastoral Care.* Louisville: Westminster John Knox, 1994.

Garcia-Preto, N. "Latino Families: An Overview." In *Ethnicity and Family Therapy*, edited by Monica McGoldrick et al., 153–65. New York: Guilford, 2005.

Gilbert, Roberta M. *Extraordinary Relationships: A New Way of Thinking about Human Interactions.* Minneapolis: Chronimed, 1992.

Gottman, J. M. *What Predicts Divorce?* Hillsdale, NJ: Lawrence Erlbaum Associates, 1994.

———. *Why Marriages Succeed or Fail, and How You Can Make Yours Last.* New York: Simon & Schuster, 1995.

Gottman, J. M., et al. "Predicting Marital Happiness and Stability from Newlywed Interactions." *Journal of Marriage and the Family* 60 (1998) 5–22.

Graham, Elaine, et al. *Theological Reflection: Methods.* London: SCM, 2005.

———. *Theological Reflection: Sources.* London: SCM, 2007.

Grant, Brian W. *A Theology for Pastoral Psychotherapy: God's Play in Sacred Spaces.* New York: Haworth Pastoral, 2001.

Guillemin, M., and L. Gillam. "Ethics, Reflexivity, and Ethically Important Moments in Research." *Qualitative Inquiry* 10 (2004) 261–80.

Gullickson, A. "Black/White Interracial Marriage Trends: 1850–2000." *A Journal of Family History* 31 (2006) 289–312.

Gurman, Alan. S. *Clinical Handbook of Couple Therapy.* 4th ed. New York: Guilford, 2008.

Gurung, R. A. R., and T. Duong. "Mixing and Matching: Assessing the Concomitants of Mixed-Ethnic Relationships." *Journal of Social and Personal Relationships* 16 (1999) 639–57.

Halford, W. Kim. *Marriage and Relationship Education: What Works and How to Provide It.* New York: Guilford, 2011.

Halford, W. Kim, et al. "Best Practice in Couple Relationship Education." *Journal of Marital and Family Therapy* 29 (2003) 385–406.

Hamburg, S. *Will Our Love Last? A Couple's Road Map.* New York: Scribner, 2001.

Hardy, K. V., and T. A. Laszloffy. "Couple Therapy Using a Multicultural Perspective." In *Clinical Handbook of Couple Therapy*, edited by A. S. Gurman and N. S. Jacobson, 569–93. New York: Guilford, 2002.

———. "The Dynamics of a Pro-Racist Ideology." In *Revisioning Family Therapy: Race, Culture, and Gender in Clinical Practice*, edited by M. McGoldrick, 118–28. New York: Guilford, 1998.

———. "Training Racially Sensitive Family Therapists: Context, Content, Contact." *Families in Society* 73 (1992) 364–70.

Helms, J. E. "Toward a Theoretical Explanation of the Effects of Race on Counseling: A Black and White Model." *The Counseling Psychologist* 12 (1984) 153–65.

Herman, M. R., and M. E. Campbell. "I Wouldn't, But You Can: Attitudes Toward Interracial Relationships." *Social Science Research* 41 (2012) 343–58.

Hervis, Olga E., et al. "Brief Strategic Family Therapy." In *Multicultural Couple Therapy*, edited by Mudita Rastogi and Volker Thomas, 167–86. Los Angeles: Sage, 2009.

Hidalgo, D. A., and C. L. Bankston. "Blurring Racial and Ethnic Boundaries in Asian American Families: Asian American Family Patterns." *Journal of Family Issues* 31 (2010) 280–300.

Hiltner, Seward. *Preface to Pastoral Theology*. Nashville: Abingdon, 1958.

Ho, M. K. *Intermarried Couples in Therapy*. Springfield, IL: Charles Thomas, 1990.

Holified, E. Brooks. *A History of Pastoral Care in America: From Salvation to Self-Realization*. Nashville: Abingdon, 1983.

Holman, T. B., et al. "Assumptions and Methods." In *Premarital Prediction of Marital Quality or Breakup*, edited by B. Holman, 29–45. New York: Plenum, 2001.

Hopkins, Dwight N. *Being Human: Race, Culture, and Religion*. Minneapolis: Fortress, 2005.

Houser, Rick, et al., eds. *Culturally Relevant Ethical Decision-Making in Counseling*. Thousand Oaks, CA: Sage, 2006.

Hsu, J. "Marital Therapy for Intercultural Couples." In *Culture and Psychology: A Guide to Clinical Practice*, edited by Wen-Shing Tseng and Jon Streltzer, 225–42. Washington, DC: American Psychiatric, 2001.

Hunsinger, Deborah Van Deusen. *Theology and Pastoral Counseling: A New Interdisciplinary Approach*. Grand Rapids: Eerdmans, 1995.

Hunter, Rodney J., editor. *Dictionary of Pastoral Care and Counseling*. Nashville: Abingdon, 1990.

Inman, A. G., et al. "Cultural Intersections: A Qualitative Inquire Into the Experience of Asian Indian-White Interracial Couples." *Family Process* 50 (2011) 248–66.

Ivey, A. E. *Intentional Interviewing and Counseling: Facilitating Client Development in a Multicultural Society*. 3rd ed. Pacific Grove, CA: Brooks Cole, 1994.

Ivey, A. E., et al. *Counseling and Psychotherapy: A Multicultural Perspective*. 4th ed. Boston: Allyn & Bacon, 1997.

———. *Theories of Counseling and Psychotherapy: A Multicultural Perspective*. 5th ed. Boston: Allyn & Bacon, 2002.

James, R. K., and B. E. Gilliland. *Theories and Strategies in Counseling and Psychotherapy*. 5th ed. Boston: Allyn & Bacon, 2003.

Jethwani, T. "Revisioning Boundaries: A Study of Interracial Marriage among Second Generation Asian Indian Women in the U.S." *Dissertations Abstracts International: A Humanities and Social Services* 23 (2002) 3198–99.

Johnson, Allan G. *Privilege, Power, and Difference*. 2nd ed. Boston: McGraw Hill, 2006.

Johnson, J. "Interracial Friendship and African American Attitudes about Interracial Marriage." *Journal of Family History* 36 (2006) 201–20.

Johnson, Luke Timothy, and Mark D. Jordan. "Uneasy Embodiment, Sexual Ambivalence, and the Incarnated and Resurrected Christ." In *Sex, Marriage and Family in World Religions*, edited by Don S. Browning et al., 86–88. Columbia: Columbia University Press, 2009.

Jones, E. *Family Systems Therapy: Developments in the Milan-Systemic Therapies*. New York: Wiley, 1993.

Karis, Terri A., and Kyle D. Killian, eds. *Intercultural Couples: Exploring Diversity in Intercultural Relationships*. New York: Routledge, 2009.

Kennedy, S., et al. "Our Monocultural Science." *American Psychologist* 39 (1984) 996–97.

Killian, Kyle D. "Couple Therapy and Intercultural Relationships." In *Clinical Handbook of Couple Therapy*, edited by A. S. Gurman et al., 512–15. New York: Guilford, 2015.

———. *Interracial Couples, Intimacy and Therapy: Crossing Racial Border*. Columbia: Columbia University Press, 2013.

Kim, Young Y. *Becoming Intercultural: An Integrative Theory of Communication and Cross-Cultural Adaptation*. Thousand Oaks, CA: Sage, 2001.

Kimmel, M. S. "Toward a Pedagogy of the Oppressor." In *Privilege: A Reader*, edited by M. S. Kimmel and A. L. Ferber, 1–10. Boulder, CO: Westview, 2003.

Kitano, H. L., et al. "Asian-American Interracial Marriage." *Journal of Marriage and the Family* 46 (1984) 179–90.

Kluckhohn, C., and H. A. Murray, eds. *Personality in Nature, Society and Culture*. New York: Knopf, 1948.

Kohut, Heinz. *The Analysis of the Self*. New York: International Universities Press, 1971.

———. "Introspection, Empathy and Psychoanalysis: An Examination of the Relationship between Mode of Observation and Theory." *Journal of the American Psychoanalytic Association* 7 (1959) 459–83.

———. "Introspection, Empathy, and the Semi-Circle of Mental Health." *International Journal of Psycho-Analysis* 63 (1982) 395–407.

———. *The Restoration of the Self*. New York: International Universities Press, 1977.

Krathwohl, David R., and Nick L. Smith. *How to Prepare a Dissertation Proposal: Suggestions for Students in Education and Behavioral Sciences*. New York: Distributed by Syracuse University Press, 2005.

Laird, J. "Theorizing Culture: Narrative Ideas and Practice Principles." In *Re-Visioning Family Therapy: Race, Culture, and Gender in Clinical Practice*, edited by Monica McGoldrick, 20–36. New York: Guilford, 1998.

Lareau, Annette. *Unequal Childhoods: Class, Race, and Family Life*. Los Angeles: University of California Press, 2003.

Larson, J. H. "Clinical Update: Premarital Assessment." *Family TherapyMagazine* 13 (2002) 36–42.

Lartey, Emmanuel Y. *In Living Color: An Intercultural Approach to Pastoral Care and Counseling*. 2nd ed. London: Jessica Kingsley, 2003.

———. "Pastoral Counseling as Faithful Practice amid Liminality, Uncertainly, and Multiplicity." *Quarterly Review: A Journal of Theological Resources for Ministry* 25 (2005) 366–76.

———. *Pastoral Theology in an Intercultural World*. Cleveland, OH: Pilgrim, 2013.

———. "Practical Theology as a Theological Form." In *The Blackwell Reader in Pastoral Theology*, edited by James Woodward and Stephen Pattison, 128–34. Malden: Blackwell, 2000.

Lee, Larry Jin. "The Unspoken Power of Racial Context: What's Race Gotta Do With It?" In *Multicultural Couple Therapy*, edited by Mudita Rastogi and Volker Thomas, 77–102. Thousand Oaks, CA: Sage, 2009.

Levinas, Emmanuel. *Totality and Infinity: An Essay on Exteriority*. Translated by Alphonso Lingis. Pittsburgh: Duquesne University Press, 1969.

Litchman, M. *Qualitative Research in Education: A User's Guide*. Thousand Oaks, CA: Sage, 2006.

Markman, H., et al. *Fighting for Your Marriage*. San Francisco: Jossey-Bass, 1994.

Maruskin, Joan M. *Immigration and the Bible: A Guide for Radical Welcome*. New York: Women's Division, The General Board of Global Ministries, The United Methodist Church, 2012.

May, Rollo. *The Art of Counseling*. New York: Abingdon, 1967.

———. *Love and Will*. New York: Norton, 1969.

———. *The Meaning of Anxiety*. New York: Washington, 1950.

May, Rollo, et al., eds. *Existence*. New York: Rowman & Littlefield, 1958.

McFadyen, Alistair I. *The Call to Personhood: A Christian Theory of the Individual in Social Relationships*. New York: Cambridge University Press, 1990.

McGeorge, C. R., and T. S. Carlson. "Premarital Education: An Assessment of Program Efficacy." *Contemporary Family Therapy* 28 (2006) 165–90.

McGoldrick, Monica. "Culture: A Challenge to Concepts of Normality." In *Normal Family Processes*, edited by F. Walsh, 235–59. New York: Guilford, 2007.

———. *Pastoral Theology in an Intercultural World*. Cleveland: Pilgrim, 2006.

McGoldrick, Monica, and Kenneth V. Hardy. "Introduction: Re-Visioning Family Therapy from Multicultural Perspective." In *Re-Visioning Family Therapy: Race, Culture, and Gender in Clinical Practice*, edited by Monica McGoldrick and Kenneth V. Hardy, 3–24. 2nd ed. New York: W. W. Norton, 2008.

———, eds. *Re-Visioning Family Therapy: Race, Culture, and Gender in Clinical Practice*. 2nd ed. New York: Guilford, 2008.

McGoldrick, Monica, et al. *Genograms: Assessment and Intervention*. 3rd ed. New York: W. W. Norton, 2008.

McGoldrick, Monica, et al., eds. *Ethnicity and Family Therapy*. 3rd ed. New York: Guilford, 2005.

McWilliams, Nancy. "What Defines a Psychoanalytic Therapy?" *Psychoanalytic Psychotherapy: A Practitioner's Guide*, 1–26. New York: Guilford, 2004.

Miller, Nancy Katz. *Being Both: Embracing Two Religions in One Interfaith Family*. Boston: Beacon, 2013.

Miller-McLemore, Bonnie J. "Feminist Theory in Pastoral Theology." In *Feminist and Womanist Pastoral Theology*, edited by Bonnie J. Miller-McLemore and Brita L.Gill-Austern. Nashville: Abingdon, 1999.

———. "The Living Human Web: Pastoral Theology at the Turn of the Century." In *Through the Eyes of Women: Insights for Pastoral Care*, edited by Jeanne Stevenson Moessner, 9–26. Minneapolis: Fortress, 1996.

———. "Pastoral Theology as Public Theology: Revolutions in the 'Fourth Area.'" In *Pastoral Care and Counseling: Redefining the Paradigms*, edited by Nancy J. Ramsay, 44–64. Nashville: Abingdon, 2004.

Min, Anselm Kyongsuk. *The Solidarity of Others in a Divided World: A Postmodern Theology after Postmodernism*. New York: Continuum, 2004.

Minuchin, S. *Families and Family Therapy*. Cambridge, MA: Harvard University Press, 1974.

Mishne, Judith. *Multiculturalism and the Therapeutic Process*. New York: Guilford, 2002.

Mitchell, Stephen A., and Margaret J. Black. *Freud and Beyond: A History of Modern Psychoanalytic Thought*. New York: Basic, 1995.

Merriam, S. B. *Qualitative Research in Practice: Examples for Discussion and Analysis*. San Francisco: Jossey-Bass, 2002.

Molina, B., et al. "Cultural Communities: Challenges and Opportunities in the Creation of 'Happily Ever After' Stories of Intercultural Couplehood." *The Family Journal: Counseling and Therapy of Couples and Families* 12 (2004) 139–47.

Moore, Zoe Bennett. *Introducing Feminist Perspectives on Pastoral Theology*. Cleveland: Pilgrim, 2002.

Moreton-Robinson, Aileen. *Talkin' Up to the White Woman: Indigenous Women and Feminism*. Brisbane: University of Queensland Press, 2002.

Moschella, Mary Clark. *Ethnography as a Pastoral Practice: An Introduction*. Cleveland: Pilgrim, 2008.

Muran, J. Christopher, ed. *Dialogues on Difference: Studies of Diversity in the Therapeutic Relationship*. Washington, DC: American Psychological Association, 2007.

Murray, C. E. "Professional Responses to Government-Endorsed Premarital Counseling." *Marriage and Family Review* 40 (2006) 53–67.

Neuger, Christie C. *Counseling Women: A Narrative Approach*. Minneapolis: Fortress, 2001.

Nichols, Michael P. *Family Therapy: Concepts and Methods*. 9th ed. Boston: Allyn & Bacon, 2010.

Orange, Donna M., et al. *Working Intersubjectively: Contextualism in Psychoanalytic Practice*. New York: Routledge, 2009.

Osmer, Richard R. *Practical Theology: An Introduction*. Grand Rapids: Eerdmans, 2008.

Pargament, Kenneth. *Spiritually Integrated Psychotherapy: Understanding and Addressing the Sacred*. New York: Guilford, 2007.

Patton, John. *Pastoral Care in Context: An Introduction to Pastoral Care*. Louisville: Westminster John Knox, 1993.

Penas, Ibanez B., and Carmen López Sáenz. *Interculturalism: Between Identity and Diversity*. Bern: Peter Lang AG, 2006.

Perel, E. "A Tourist's View of Marriage: Cross-Cultural Couples—Challenges, Choices, and Implications for Therapy." In *Couples on the Fault Line: New Directions for Therapists*, edited by P. Papp, 178–204. New York: Guilford, 2000.

Ponterotto, Joseph G. *Handbook of Multicultural Counseling*. Los Angeles: Sage, 2001.

Pope, Kenneth S., and Melba J. T. Vasquez. *Ethics in Psychotherapy and Counseling: A Practical Guide for Psychologists*. San Francisco: Jossey-Bass, 1991.

Prashantham, B. J. *Indian Case Studies in Therapeutic Counseling*. Vellore: Christian Counseling Center, 2001.

Ramsay, Nancy J. *Pastoral Care and Counseling: Redefining the Paradigms*. Nashville: Abingdon, 2004.

Rastogi, Mudita, and Volker Thomas, eds. *Multicultural Couples Therapy*. Los Angeles: Sage, 2009.

Richardson, Brenda Lane. *Guess Who's Coming for Dinner: Celebrating Interethnic, Interfaith, and Interracial Relationships*. N.d.: Wildcat Canyon, 2000.

Ridley, C. R. *Overcoming Unintentional Racism in Counseling and Therapy: A Practitioner's Guide to Intentional Intervention*. Thousand Oaks, CA: Sage, 1995.

Riley, Naomi Schaefer. *Till Faith Do Us Part: How Interfaith Marriage Transforming America*. New York: Oxford University Press, 2013.

Robinson, Lena. *'Race,' Communication and the Caring Professions*. 1st ed. Abingdon: Taylor and Francis Group, 1998.

Romano, Dugan. *Intercultural Marriage: Promises and Pitfalls*. 3rd ed. Boston: Intercultural, 2008.

Rosenbaum, Mary Helene, and Stanley Ned Rosenbaum. *Celebrating our Differences: Living Two Faiths in One Marriage.* Rev. ed. New York: Ragged Edge, 2001.
Ruether, Rosemary Radford. *Sexism and God-Talk.* 3rd ed. Boston: Beacon, 1993.
Rumbaut, Ruben G. "Ages, Life Stages, and Generational Cohorts: Decomposing the Immigrant First and Second Generation in the United States." *International Migration Review* 38:3 (2004) 1160–205.
Rumbaut, Ruben G., and Alejandro Portes, eds. *Ethnicities: Children of Immigrants in America.* New York: Russell Sage Foundations, 2001.
Schreiter, Robert J. *Constructing Local Theologies.* New York: Orbis, 1999.
Scott, Kieran, and Michael Warren, eds. *Perspectives on Marriage: A Reader.* 3rd ed. NewYork: Oxford University Press, 2007.
Seeley, Karen M. *Cultural Psychotherapy: Working with Culture in the Clinical Encounter.* Lanham: Jason Aronson, 2000.
Seshadri, G., and C. Knudson-Martin. "How Couples Manage Interracial and Intercultural Differences: Implications for Clinical Practice." *Journal of Marital and Family Therapy* 39 (2013) 43–58.
Shelling, G., and J. Fraser-Smith. *In Love but World's Apart: Insights, Questions, and Tips for the Intercultural Couple.* N.d.: AuthorHouse, 2008.
Shibusawa, Tazuko. "Interracial Asian Couples: Beyond Black and White." In *Re-Visioning Family Therapy: Race, Culture, and Gender in Clinical Practice,* edited by Monica McGoldrick and Kenneth V. Hardy, 378–88. New York: Guilford, 2008.
Silliman, B., and W. R. Schumm. "Improving Practice in Marriage Preparation." *Journal of Sex and Marital Therapy* 25 (1999) 23–43.
Skurtu, Angela. *Premarital Counseling: A Guide for Clinicians.* New York: Routledge, 2016.
Snyder, I. B., et al. *Assessing Perceived Marriage Education Needs and Interest of Latino individuals in Utah county Utah.* MS diss., Brigham Young University, 2006.
Sodowsky, G., P. Jackson, and G. Loya. "Outcome of Training in the Philosophy of Assessment: Multicultural Counseling Competencies." In *Multicultural Counseling Competencies: Assessment, Education, Training and Supervision,* edited by D. Pope-Davis and H. Coleman, 3–42. Thousand Oaks, CA: Sage, 1997.
Sohier, R. "The Dyadic Interview as a Tool for Nursing Research." *Applied Nursing Research* 8 (1995) 96–101.
Sollod, Robert N., et al. *Beneath the Mask: An Introduction to Theories of Personality.* Chennai: Wiley & Sons, 2009.
South, S. J. "Racial and Ethnic Difference in the Desire to Marry." *Journal of Marriage and the Family* 55 (1993) 357–70.
Stahmann, R. F. "Premarital Counseling: A Focus for Family Therapy." *The Association for Family Therapy and Systemic Practice* 22 (2000) 104–16.
Stanley, S., et al. *A Lasting Promise.* San Francisco: Jossey-Bass, 1998.
Stevenson-Moessner, Jeanne, and Teresa Snorton. *Women Out of Order: Risking Change and Creating Care in a Multicultural World,* Minneapolis: Fortress, 2010.
Sue, D. W., and D. Sue. *Counseling the Culturally Different: Theory and Practice.* New York: Wiley, 1999.
Sumari, Melati, and Fauziah Hanim Jalal. "Cultural Issues in Counseling: An International Perspective, Counselling, Psychotherapy, and Health." *Counseling in the Asia Pacific Rim: A Coming Together of Neighbors Special Issue* 4 (2008) 24–34.
Surra, C. "Research and Theory on Mate Selection and Premarital Relationships in the 1980s." *Journal of Marriage and the Family* 52 (1990) 844–65.

Swinton, John, and Harriet Mowat. *Practical Theology and Qualitative Research*. London: SCM, 2006.

Taylor, Charles W. *Premarital Guidance: Creative Pastoral Care and Counseling Series*. Minneapolis: Fortress, 1999.

Ting-Toomey, S. *Communicating Across Cultures*. New York: Guilford, 1999.

Tipton, Steven M., and John Witte Jr., eds. *Family Transformed: Religion, Values, and Society in American Life*. Washington, DC: Georgetown University Press, 2005.

Tracy, David. *The Analogical Imagination: Christian Theology and the Culture of Pluralism*. London: SCM, 1981.

Turabian, Kate L. *A Manual for Research Papers, Theses, and Dissertations*. 8th ed. Chicago: University of Chicago Press, 2013.

———. *A Manual for Writers of Term Papers, Theses, and Dissertations*. 6th ed. Chicago: University of Chicago Press, 1996.

VandeCreek, Larry, et al. *Research in Pastoral Care and Counseling: Quantitative and Qualitative Approaches*. Eugene, OR: Wipf & Stock, 2008.

Volf, Miroslav. *Exclusion and Embrace: A Theological Exploration of Identity, Otherness and Reconciliation*. Nashville: Abingdon, 1996.

Waldegrave, C. "Cultural, Gender and Socioeconomic Contexts in Therapeutic Social Policy Work." *Family Process* 48 (2009) 85–111.

Walsh, Froma, ed. *Normal Family Processes: Growing Diversity and Complexity*. 3rd ed. New York: Guilford, 2003.

———. "Religion, Spirituality and the Family: Multifaith Perspectives." In *Spiritual Resources in Family Therapy*, edited by Froma Walsh, 3–30. New York: Guilford, 2009.

Watters, Ethan. *Crazy Like Us: The Globalization of the American Psyche*. New York: Free, 2010.

Weeks, Greald, et al. *If Only I Had Known . . . Avoiding Common Mistakes in Couples Therapy*. New York: W. W. Norton, 2005.

Weston, Anthony. *A Practical Companion to Ethics*. 3rd ed. New York: Oxford University Press, 2006.

Whitehead, J. D., and E. E. Whitehead. *Method in Ministry: Theological Reflections and Christian Ministry*. San Francisco: Harper & Row, 1990.

Whyte, Martin King, ed. *Marriage in America: A Communitarian Perspective*. New York: Rowman & Littlefield, 2000.

Wimberly, Anne Streaty, and Edward Powell Wimberly. *Language of Hospitality: Intercultural Relations in the Household of God*. Nashville: Cokesbury, 1991.

Wimberly, Edward P. *Counseling African American Marriages and Families*. Louisville: Westminster John Knox, 1997.

Witte, John, Jr., et al., eds. *The Equal-Regard Family and Its Friendly Critics: Don Browning and the Practical Theological Ethics of the Family*. Grand Rapids: Eerdmans, 2007.

Woodward, James, and Stephen Pattison, eds. *The Blackwell Reader in Pastoral Theology*. Malden: Blackwell, 2000.

Yancey, George A., and Sherelyn Whittum Yancey, eds. *Just Don't Marry One: Interracial Dating, Marriage and Parenting*. Valley Forge: Judson, 2002.

Zagelbaum, Adam, and Jon Carlson. *Working with Immigrant Families: A Practical Guide for Counselors*. New York: Routledge, 2011.

Zhenchao, Q. "Changing Patterns of Interracial Marriage in a Multiracial Society." *The Journal of Industrial Economics* 59 (2011) 1065–84.

www.ingramcontent.com/pod-product-compliance
Lightning Source LLC
Chambersburg PA
CBHW070253230426
43664CB00014B/2521